"This book is rich in inspiration and information. Reading it opened my eyes, broadened my vision, and challenged my faith. I highly recommend it to both men and women!"

—**Warren W. Wiersbe**,
author and former pastor of the
Moody Church, Chicago

"How does a mom raise a daughter in an age that believes the sum of her appearance must fit into a teeny, tiny, little size 0 box with its edges tightly, perfectly manicured shut? Maybe she shares example after example of what living, breathing, change-the-world courage looks like from the women who've come before us. I know that from now on when I'm looking for heroes for my daughter, I will be bookmarking the pages of Michelle's book for years to come. Fifty women who teach us that famous isn't about how many people know your name and that brave often looks like pressing on even when you're afraid. My daughter and I are both indebted to Michelle for introducing us to many women we'd never met before and are sure never to forget."

—**Lisa-Jo Baker**,
community manager for (in)courage and
author of *Surprised by Motherhood*

"We are, indeed, surrounded by such a great cloud of witnesses. In the pages of this book, Michelle DeRusha skillfully introduces us to extraordinary women who lived boldly and bravely and who planted their feet solidly on faith. Often their unwavering belief resulted in excommunication, mistreatment, torture, or even death. In the face of some of the same questions, temptations, and doubts we encounter today, these women were pioneers. Their stories give the church of today—men and women alike—a courageous and brave example of living faith and of living out faith, the evidence of things unseen."

—**Deidra Riggs**,
managing editor of *The High Calling*
and founder of *Jumping Tandem*

"This beautiful book is an invitation to a journey—a journey that moves from kitchens to slums to plantations . . . and always straight to the heart of God. Pick up this book and let your very soul brush up against the fringes of the hearts of our sisters, whose stories span centuries of our collective faith. In this thoroughly researched and well-written work, Michelle DeRusha invites us into the lives of fifty women whose stories are *our* stories. This book inspired me, challenged me, and made me feel so proud to be a woman who belongs to Jesus."

—Jennifer Dukes Lee,
author of *Love Idol*

"Beautifully written, accessible, inspiring, and relevant, this book is a welcome reminder and celebration of the everyday women of valor who came before us. It is a gift to the whole church."

—Sarah Bessey,
author of *Jesus Feminist*

"I love it when a woman champions other women. Through Michelle's stories, I am reminded of how our generations of women stand on the shoulders of so many giants in our faith."

—Idelette McVicker,
founder and editor-in-chief at
SheLoves Magazine

50 WOMEN
Every Christian
Should Know

50 WOMEN
Every Christian
Should Know

LEARNING FROM HEROINES OF THE FAITH

MICHELLE DERUSHA

BakerBooks

a division of Baker Publishing Group
Grand Rapids, Michigan

Published by Baker Books
a division of Baker Publishing Group
P.O. Box 6287, Grand Rapids, MI 49516-6287
www.bakerbooks.com

Printed in the United States of America

Library of Congress Cataloging-in-Publication Data

De Rusha, Michelle.
    50 women every Christian should know : learning from heroines of the faith / Michelle DeRusha.
        pages cm
    Includes bibliographical references.
    ISBN 978-0-8010-1587-8 (pbk.)
    1. Christian women—Biography. I. Title. II. Title: Fifty women every Christian should know.
  BR1713.D47 2014
  270.092'52—dc23   2014012774
  [B]

Published in association with the Books & Such Literary Agency.

14 15 16 17 18 19 20   7 6 5 4 3 2 1

To my mother, Maureen—
my own personal heroine of the faith

And in memory of my grandmothers,
Elizabeth and Eileen

Contents

Contents

Contents

Acknowledgments

As you might imagine, a book featuring fifty women and spanning more than nine hundred years requires a fair bit of research and work to bring to fruition. I am grateful to a number of people who helped enormously along the way, including:

Chad Allen, editorial director at Baker Books, who took a significant leap of faith when he hired an unpublished writer to tackle a formidable project.

Anne Marie Miller, for your editing expertise and your excellent eye for detail.

The entire Baker Books team, including Jessica English, Ruth Anderson, Brianna DeWitt, Elizabeth Kool, and Lauren Carlson.

My agent, Rachelle Gardner, who convinced Chad Allen that I was the woman for the job. Thank you for your faith in me as a writer.

The staff at the University of Nebraska–Lincoln Love Library and the Lincoln City Libraries.

My blog readers, for encouraging me and cheering me on, especially when I hit the wall at thirty women.

Warren Wiersbe, for graciously reading an early draft of the manuscript and offering his blessing.

Deidra Riggs, for delivering a double chocolate cupcake to my door when I discovered, five days before the final manuscript was due, that I'd written about only forty-nine instead of fifty women.

My dad, who encouraged me to quit my day job before I had a book contract in hand. Thanks for your faith and confidence in me, Dad.

My boys, Noah and Rowan, who asked every day when I picked them up at school, "What number are you on? Did you finish yet?" Thanks for keeping me on task, guys.

My husband, Brad, who listened to me rattle on about fifty different women for eight months, encouraged me when I wanted to quit, and took the kids on countless hikes while I hunkered down in the library.

To my mom, Maureen; my aunts, Kathy, Maureen, Pat, and JoAnn; and my grandmothers, Elizabeth and Eileen—*you* are my personal heroines of the faith. Thank you for showing me how it's done.

And finally, to the fifty women featured in this book. You are my sisters in faith, women of valor, heroines all. Thank you for your courage, your inspiration, your determination. Thank you for paving the way. *Eshet Chayil!*

Introduction

Before I started to write this book, I had already set each of these fifty women on a pedestal, in a place of honor and respect. I admired them, even revered them. Their names alone left me a little bit awestruck. But would I relate to them? I wondered. Would they speak to me personally? Would their stories resonate with me right now, here in the middle of my everyday, ordinary life? I assumed no. I assumed this was merely history, not applicable to me.

And I was wrong.

I knew the life stories of the following fifty women would be fascinating and inspiring, but I didn't expect their stories to impact my personal twenty-first-century life. I didn't expect to relate to these women as real people. After all, as the subtitle states, the fifty women included in this book are *heroines* of the Christian faith. These women saved lives. They founded new denominations. They walked new paths. They advocated for the poor, the sick, the dying, and the neglected. Some even died for their faith. Their stories and contributions span nine hundred years of Christian history. They were missionaries, preachers, writers, abolitionists, doctors, educators, and activists—true leaders in every sense of the word. They are women who are known far and wide and whose very lives are a testament to the Christian faith: Teresa of Ávila. Florence Nightingale. Catherine Booth. Amy Carmichael. Harriet Tubman. Corrie ten Boom. Dorothy Day. We know their names.

As I researched each of these women, my preconceived assumptions were dismantled one by one. I assumed these spiritual giants never struggled in their faith, but Lottie Moon, Mother Teresa, Madeleine L'Engle, and several others proved me wrong. I assumed these women were never swayed by earthly temptations or materialistic desires, but Teresa of Ávila and Elizabeth Fry set me straight. I assumed these Christian heroines never questioned their God-given calling, but Hannah More, Ruth Bell Graham, and Ida Scudder turned that notion on its head. I assumed these leaders were all born and bred die-hard Christians from the start, but Edith Stein, Pandita Ramabai, and Simone Weil demonstrated that age and history are no match for God's transformative power. I assumed each of these women was virtually flawless and morally spotless, yet every one of them turned out to be fallible, just like me.

What I discovered in researching and writing this book is that the stories of these fifty women are our stories too. True, many of them lived centuries ago, in places, times, and circumstances far removed from our own. But their battles are our battles. Their grief is our grief. Their doubts and questions are our doubts and questions. We walk similar valleys. We scale similar mountains. We weep the same tears of anguish and triumph in similar moments of joy. Their love for God mirrors our own. Behind the long list of accomplishments and contributions are real women with fears, struggles, challenges, distractions, and sorrows much like ours.

While we have never suffered through the atrocities of life in a concentration camp, we can understand something of Corrie ten Boom's anguish and loss. Although we haven't forged an unmarked path as the first ordained female minister, we can relate to the insecurity and fear Antoinette Brown Blackwell faced along the way. While most of us haven't founded a mission or preached to thousands worldwide, we might identify with Catherine Booth's unrelenting determination.

In the end, I was surprised by how well I related to many of the women included in this book. The fact that they lived decades or even centuries ago didn't matter. The fact that their vocations and their callings varied dramatically from mine was irrelevant. The fact that many of their names are known and esteemed was not important. In short, I observed my own struggles, flaws, desires, and joys reflected in their stories and in their lives. I finally understood that these women are not only our heroines, they are also our sisters in faith.

1

Hildegard of Bingen

"Say and Write What You See and Hear"

$(1098-1179)$

At first she ignored it entirely. Although she had heard the message loud and clear, she didn't pay any attention. After all, the order was a radical one. *Say and write what you see and hear*, he had said. But she ignored him. What was she—a nun sequestered in a German convent, a woman living in the twelfth century—supposed to do with that message? How could she follow a command so counter-cultural, so revolutionary? Not knowing how to respond, she ignored God's call . . . until the day came when she could ignore it no longer.

"Say and Write What You See and Hear"

As her parents' tenth child, Hildegard was dedicated to the church as a tithe when she was eight years old. At age sixteen she officially "took the veil" and entered the convent of Disibodenberg, near Bingen,

Germany, as a Benedictine nun. Hildegard was elected abbess of the convent in 1136, and it was around this time that the visions she had experienced since she was a young child began to intensify and were clearly revealed to her as interpretations of the Scriptures.

"And it came to pass in the eleven hundred and forty-first year of the Incarnation of Jesus Christ, Son of God, when I was forty-two years and seven months old, that the heavens were opened and a blinding light of exceptional brilliance flowed through my entire brain," wrote Hildegard in the preface of her first major visionary work, *Scivias*. "And so it kindled my whole heart and breast like a flame, not burning but warming. . . . And suddenly I understood the meaning of the expositions of the books, that is to say of the Psalter, the evangelists and other catholic books of the Old and New Testaments."[1]

Not long after this vision, Hildegard received a more specific communication from God, encouraging her to take up the pen: "O fragile one, ash of ash and corruption of corruption, say and write what you see and hear."[2] And just so there was no mistaking the command, this particular vision was repeated three more times to Hildegard on three separate occasions. Initially she resisted, and you can imagine why. God seemed to be instructing Hildegard to do what virtually no other woman was doing at the time. As a woman and a nun living during a time in which most women were illiterate and certainly not encouraged to write or preach, she was terrified and overwhelmed by the directive.

Hildegard did her best to ignore God's command until finally he made it impossible for her to do so any longer. She succumbed to illness, an illness she believed was a direct result of her disobedience: "Although I heard and saw these things, because of doubt and a low opinion (of myself) and because of the diverse sayings of men, I refused for a long time the call to write, not out of stubbornness, but out of humility, until weighed down by the scourge of God, I fell onto a bed of sickness."[3]

Hildegard overcame two major obstacles in order to produce the great volume of writing for which she is remembered. First, there was the fact of her gender, a significant barrier. Second was the extent of her education. Male theologians in the twelfth century benefited from years of a classical education, including a practical and theoretical understanding of Latin, as well as music, arithmetic, geometry, astronomy, theology, and sometimes even law and medicine. Although she learned to read and write in German and Latin, Hildegard's education was rudimentary at best. As biographer Sabina Flanagan writes, "For someone to write on theology who lacked such a background and was also a woman was a bold step indeed."[4]

Yet try as she might to ignore the call to write, she couldn't suppress God's persistent command. Finally, desperate and ill, Hildegard reached out to her friend and confidant Bernard, the Abbot of Clairvaux, for advice. Not only did the abbot reassure her, he was also instrumental in gaining Pope Eugenius's official sanction of her writing. And with that, Hildegard was free to record the visions that would eventually comprise three comprehensive theological works: *Scivias* (*Know the Ways*), *Liber Vitae Meritorum* (*The Book of Life's Merits*), and *Liber Divinorum Operum* (*The Book of Divine Works*).

Sin, Sex, Science, and Everything In Between

Hildegard wrote the six-hundred-page *Scivias* over a period of ten years, juggling the writing and editing with her many duties as head of the convent. *Scivias* is divided into three books, with each book following a similar format: a description of the visions and then the explanation that Hildegard received from God. Vacillating between concrete and abstract language, *Scivias* covers a wide range of topics, including creation, the fall of Lucifer and Adam, the church and its sacraments, and redemption, concluding with an apocalyptic ending of the last judgment and the creation of the new heaven and earth.

Hildegard's *Liber Vitae Meritorum* (*The Book of Life's Merits*) was written between 1158 and 1163 and is primarily concerned with the vices that plague humans over the course of their lives. The book is comprised of six visions encompassing thirty-five sins, with a corresponding punishment and penance for each. Because of this emphasis on punishment, some critics view this work as a preface to the development of the theology of purgatory that would become more prevalent later in the Middle Ages.

Part three of her theological trilogy, *Liber Divinorum Operum* (*The Book of Divine Works*), is considered her most mature and impressive achievement. The book is comprised of ten visions, with the central part of the work focused on the opening chapter of the Gospel of John.

Hildegard didn't limit herself to theological writings, and in some ways, her medical and scientific writings are even more intriguing than her theological works. Because they are not written in her typical visionary format, don't contain any reference to a divine source, and are written in a mix of Latin and German, some scholars question whether Hildegard is even the author of these works, which include *Physica* (*Natural History*) and *Causae et Curae* (*Causes and Cures*). Many also question whether they were based on her actual medical experience and observations or were simply a compilation of ancient practices and local medical lore.

Physica includes two hundred short chapters on plants, followed by sections about the elements, jewels and precious stones, fish, birds, mammals, and reptiles. Throughout the book Hildegard gives practical medical, dietary, and other advice mixed with bits of local color. For instance, she tells us that the peach tree was more useful for medicine than for food, with its bark, leaves, and kernels used in remedies for skin infections, bad breath, and headaches. Cherry seeds, on the other hand, when pounded and mixed with bear fat, were used to treat skin disorders and, when ingested without the bear fat, to kill intestinal worms.

Causae et Curae differs from *Physica* in its discussion of more than two hundred specific diseases and maladies—including baldness, migraines, asthma, nosebleeds, epilepsy, and sterility—and their cures. Rather than avoiding the topic of human sexuality altogether, Hildegard approached it both pragmatically and poetically, without a hint of prudishness. Not only did she describe sexual intercourse and conception, she also included a rare account of the nature of sexual pleasure from the woman's point of view. The result was that *Causae et Curae* addressed the topic of human sexuality more comprehensively than any writings by her contemporaries.

While she worked on *Liber Divinorum Operum*, Hildegard also wrote a number of musical works, poetry, dozens of letters, and a play, *Ordo Virtutum* (*Play of Virtues*), which was performed at her convent. During this time she also traveled to monastic communities in Wurzburg and Kitzingen to preach and, in 1160, to Trier, where she preached in public, a highly unusual act for a woman at that time. She traveled twice more to preach—to Cologne and Werden around 1163 and, in 1170, to Zwiefalten.

Listening and Obeying

The visions Hildegard received from God impacted not only her writing but her life and the lives of the nuns she managed as well. While she was writing *Scivias*, Hildegard suddenly announced one day that she had received a command from God to relocate her convent from Disibodenberg to Rupertsberg, about nineteen miles away. The monks strongly opposed this proposal, as did many of the parents of the young nuns in her convent. They couldn't fathom why Hildegard would want to move her nuns from relative comfort amid lush vineyards and rolling hills to a hardscrabble, bare-bones existence with fewer amenities. They also accused her of suffering from delusions.

Faced with such strong opposition and accusation, Hildegard collapsed into illness again. When an abbot saw the extent of her suffering, he deemed her illness a divine intervention, and Hildegard was granted permission to move the convent. She purchased the site, and she and twenty of her nuns traveled on foot over a day's journey from the well-established, stone-built monastery to the dilapidated quarters at Rupertsberg.

"They said, 'What is the point of this, that noble and wealthy nuns should move from a place where they wanted for nothing to such

23

great poverty?'" wrote Hildegard later. "But we were awaiting the grace of God, who showed us this place, to come to our aid. After the burden of these troubles God rained grace upon us."[5]

Toward the end of her life, when Hildegard was in her eighties, she received word from God allowing her to bury an excommunicated nobleman at the convent. Hildegard defied her superiors by hiding the grave when they ordered that the body be exhumed, and as a result, the entire convent community was excommunicated, and—most disturbing to Hildegard—banned from singing. While she complied with the punishment and avoided singing and communion, she ignored the order to exhume the corpse. Instead, Hildegard appealed to higher church authorities and succeeded in having the punishment lifted just six months before her death in 1179.

Feminist, Saint, or Both?

Hildegard von Bingen was a writer, composer, naturalist, theologian, abbess, and visionary. She founded a convent; traveled the countryside as a preacher; corresponded and interacted with the pope, bishops, and other ecclesiastical leaders; and produced a body of written work that far exceeded most of her male contemporaries. While her list of accomplishments may read like an accomplished twenty-first-century résumé, the reality is that she was born more than nine hundred years ago, during a time when most women could neither read nor write. Today Hildegard of Bingen is celebrated by many as a feminist.

Although the Roman Catholic Church recognized Hildegard as a "prophetess," she was not officially made a saint in the church until May 2012, when Pope Benedict XVI ordered her name inscribed in the "catalogue of saints." In October 2012, Pope Benedict also named Hildegard a Doctor of the Church (meaning her teachings are recommended doctrine), making her one of only four women—including Teresa of Ávila, Catherine of Siena, and Thérèse of Lisieux—to be so honored.

24

Whether you consider her a feminist, a saint, or a little bit of both, one thing is certain: Hildegard of Bingen serves us well as a woman of faith, even today, more than nine centuries after her death. She is an example of courage, perseverance, and trust in the face of daunting obstacles and against steep odds. When Hildegard heard the voice of God, she listened and obeyed in faith.[6]

2

Saint Birgitta (Bridget) of Sweden

God's Emissary

(1303 – 1373)

Birgitta Persson made a name for herself before she even entered the world.

When her mother, Ingeborg, was several months pregnant with Birgitta (who was named after her father, the knight Birger Persson), she was miraculously rescued from a shipwreck by the king's brother. Although dozens died in the wreck, Ingeborg survived the tragedy. In a vision she experienced the night following her rescue, a person dressed in brilliant, glowing clothing informed Ingeborg that she had been saved because of the good she bore in her womb, a gift given to her from God. A few months later, on the night of Birgitta's birth, an elderly priest in the local parish experienced a vision as well, in which Mary appeared to him with a book in her hands, informing him that a girl had been born "whose voice will be heard throughout the world with admiration."[1]

The Impediment of Marriage

Despite her auspicious beginnings, the girl who later became known as Saint Birgitta of Sweden (and by English speakers as Saint Bridget of Sweden) did not immediately show signs of the mysticism that would eventually lead to her canonization. In fact, for the first three years of her life she didn't speak a single syllable, leading her parents to fear she was a mute. Finally, when she was nearly four years old, Bridget began to talk, surprising everyone by uttering not rudimentary words and phrases but fully articulated sentences.

By the time she was a young teenager, Bridget aspired to lead the life of a holy woman. But as she was one of only two surviving daughters of an eminent Swedish family, religious life wasn't an option. Despite her reluctance, when she was thirteen years old Bridget wed the eighteen-year-old nobleman Ulf Gudmarsson.

Bridget landed in a tricky position. In the fourteenth century, the Roman Catholic Church still maintained that marriage was an inferior state. The traditional view of the three states of womanhood—virginity, marriage, and widowhood—emphasized virginity first and foremost as the only state in which women could achieve true union with Christ, as well as be recognized as a saint by the church itself. As biographer Bridget Morris notes, "Marriage, which involves sexual activity, was regarded by the Church as incompatible with a woman's aspirations to live a godly life of the highest kind."[2]

There were, however, a few exceptions to this doctrine: if the girl had been forced into marriage or sexual activity against her will, if her marriage was not consummated, or if she lived with her husband in partial or complete abstention from sexual activity. Bridget chose the latter option. The couple lived chastely for at least one year after their marriage, and then, when they did engage in sexual relations, it was always with the goal of pregnancy. The couple prayed diligently for a child, and they were generously rewarded—Bridget bore eight children, all of whom lived beyond infancy, a rarity in the Middle Ages.

Although marriage had gained a level of acceptability by the time Bridget was canonized, the church still reserved the highest state of sanctity for virgins. In fact, during the canonization process for Bridget's contemporary, Saint Catherine of Siena, a Dominican advocate for the saint argued that given her unmarried state, Catherine was superior to Bridget.[3]

Bridget and Ulf were married for twenty-eight years, and while it was an affectionate and loving marriage, it's clear from her own writing that Bridget was also at least somewhat relieved when her husband died. "When I buried my husband, I buried him with all bodily love," she wrote, "and although I loved him with all my heart, I should not wish to buy back his life, not with the least money."[4] With that pronouncement, Bridget discarded the ring her husband had given her, declaring that it reminded her too much of her earthly ties. She was now free to pursue the holy life and the path to sainthood that she had always desired.

"My Bridge and My Channel"

A few days after her husband's death, Bridget experienced a vision calling her to religious life. As she prayed in her private chapel, she witnessed a bright cloud, within which was suspended the likeness of a human being. "Woman, hear me; I am your God, who wishes to speak with you," the voice said. "Fear not, for I am the Creator of all, and not a deceiver. I do not speak to you for your sake, but for the sake of the salvation of others. . . . You shall be my bridge and my channel, and you shall hear and see spiritual things, and my Spirit shall remain with you even until your death."[5]

Up to this point, Bridget had wrestled with whether to fulfill her calling as a cloistered monastic or as a religious figure who would remain in contact with the world. The specificity of this vision may have allowed Bridget the flexibility to pursue a religious life in which she was very much out in the world. While many of her predecessors experienced personal, intimate visions in which they were united with Christ in transcendent love, Bridget's vision was a call to action, a command to serve as a conduit—a "bridge and a channel"—of God's love for others.

This specific calling fit well with the role to which Bridget was already accustomed. In fact, earlier in her life, she'd not only taught her husband to read and use the Franciscan Little Office of the Blessed Virgin Mary, she was also entrusted with the education of the young King Magnus Eriksson of Sweden and his wife, Queen Blanca, despite that she was only three years older than the king himself.

Bridget was related to the king through her mother's side of the family and benefited greatly from that connection during her lifetime. In 1346, when she founded the Order of the Brigittines after the death of her husband (an order still in existence today), King Magnus donated his former castle, on the shores of Lake Wettern in Vadstena, Sweden, as a residence for the nuns. Bridget, however, did not enter her own convent. She embarked on a different mission altogether.

Radical Revelations

In 1349, Bridget received a vision from God that determined the course of the rest of her life: "Go to Rome . . . and you are to stay there in Rome until you see the supreme pontiff and the emperor there at the same time in Rome, and you shall announce my words to them."[6] She heeded the calling and set out for Rome that same year, never to return to her native country of Sweden.

In a time when mystics were often deemed heretics and messengers of the devil, Bridget's visions and her subsequent writings were nothing short of radical. Her messages were directed specifically at powerful, influential men and often predicted dire outcomes if they did not take note of God's commands. For example, in Book IV of her *Revelations*, Bridget attacked the corrupt and decayed moral state of Rome. She compared the city to a meadow overgrown with thistles, desperately in need of a thorough weeding with a sharp iron, a cleansing with fire, and plowing by a pair of oxen.[7] She described the shocking, immoral behavior of the canons, priests, and deacons, whom she called "the devil's whoremongers,"[8] for abandoning clerical dress and customs and living in sin with mistresses in their own homes while still conducting daily Masses. She compared nunneries to brothels, accused monks of failing to follow their own rules, and criticized laypeople for practicing such rampant polygamy that wives and mistresses were giving birth at the same time in the same house. She also blamed the demise of the church and society on the fact that the pope had abandoned Rome to live in a luxurious palace in Avignon, France. "Don't be surprised, my Lord, that I call Rome unfortunate," she wrote in *Revelations*. "The Catholic faith may soon go under. . . . Some of the priesthood still love God, but with the pope not being there, they feel fatherless."[9]

These searing criticisms of noblemen and the clergy were extraordinarily courageous, especially given her status as a widowed woman. As a result, Bridget was not immune from vicious attacks against her character, as well as accusations of heresy. It's said that at one point, as she walked down a narrow alley in Rome, a nobleman whom she'd lambasted a few days earlier intentionally dumped the dirty water from his washbasin out the window and onto Bridget's head. While she had friends in Rome, she was generally viewed with suspicion or outright hatred and was constantly threatened with imprisonment and even death by burning at the stake. Most likely she was spared such a death because her criticisms were directed at individual popes and the state of Rome in general, rather than at the institution of the Roman Catholic Church itself.

Bridget was determined to succeed in her calling, and her wish was fulfilled—albeit temporarily—when Pope Urban V returned to Rome in 1368, parading into the city at the side of Emperor Charles IV. By 1370, however, Urban had retreated to Montefiascone, where Bridget was granted permission to appeal to him in person. Ultimately she failed to persuade him to return to Rome.

30

In Book IV of *Revelations* she also detailed the vision she received from the Virgin Mary, noting that if the pope returned to Avignon, he would "receive a blow or a puff of wind so that his teeth will gnash or be knocked out, his sight will become dim and dark and his limbs will tremble."[10] When Pope Urban succumbed to a sudden illness and died in Avignon just days after his return, Bridget's prophecy was deemed fulfilled.

Perseverance in Trust

Bridget's determination to see the papacy restored to Rome did not diminish over the remainder of her life. Just five days before her death in 1373, she appealed to Pope Gregory XI for the last time, despite the fact that she'd been told by God in a vision that she would not live to see the pope's return to Rome. "If Gregory asks for signs, give him three," she wrote to her confessor, the priest Alfonso Pecha. "That God has spoken wonderful words through a woman. To what purpose is not for the salvation of souls and their bettering. . . . It is my will that he come now, this fall, and that he comes to stay. Nothing is dearer to me than this: that he come to Italy."[11]

Some might say Bridget ultimately failed in her God-given calling. After all, she dedicated much of her life to restoring the pope to Rome, yet she didn't live to see that mission come to fruition. Likewise, she founded her monastic order at Vadstena, yet she was never a true member of the order herself, nor did she ever return to Sweden to see the results of her vision.

However, Bridget served in an extraordinarily unique capacity during her life, not only as a prophetic visionary but also as a political and social emissary who courageously criticized the moral decline of society, even at the risk of ostracism, excommunication, and death.

Even more important, perhaps, is that Bridget never wavered in her faithful trust in God. Despite the fact that she witnessed few concrete results after nearly three decades of effort, she persevered in obedience and trusted God's calling for her. Pope Gregory XI eventually made his solemn reentry into Rome on January 17, 1377, four years after Bridget's death, and while she did not witness the historic event in her own lifetime, she never doubted God's word that it would eventually come to be. Bridget of Sweden reminds us that although we may not always see God's promises entirely fulfilled in our own lifetime, the contributions we make in faith and trust are a necessary and important part of his ultimate plan.[12]

3

Julian of Norwich

"And All Shall Be Well"

(*c. 1342 – c. 1416*)

The solemn group processed to the cell as the final notes of the somber requiem hung in the air. Making the sign of the cross, the bishop blessed the space and led the woman inside, sprinkling ashes over her head and shoulders and scattering them across the cold, stone floor. Then, leaving the woman inside the tiny, barren room, he stepped across the threshold, shutting the heavy wooden door behind him and bolting the lock from the outside. Julian of Norwich, the woman who remained alone behind the locked door, would spend more than forty years in the small room, crossing the threshold only one time—when her corpse was carried over it to the grave.

The Life of an Anchoress

Julian of Norwich was a medieval anchoress—a holy woman who sequestered herself in order to devote her entire life to God. The

33

practice of such extreme solitude was rooted in the traditions of the fourth-century Desert Fathers, who retreated from the cities to live alone in poverty and austerity in order to nurture a deep connection with God. The English word *anchorite* is derived from the Greek verb meaning "to retire." An anchoress literally retired from the world, sealing herself into a small enclosure, called an anchorhold, which was usually adjacent or connected to the village church. The rite of enclosure, with the sprinkling of dust, the final blessings, and the bolting of the door, symbolized the death of the anchoress—she was considered dead to the world, entombed with Christ.[1]

The anchoress, though confined, was not entirely secluded. Julian's anchorhold had at least two windows, as was typically the case. One window opened to the inside of the chapel so that she could follow the daily Mass and receive Holy Communion. A second window opened to either the outside or a parlor so that the anchoress could counsel visitors who sought her guidance. And then finally the door opened to a separate room in which a servant stayed. (This room was connected to the outside world so the servant could come and go.) The servant was responsible for the real-world necessities of the anchoress—cooking, cleaning, emptying the chamber pot, shopping, and other chores that the anchoress was not allowed to do for herself.

Julian never mentioned her role as counselor or spiritual advisor in her own writing, but we know from her medieval contemporary Margery Kempe that she performed this duty. Kempe wrote in her memoir about visiting the anchoress in 1412 or 1413 to seek advice and spiritual counsel regarding her own dramatic visions. Modern scholars surmise that while most of her daily hours were devoted to prayer and contemplation, Julian probably spent a few hours a week counseling visitors through her window.

Contemporary scholars know little about Julian's personal life, including her birth name, birth year, and year of death, though it's estimated that she was born around 1342–43 and died in approximately 1416. Nor do they know the exact date and the reason for her entry into the anchorhold. Some speculate that she was a laywoman, perhaps a widow whose husband and children had perished in the

Black Death, which is thought to have decimated up to a third of Norwich's population at that time. Other scholars suggest she may have been a nun. What we can conclude is that Julian likely considered the life of an anchoress to be the best way to devote her life to prayer and God.

The Visions

As a young girl, Julian prayed specifically for three rather unusual gifts from God: to see and experience Christ's crucifixion as if she were actually present, to suffer from a near-death illness, and to be afflicted with "three wounds"—contrition, compassion, and a full-hearted longing for God.[2]

Her prayers were answered in the spring of 1373, when, at the age of thirty, Julian lay on her deathbed for seven days. A priest was summoned to administer last rites, and when he placed a crucifix at eye level, he urged her to fix her gaze on the form of Jesus as she journeyed from this life to the next. As her breathing became painful and labored, she looked steadily at the cross, until "suddenly in that moment all of my pain left me, and I was as sound, particularly in the upper part of my body, as ever I was before or since."[3] Julian concluded that she was experiencing a miraculous relief from the pain in death, and those around her assumed she was on the verge of dying as well. At one point, her mother, thinking her daughter had passed, reached out to close her eyes.

But Julian didn't die. Instead, over a period of days, she experienced a series of sixteen visions, which she would later refer to as "shewings" in *The Short Text* and *The Long Text*, the writings that would compose *The Revelations of Divine Love*. She saw the bloody body of Christ on the cross—not static and immobile, but in full color, as if he were suffering right there before her eyes. Later she witnessed another vision as Christ's countenance transformed from the pall of death into one of joy and peace. She also marveled as she was shown "something small, no bigger than a hazel-nut, lying in the palm of my hand," a vision on which she would later base her theology of creation.[4] During these visions, Julian was also assaulted by the devil, whom she described as appearing in a foul stench, a great heat, smoke, and chatterings and mutterings in her ears.

Initially Julian chalked up these visions as illness-induced hallucinations—"rantings," as she called them. It wasn't until a priest defined them as spiritual visions that she began to have second thoughts about their nature and source. Still, she was quick to point out later that it was not the revelations themselves that singled her out as special or holy, but the fact that these visions helped her to love God more deeply and fully, and thus, through her, helped others do the same. "I am not good because of the revelations," wrote Julian in *The Long Text*, "but only if I love God better. . . . For I am sure there are many who never had revelations or visions, but only the common teaching of Holy Church, who love God better than I."[5]

Love Was His Meaning

Despite the fact that Julian lived in a time of rampant disease, death, and turmoil, her theology was surprisingly optimistic. As biographer Grace Jantzen points out, although Julian experienced sixteen separate "shewings," all sixteen—from the opening words of the first book to the last chapter—revolved around a single consistent theme: God's everlasting and ever-present love. "Know it well, love was his meaning," she wrote in *The Revelations*. "Who reveals it to you? Love. What did he reveal to you? Love. Why does he reveal it to you? For love. Remain in this, and you will know more of the same."[6] The passion—Christ's crucifixion—was, as Julian understood it, the supreme manifestation of God's love.

Julian's liberal theology was far from typical for the time, but her status as an anchoress protected her from accusations of heresy. While many of her contemporaries argued that the Black Death was a sign of God's punishment of the wicked, Julian believed in a broader, more merciful theology, suggesting that God demonstrated only love, never wrath, for his people. Julian even applied her understanding of God's love to sin, which, contrary to the medieval Roman

Catholic Church's stance, she viewed not as evil or the work of the devil but as a necessity for bringing one to self-knowledge. Sin, she argued, was a necessary part of free will because it created a greater understanding of the need for God's grace. She even went as far as to claim that God did not forgive our sins. "I saw truly that our Lord was never angry, and never will be," she wrote. "Because he is God, he is good, he is truth, he is love, he is peace; and his power, his wisdom, his charity and his unity do not allow him to be angry. . . . And between God and our soul there is neither wrath nor forgiveness in his sight. For our soul is so wholly united, through his own goodness, that between God and our soul nothing can interpose."[7]

Delving Deeply

While Julian was certainly grateful for her revelations, she didn't simply accept them complacently without further exploration. She didn't hesitate to ask God specific questions about her visions from him, and she often grappled with his words in an attempt to uncover his truth. When God said something that puzzled her, Julian dug into it, probing for greater understanding.

For instance, in one of her visions, God said this to her: "All shall be well, and all shall be well, and all manner of thing shall be well" (an oft-quoted phrase and, incidentally, incorporated five centuries later by T. S. Eliot into his poem *Little Gidding*). For Julian, living in a plague-infested, war-torn, suffering society rife with illness, death, and dissent, this statement didn't make any sense at all. When God told Julian, "All shall be well," she questioned him, probing for a sufficiently concrete answer that could be applied practically in everyday life. She received an answer from God, but it wasn't as specific as she would have liked. "I saw hidden in God an exalted and wonderful mystery, which will make plain and we shall know in heaven," she wrote about her vision. "In this knowledge we shall truly see the cause why he allowed sin to come, and in this sight we shall rejoice forever."[8] Sometimes, as in this case, Julian was forced to accept that a concrete answer couldn't always be uncovered, and that

God's proclamations required faith rather than a practical, rational understanding.

You Will Not Be Overcome

Julian wrestled with and contemplated the meaning of her visions over her entire lifetime, and *The Revelations of Divine Love* was her attempt to communicate God's message to her fellow Christians. Although many questions remained unanswered, Julian's conclusion—her final words in *The Revelations*—offered light and hope:

> And this word: Thou shalt not be overcome, was said full clearly and full mightily, for assuredness and comfort against all tribulations that may come. He said not: Thou shalt not be tempested, thou shalt not be travailed, thou shalt not be afflicted; but He said: Thou shalt not be overcome. God willeth that we take heed to these words, and that we be ever strong in sure trust, in weal and woe. For He loveth and enjoyeth us, and so willeth He that we love and enjoy Him and mightily trust in Him; and all shall be well.[9]

While she didn't always find a concrete answer, especially to her questions about the existence of sin and suffering, she did offer a convicting example of the depth and breadth of God's love—words as deeply compelling to modern readers as they were to her contemporaries more than five hundred years ago.[10]

4

Catherine of Siena

A Holy Resolution of the Heart

(1347–1380)

When she was twelve years old, Catherine Benincasa's parents began to make arrangements for her, their youngest of twenty-four children, to be married. Catherine, however, had other plans. Unbeknownst to them, she had taken a private vow of chastity five years earlier, and she had every intention of entering the convent and dedicating her life to Christ.

"It would be easier to melt a stone than to tear this holy resolution out of my heart," Catherine told her parents. "You only waste time in trying to fight against it."[1] Her parents were devastated. But after they'd both wept bitterly over Catherine's fierce declaration, her father, Giacomo, surprised everyone by acquiescing to his daughter's resolution. "My dearest daughter, it is far from us to set ourselves against the will of God in any way, and it is from Him that your purpose comes," he told Catherine. "Keep your promise and live as the Holy Spirit tells you to live. We shall never disturb you again in your life of prayer and devotion, or try to tempt you from your sacred work."[2] He then warned his wife and children not to lay any obstacles in Catherine's spiritual path.

Giacomo, a dye-maker, arranged a small space for Catherine near his workrooms in the basement of their home, a place where she could be quiet amid the bustle of a busy house. Catherine used a wood plank for a bed and a wooden log for a pillow. A few stone steps led from the 10-by-16-foot room to a small, barred window that overlooked the narrow lane behind the Benincasa home. Catherine spent three years in this cell, emerging only to attend early morning Mass at the Dominican church in the village. She prayed relentlessly; ate only herbs, bread, and water; and slept only two hours each night. She also scourged herself with an iron chain three times a day—once for her sins, once for the sins of all living people, and once for the souls in purgatory—as was the custom of her spiritual father, Saint Dominic. Catherine's mother, Lapa, appalled by her daughter's extreme self-denial and punishment, tried every means possible to subdue her, but her efforts were futile. In the tradition of the Desert Fathers, whom she had read so much about in her youth, Catherine's underground cell-like chamber became her desert. She was steadfast and immovable in her discipline.

Going Forth without Fear

After three years in the underground room, Catherine rejoined her family, resumed her domestic duties in her father's home, and officially joined the Third Order of Saint Dominic. As a Dominican tertiary, Catherine was not required to live in the convent. Instead, she remained at home and dedicated her time to caring for victims of the Black Plague, which killed 80,000 in Siena alone, including her own brother and sister and eight nieces and nephews. She also visited local prisons and attended public executions, where she consoled the accused with prayer.

Catherine continued to communicate constantly with God, and as she entered her late twenties, she began to hear a recurring command from him to serve the greater public—a command she initially questioned. "Go forth without fear, in spite of reproach," God told her. "I have a mission for thee to fulfill. Wheresoever thou goest I will be with thee. I will never leave thee but will visit thee and direct all thy actions."[3] The mission, Catherine would soon learn, was to reform the church and restore the papacy to Rome.

Like her contemporary, Bridget of Sweden, Catherine dedicated the remainder of her life to relocating the papacy from Avignon, where it had resided for nearly seventy-five years, to its rightful place in Rome. She launched her campaign by writing bold letters to Pope Gregory XI, urging him forward on this holy crusade:

> Press on, and fulfill with true zeal and holy what you have begun with holy resolve, concerning your return, and the holy and sweet crusade. And delay no longer, for many difficulties have occurred through delay, and the devil has risen up to prevent these things being done, because he perceives his own loss. Up, then, father, and no more negligence! . . . Pardon me, father, that I have said so many words to you. You know that through the abundance of the heart the mouth speaketh. I am certain that if you shall be the kind of tree I wish to see you, nothing will hinder you.[4]

In 1376 Catherine traveled from Siena to Avignon to visit Pope Gregory in person. Though without education, wealth, or rank, she entered the palace confidently and spoke to the pope through an interpreter, exhorting Gregory to lay aside his own self-interest and return to Rome. "Do not be a boy, be a man," Catherine boldly cajoled him.[5] Her rhetoric, though risky, was ultimately successful. Several weeks after her visit, Pope Gregory sailed from Avignon to Genoa, where he stalled, hesitant and fearful, unwilling to continue to Rome until he spoke with Catherine again. She complied, and although their conversation was not recorded, it's evident from the fact that Pope Gregory continued on to Rome that Catherine was again successful in persuading him. With Pope Gregory safely back in Rome, Catherine turned her attention to rallying support for him.

This was a time of rampant corruption within the Roman Catholic Church. With the republics and principalities of Italy revolting against the papacy, Catherine's mission was a dangerous one. In fact, at one point Catherine was nearly murdered by an incensed mob when she was sent by Pope Gregory as a peace envoy to Florence. As a group of men descended on her and her small entourage in a garden, swinging swords and clubs and bellowing her name in rage, she kneeled before them and spoke fearlessly: "I am Catherine. Do to me whatever thou wilt. But I charge you, in the name of the Almighty, to hurt none of these who are with me."[6] Confused by her lack of resistance, the men sheathed their swords, but Catherine remained kneeling, calmly stating, "I have always longed to suffer for God and His church, so if you have been appointed to kill me do not be afraid to do so."[7] Unnerved, the men dispersed, and shortly thereafter, the Florentine rulers signed a peace treaty with the pope.

Truth be told, Catherine was disappointed that she had not been allowed to give her life for God in the garden that day. "I burned with desire to suffer for the glory of God and the salvation of souls, for the reform and welfare of the Holy Church," she wrote to her confessor, Fra Raimondo delle Vigne, a few days after the dramatic scene. "My heart almost burst with the desire to give my life."[8] Yet she also realized and accepted that martyrdom was not God's will for her. It was clear to Catherine that God's mission for her was within the maelstrom of world politics.

Gregory's successor, Pope Urban VI, was equally dependent on Catherine's negotiation and peacemaking skills. He summoned her to Rome in the midst of the Great Western Schism of 1378, during which he and Pope Clement VII, who had reestablished a papacy in Avignon, fought for control. Catherine dedicated the remainder of her life to working strenuously in support of Pope Urban VI for the reformation of the church.

The fact that a woman served as a political envoy during this tumultuous time is nothing short of astounding. Her letters—more than three hundred of which have been preserved and published— illustrate her fierce determination and fearless conviction, as well as her savvy negotiation skills and her ability to influence even the most fiery and powerful political figures of the time. It was no secret that Pope Urban VI was a difficult man, prone to volatile and even violent outbursts. Catherine's ability to appease yet also persuade Pope Urban VI, as well as dozens of other high-level officials, is a remarkable testament to her steely determination and her peace-making skills.

Determined until Death

Shortly before her death at the age of thirty-three, Catherine dictated what became known as her *Dialogue*, a series of visions and reflections that came to her directly from God while she was in a state of ecstasy. Before she succumbed to the visions, she instructed her secretary to listen to the words that streamed from her mouth while she was in the throes of intimate communication with Jesus. The result, after four consecutive days of transcription, during which Catherine was physically incapacitated in an ecstatic state, was a manuscript centered on the theme of God's mercy. In Catherine's lifetime the book was circulated only among her friends and disciples, but after her death, it was printed and distributed to a wider audience. *The Dialogue* was recognized as teaching divinely inspired by the Holy Spirit, and Catherine herself came to be valued as a teacher of divine knowledge.

Throughout her thirty-three years Catherine had continued the spiritual practice of self-denial, abstaining from food and drink and often ingesting only the Eucharist as her solitary meal in an entire day. Scholars today suggest that she suffered from anorexia. Constantly weak, ill, malnourished, and rail-thin, she declined rapidly until she was bedridden, rising only to attend Mass each morning in the oratory of her home. Too weak to walk the few steps back to her bedroom herself, Catherine's skeletal body was often carried to her bed—she still slept on only a rough, wooden plank—after church.

Still, Catherine was determined to fulfill her God-given mission. Her last political push was made from her deathbed, when she wrote

Pope Urban VI a final letter, begging him to be strong and stand firm against those bent on destroying the church. "May Your Holiness understand what has to be done!" she implored the pope. "Courage, courage, for God does not despise your desire and the prayers of His servants." She signed her last letter to the pope with her standard valediction: "Sweet Jesus, Jesus love."[9] Three months later she died, praying audibly until the last moment for the church and Pope Urban VI.

Today Catherine is honored as a saint in the Roman Catholic Church and is remembered for her numerous contributions to Christianity, including her voluminous and articulate letters, her mystical revelations from God, and her unique ability to influence the most powerful political and religious men of the time. Even beyond her historical contributions, though, we admire Catherine of Siena for her strong-willed determination, her courage, and her obedience to God, no matter what the cost. God instructed his disciple to go forth without fear. Catherine never wavered in heeding that command.[10]

5

Margery Kempe

Medieval Memoirist

(c. 1373–c. 1438)

In 1934, when Colonel William Butler-Bowdon discovered an original manuscript crushed amid the historic volumes in the library of his English country house, he suspected he had uncovered a rare treasure. Little did he know that the pages he had pulled from the stacks would come to be considered the first autobiography ever written in the English language. *The Book of Margery Kempe*, lost for centuries before it was unearthed in the colonel's family library, was dictated in the early fifteenth century to two scribes by the illiterate Margery Kempe—daughter of an English mayor and Parliament member, wife of a medieval merchant, and mother to fourteen children.

Not Forsaken

Margery Kempe's narrative opens with a description of her difficult first pregnancy. Gravely ill and fearing imminent death, she summoned a priest to hear her confession. The problem, however, was that Margery hid a deep secret of a sin so atrocious she was unable to bring herself to confess it to her priest. Fearing eternal damnation as the result of her unconfessed sin, Margery was overcome by hallucinations. As images of fire-breathing devils tortured her day and night, she threatened to commit suicide, thrashing in the bed and scratching and biting herself so violently that her husband tied her to the bedposts for weeks at a time. Then, almost as abruptly as the delusions began, Christ appeared to Margery. Clad in purple silk, he sat on the edge of her bed and gently asked her, "Daughter, why hast thou forsaken me, and I forsook never thee?"[1] Before she could answer, he ascended to heaven on a beam of light, leaving Margery with a profound sense of peace and joy, as well as the desire to devote her life fully to God. This was the first of many visions Margery experienced over her lifetime.

Margery Kempe considered herself a mystic first and foremost, even above her duties as a mother and a wife. Although she bore fourteen children, she eventually negotiated a bishop-sanctioned vow of chastity with her husband after sexual relations with him became abhorrent to her. She also modeled her life after saints like Bridget of Sweden and holy women like the anchoress Julian of Norwich, who lived nearby and whom Margery met in person. She often fasted for days at a stretch, frequently waking at 2:00 a.m. to walk in the darkness to church, where she would pray on her knees until noon. As a daily penance she wore a haircloth, a rough garment made of goat's hair, beneath her gown and hid it from her husband, even when they still shared the same bed.

Margery was not a quiet mystic. Her visions prompted her to weep and wail and fall prostrate on the ground, her arms spread wide in the form of a cross, moaning, sobbing, and "roaring," as she described herself, for hours at a time. Embarrassed by his wife's outbursts, her husband would often pretend he didn't know her or slink away to a tavern or inn while they were traveling until she regained her composure. The public didn't appreciate Margery's visions either. Most of her contemporaries assumed she was intentionally creating a disturbance. As biographer Louise Collins notes, the public concluded "there was a devil in her, or else she was putting it on. She was some sort of heretic. She ought to be thrown out, arrested, got rid of."[2] As a result, public criticism and the charge of heresy dogged Margery Kempe for much of her life.

Jerusalem Journey

When she entered middle age, Margery struck a deal with her husband: she would pay off his debts with the inheritance left from her father, and he would grant her a chaste marriage and permission to travel to Jerusalem. Margery departed on the Jerusalem Journey, as it was often called, in the winter of 1413–14. While the Holy Land was considered the greatest tourist attraction of medieval times, the trip was also fraught with danger. Pilgrims were frequently attacked by robbers and often succumbed to illness and even death during the months it took to cross roiling seas, scale treacherous mountains, and traverse barren deserts as they clutched the back of a donkey and stumbled on foot to reach the final destination.

As a woman traveling without the protection of her husband, Margery also faced the unique threat of abandonment by her fellow travelers. In short, her constant chatter about religion, her pious refusal to eat meat or drink wine, and her frequent fainting and prolific tears of devotion irritated her companions. After weeks of friction and frayed patience, the group parted ways in Constance, Italy, at the foot of the Alps. Margery was left with only one companion, a feeble, elderly man whom she paid to accompany her over the formidable mountains. When the two finally descended through the deep, rocky ravines and emerged in the village of Bolzano, Italy, her former traveling companions eagerly reunited with Margery, convinced that only a God-given miracle could have protected her and the elderly man on such a punishing trip.

Ultimately, Margery made it to the Holy Land, where she toured dozens of sacred spots and shrines, including the room where Christ and his disciples ate the Last Supper together, the Pool of Siloam, the mount where Christ delivered his sermon, and finally the Church of the Holy Sepulcher, where Margery experienced her most violent and dramatic vision yet. She glimpsed the crucified Jesus himself, suspended on the cross before her eyes:

> It was granted this creature to behold so verily his precious tender body, completely rent and torn with scourges, more full of wounds than ever was a dove house of holes, hanging upon the cross with the crown of thorns upon his head, his blissful hands, his tender feet nailed to the hard tree, the rivers of blood flowing out plenteously from every member, the grisly and grievous wound in his precious side shedding out blood and water for her love and salvation, then she fell down and cried with loud voice, wonderfully turning and twisting her body on every side, spreading her arms abroad as if she should have died, and could not keep herself from crying or from these bodily movings, for the fire of love that burnt so fervently in her soul with pure pity and compassion.[3]

While weeping and praying aloud was customary behavior at the sacred sites, Margery's extreme, screaming hysteria startled the pilgrims around her. "The crying was so loud and so wonderful that it made people astonished," she wrote.[4] Later, when she returned to England, the shrill cry accompanied her, first occurring once or twice a month, then once or twice a week, and then finally multiple times each day. On one particular day, she screamed fourteen times, and she could never anticipate when the piercing sound would burst from her mouth: "Sometime in the church, sometime in the street, sometime in the chamber, sometime in the field God would send them, for she never knew time nor hour when they would come."[5]

Trials of Heresy

Margery's violent spiritual outbursts and the fact that she dressed all in white like a nun, despite that she was officially still a married woman, drew the attention of the public and both church and government officials. She was accused of being a Lollard, part of the group who proclaimed the Catholic Church to be corrupt and advocated for the reduction of the priests' authority in favor of an emphasis on Scripture alone.

En route from a pilgrimage in Spain to her own village of Lynn, Margery was overcome by an extreme vision in a Leicester church. Appalled by her dramatic display and leery that she might be a heretic, officials seized her and turned her over to the mayor, who lambasted her as a "false strumpet, a false Lollard and a false deceiver of the people" and threatened to imprison her, to which Margery responded, "I am as ready, sir, to go to prison for God's love as I am ready to go to church."[6] In the end, neither the Leicester court nor the Abbot of Leicester could find ample evidence to convict her as either a political agitator or a heretic, and she was allowed to continue her journey home.

Still, Margery couldn't refrain from speaking about her God-inspired visions at every available opportunity. Only a few days after the inquiry in Leicester, she was detained again and required to appear at a hearing before the archbishop of York. Initially she wasn't the least bit dismayed or intimidated. After all, these were the kinds of situations saints faced throughout their lives, and to be beatified as a saint was Margery's greatest ambition. However, the archbishop proved to be a formidable opponent, and at one point Margery trembled with fear at the increasingly real possibility of being burned at the stake, which was the standard medieval punishment for heretics. Yet she held her ground. When the archbishop demanded that she swear not to teach or challenge the people in his diocese, she refused, stating, "No, sir, I shall not swear, for I shall speak of God and reprove those who swear great oaths wherever I go." She also differentiated between speaking and preaching, insisting that she did not engage in the latter: "I preach not, sir, I go in no pulpit. I use but communication and good words, and that I will do while I live."[7]

The archbishop of York finally released Margery, but she continued to endure trials during her journey home and even in Lynn, when she finally returned from her pilgrimage to Spain. It wasn't until the townspeople credited her prayers with saving Lynn from a devastating fire in 1421 that she began to earn the lasting respect of both the people and the village officials.

The Book

Margery was familiar with the medieval tradition of monks, priests, nuns, and other holy people who left a record of their lives as a testament of their faith. Aspiring to follow in their footsteps on her way toward possible sainthood, Margery embarked on a similar project after hearing directly from God that he approved of her writing. "Dread you not, daughter. . . . He who writes pleases me right much," wrote Margery in Book One. "You should not please me more than you do with your writing, for daughter, by this book many a man shall be turned to me and believe therein."[8]

It's unclear exactly when Margery wrote her book, although we do know she began it long after she returned from her pilgrimages. The book is divided into two parts—the first two-thirds dictated to a scribe who died before it was finished, and the last third dictated to a priest who was initially reluctant to collaborate with such an infamously troublesome woman. Even after receiving his own vision regarding his role in writing the book, the priest constantly bemoaned the labor that was required to shape the book into publishable prose.

With its detailed descriptions of Margery's visions and prayers, the book clearly emulates the genre. But what makes it unique are the insights it offers into the life of a medieval woman, atypical though she was. Margery had the gift of storytelling, and her book brings real-world medieval characters—from the archbishop of York to her irascible traveling companions to her henpecked husband—to life.

Margery Kempe did not achieve her lifelong aspiration: the Roman Catholic Church never canonized her, and she is not considered a saint today. In fact, many contemporary scholars don't even consider her a mystic. Nonetheless, Margery and her story remain an important contribution to Christian history, not because of her status or her holiness, but because of her authenticity.

We relate to Margery because she is real and human—flawed and sometimes foolish, just like the rest of us. We see ourselves in Margery, a relatively average wife and mother, someone who wasn't born into nobility and who didn't benefit from the privilege of education or wealth, yet who strove in her daily life to heed what she heard from God. It's true, Margery Kempe isn't a saint. But that's exactly what makes her so approachable and so appealing today.[9]

6

Katharina Luther

The Deeper Story

(1499 – 1550)

The Danish philosopher Søren Kierkegaard once noted that Martin Luther might as well have married a wood plank. His point was that the famed leader of the Protestant Reformation had married Katharina von Bora for one reason only: to prove that he condoned clerical marriage. Katharina, according to Kierkegaard, was but one tiny plank in Luther's Reformation platform.[1]

A closer look at Katharina's life and personality, however, reveals a deeper story. After all, Katharina was a nun who courageously abandoned the convent during one of the most tumultuous periods in Christian history. She was a woman who risked marrying one of the most controversial men of the time—a man who could have very likely been burned as a heretic at any given moment. She was a woman who raised six children; ran a boardinghouse; oversaw a working farm complete with fruit orchards, livestock, and a fish pond;

and advised and cared for her husband, who was prone to illness and bouts of depression. Far from a mere plank in her husband's platform, Katharina von Bora was an integral part of the entire foundation.

Escape in a Herring Wagon

Little is known about Katharina's early life and childhood, including the exact date or place of her birth. Around the age of five, following the death of her mother, she was sent by her father to a Benedictine boarding school. Later, at age nine, she was placed in a Cistercian convent in Nimbschen, Germany. In 1515, two years before Luther would nail his ninety-five theses to the church door in Wittenberg, Katharina officially became a nun at the age of sixteen.

By the 1520s Luther's Reformation writings had circulated around Germany and had even made their way into the convents and monasteries, inspiring a number of monks and nuns to rebel. On Easter Eve, April 5, 1523, Luther himself arranged for Katharina and eight other nuns to escape from the convent, hidden among herring barrels in a covered wagon. As the wagon lurched into Wittenberg a few days later, a local man is said to have written to a friend, "A wagon load of vestal virgins has just come to town, all more eager for marriage than for life. May God give them husbands lest worse befall."[2]

Luther felt responsible for these women and worked diligently to find appropriate homes for them. Several of the former nuns returned to their families, one took a teaching job, and the remaining women were married—with the exception of Katharina. After two years and two failed engagements, Katharina finally suggested to Luther that he marry her himself.

She Married a Heretic

Luther had always claimed he would never marry, not because he was, as he put it, "a sexless log or stone," but "because I expect daily the death of a heretic." However, he reconsidered his position, especially after he consulted with his parents, who were overjoyed at the prospect of possible grandchildren. He also delighted in the fact that his marriage would surely "rile the pope, make the angels laugh and the devils weep, and would seal his testimony."[3] Neither Luther nor Katharina made any pretense that their marriage was for love—he married for conviction, she for convenience.

Their marriage was nothing short of scandalous at the time. Katharina, though she'd fled the convent, was, for all intents and purposes, a nun, while Luther himself was a monk. Both had taken vows of chastity. The union of a clergyman and a nun was radically revolutionary.

Luther wasn't the only one who was openly criticized for marrying. Rumors flew wildly around Wittenberg and beyond, some claiming that the two lived together before actually marrying. Even two years after their marriage, Katharina was the subject of a ruthless printed pamphlet, accusing her of acting like a chorus girl, leading a "damnable, shameful life," being "despised of all men," and forsaking Christ and earning his disfavor.[4]

There was also the fact that Luther led a dangerous life. He was honest with his wife from the start, stating matter-of-factly that if he were burned as a heretic, she would likely receive the same punishment. And then there was the age difference to consider—with nearly twenty years between them, Katharina was aware that she would likely be left a widow, even if her husband didn't die prematurely as a religious heretic. In short, marrying Martin Luther in 1525 was not only a radical, controversial, history-altering decision on Katharina's part, it was also a courageous one.

His Better Half

The union may have begun as one of conviction and convenience, but over time it grew into a marriage of mutual respect, admiration, and love for both husband and wife. Katharina affectionately referred to Luther as "Doctor," and his letters to her are peppered with pet names, including "Kitty, my rib" and "*Selbander*," which is

54

German for "better half." He also called her "My Lady," "My Lord," and, tongue-in-cheek, *"Kette,"* which is German for "chains" and a pun on her name.[5]

Although we don't have any letters written by Katharina herself, it's obvious from some of Luther's correspondence that the couple enjoyed witty repartee and a lively, lighthearted relationship. When Luther teasingly noted that polygamy was allowed in the Old Testament, Katharina retorted, "Well if it comes to that, I'll leave you and the children and go back to the cloister."[6] Even when he became gravely ill while traveling, the letters he wrote from the road revealed a teasing, tender sweetness. In 1546, on the way home from a conference with the dukes in Eisleben, Luther wrote:

> To the saintly, worrying Lady Katherine Luther, doctor at Zulsdorf and Wittenberg, my gracious dear wife: We thank you heartily for being so worried that you can't sleep, for since you started worrying about us, a fire broke out near my door and yesterday, no doubt due to your worry, a big stone, save for the dear angels, would have fallen and crushed us like a mouse in a trap. If you don't stop worrying, I'm afraid the earth will swallow us.[7]

Although Katharina and Luther shared a mutual respect and love, Katharina was also not afraid to engage in theological and political discussions with her husband and to challenge him when necessary. His colleagues, knowing how persuasive she could be, often enlisted Katharina to convince Luther of a particular action or response. And she was stubborn as well. When Luther insisted that she read the Bible cover to cover, she finally retorted, "I've read enough. I've heard enough. I know enough. Would to God I lived it."[8]

Katharina was devoted to Luther and cared for him with compassion and love during his frequent illnesses. He was prone to depression, hypochondria, and kidney stones, and it was Luther's good fortune that his wife was exceedingly skilled in medicine. She often tweaked his diet to help alleviate his kidney stones, concocted herbal remedies and poultices to quell his depression, and used massage to ease his anxiety.

Katharina was also no ordinary housewife. The family lived in an abandoned monastery called the Black Cloister, where she raised not only her own six children but, at various times, a half dozen nieces and nephews and the four orphans of a friend who had died in the plague, as well as Luther's frequent guests and student boarders. Often all forty rooms of the Black Cloister were occupied, with Katharina managing all the associated household duties, from cooking and cleaning to gardening and laundry. Although she had some domestic help, she performed much of the work herself. Katharina herded, milked, and slaughtered cattle; made butter and cheese; brewed beer; planted and harvested a garden and a fruit orchard; managed multiple livestock and poultry, including horses, cows, calves, pigs, chickens, pigeons, and geese; and caught fish from a brook that flowed through the property. Luther called her "the morning star of Wittenberg," because she rose daily at 4:00 a.m., and it's no wonder, given the amount of work she had to accomplish in a single day. He also admitted, "In domestic affairs, I defer to Katie. Otherwise I am led by the Holy Ghost."[9]

Katharina was determined to make the Black Cloister self-sustaining, not only for the present, but also because she foresaw the day when she would outlive her husband. With that fact in mind, she invested in additional real estate, snapping up another farm in Zühlsdorf, two days' travel from Wittenberg, despite the fact that Luther did not agree with her decision.

Beyond the Plank

When Luther died in 1546, many of Katharina's fears materialized. At the outbreak of the Schmalkaldic War that same year, she and the children were forced to flee Wittenberg, and when she returned, the Black Cloister was nearly destroyed. Though the building remained, the land was scorched and the livestock obliterated. Katharina was determined to rebuild, but financial constraints made living at the cloister impossible. She fled the city once again in the fall of 1552 in an effort to protect herself and her children from the Black Plague, which was ravaging Wittenberg. During that flight, she was thrown from a horse-drawn wagon, sustained massive injuries, and died three months later.

We might be tempted to diminish Katharina Luther's role in Christian history, either by overlooking her entirely or, at best, defining her, as Kierkegaard did, as nothing more than a tool Luther used to illustrate his convictions about clerical marriage. In doing so, though, we risk making a caricature of a woman who in reality was a courageous risk taker; an unsentimental, determined survivor; a savvy businesswoman; an astute advisor; a devoted wife and mother; and a woman of faith.

While she did not impact history in the public sphere as did many of the women included in this book, her legacy as the enterprising and loyal partner of Martin Luther should be acknowledged and celebrated. She may not get much credit in the history books, but Katharina Luther was an integral part of Martin Luther's success.

7

Teresa of Ávila

Afire with a Great Love for God

(1515–1582)

Teresa de Cepeda y Ahumada had a penchant for fine clothes, and her expressive fashion complemented her vivacious personality. As a young woman she draped herself in decadent fabrics and jewels, from glittering earrings, enormous brooches, and opulent rings to rich silks and exquisite lace. With her hair elaborately coiffed in the latest style and her body scented in perfume, she often spent her evenings on the town, dancing and reveling with her friends and suitors. She was equal parts effusive and temperamental, depending on the day or the hour. She also loved laughter, frivolity, gossip, and entertainment; relished lively music; and enjoyed an appetite for good food as well as the good life—"There is a time for penance, and a time for partridge," she once quipped.[1] More than anything, she craved attention and was often at the center of it.

As difficult as it is to reconcile this Teresa (bold, beautiful, materialistic, and vain) with the perception of Teresa of Ávila (mystic,

Carmelite nun, theologian, and saint), the two are indeed one and the same. So the question is, how was this fashionista socialite transformed into a faithful saint?

Wrestling Demons

Teresa de Cepeda y Ahumada was born in 1515 in Gotarrendura, Spain, the daughter of Alonso Sanchez de Cepeda and Alonso's second wife, Beatriz. She was one of twelve children in the wealthy, prestigious de Cepeda family, and she lived in a sprawling compound complete with elaborate gardens, numerous servants, and a home filled with intricate Flemish tapestries and carpets, wrought-iron chandeliers, and stately oak furniture.

Although Teresa was inclined toward the frivolous, she had a deeper, more troubled side as well. As a young girl of seven, she pored over the pages of the *Flos Sanctorum*, a popular collection of stories about the saints and martyrs. Convinced it would be more expeditious to martyr herself and go straight to heaven immediately rather than live out her entire life, she convinced her older brother to run away with her to the Moors. Once there she planned to proclaim herself a Christian and, she hoped, be beheaded for it and ascend instantly to heaven. The two siblings snuck out of the house at dawn and made it just outside the city's fortress walls before their uncle arrived on horseback and whisked them home.

After her mother died in childbirth, Teresa, by then a young teenager, put herself in the hands of the Virgin Mary, prostrating herself before Mary's statue and begging her to fill the huge gap left in her life. It was a veneration that would last a lifetime, yet it didn't wrench Teresa from the grip of frivolity just yet. In fact, if anything, her mother's death led Teresa to the brink of temptation. Fearing his daughter's honor was at stake, her father packed Teresa off to the nearby Augustinian convent, which ran a finishing school that prepared the wealthy young boarders for a devout domestic life. At Santa Maria de Gracia, Teresa wore the demeanor of a pious young woman, but on the inside, she still struggled to expel the demons that tormented her.

Two Choices

The truth was Teresa didn't want to be a nun, and she worried she wasn't suited for a life of such spiritual devotion. She watched the older nuns at Santa Maria de Gracia, noting their passionate prayers, their dedication, and their obvious love for God. But Teresa didn't feel any of the emotion she observed in her role models. She never even wept while she prayed, and that lack of emotional connection with God disturbed her. "She was a hard-praying, dry-eyed realist," writes biographer Cathleen Medwick, "with (it seemed) very little to offer God."[2] She was concerned that if she entered the convent and continued to fail at prayer, her days would yawn open one after another, an endless spiritual wasteland.

Ironically, Teresa was rescued by illness, the first bout of many afflictions she would suffer throughout her life. Forced to leave Santa Maria de Gracia, she convalesced at her uncle's home, where she engaged in long theological conversations with him. "I began to grasp that truth which I had heard as a child, that all is nothing, and that the world is vanity and on the verge of ending," she wrote. "And I began to be afraid that if I had died right then, I would have gone to hell. Even though I couldn't make myself want to become a nun, I saw that was the best and safest thing to do; and so, little by little, I decided to bully myself into doing it."[3]

As it turned out, Teresa of Ávila became a nun simply because she was terrified of damnation.

The Visions . . . and a Break from Worldliness

In 1535 Teresa entered the La Encarnacion convent in Ávila, where she remained for twenty-six years. It's no coincidence that the order she chose was significantly less demanding than the Augustinian order. In fact, Renaissance scholar Theodore Rabb notes, "This may indicate how gradually she moved from worldliness to the austerity for which she would eventually be known."[4] At La Encarnacion, Teresa lived in a two-level suite with fine furniture and its own kitchen. She was allowed to entertain friends and relatives, was encouraged to leave the convent when she needed to, and was referred to as "Dona Teresa," a nod to her social standing.

Throughout her thirties Teresa continued to suffer from worsening episodes of illness, fainting, fevers, and visions, which she interpreted as a direct reprimand from God for her sins. And while she grew into her role as a nun with surprising ease, Teresa still battled the temptation of worldly distractions. "All the things of God gave me great pleasure, yet I was tied and bound to those of the world," she wrote years later.[5] Although it most likely pained Teresa to include this account of her twenty-year battle with temptation in her *Vida*, her spiritual autobiography, she recorded her own personal struggles as a testament to God's resilient pursuit and forgiveness of even the most persistent sinners.

As she approached her fortieth birthday, Teresa began to experience some relief from her spiritual strife, namely through a new way of praying, which prompted a feeling of communion with God. These visions would become known as her raptures, the most famous of which is portrayed in Italian sculptor Gian Lorenzo Bernini's *The Ecstasy of St. Teresa* in Rome. "In his hands I saw a long golden spear and at the end of the iron tip I seemed to see a point of fire," Teresa wrote about the angel who visited her during the rapture. "With this he seemed to pierce my heart several times so that it reached my entrails. When he drew it out I thought he was drawing them out with it, and he left me completely afire with a great love of God."[6]

The problem, of course, was that some church officials suspected that Teresa's raptures were the work of the devil, or worse, her attempt to commune directly with God. In these years following the Protestant Reformation, the Roman Catholic Church was highly suspicious of even remotely unorthodox behavior—they didn't quite know what to do with a nun whose visions gave her direct contact with God. In fact, Teresa, who by this point had renounced her secular name and embraced the name Teresa de Jesus, faced resistance from the church and the Inquisition until her death in 1582.

Convent Reform

Several years after she entered La Encarnacion, Teresa began to hear a new message and direction from God. She realized that while she had devoted herself to God, she had not relinquished her comfortable life. As a result, she began to contemplate the possibility of a stricter existence for her and her nuns, including a vow of poverty. God, it seemed, agreed. Teresa felt him encourage her to develop a new convent, and she believed he even presented her with its name: San Jose.

Life at San Jose was a dramatic departure from Teresa's La Encarnacion suite and certainly from her pampered life as a child and young adult. Now, instead of luxurious fabrics and furs, she wore a threadbare habit of coarse wool and walked barefoot over the rocky terrain. Instead of rich food and drink, she abstained from red meat and ate only bread, cheese, fruit, and vegetables cultivated in the convent garden. Instead of gossip and socialization with the other nuns or visitors, there was either silence or prayer. In spite of the hardships, Teresa couldn't have been happier. She describes her five years at San Jose as the most tranquil years of her life.

In addition to enduring the physical hardships of reformed convent life and dealing with ever-worsening health crises, Teresa also faced enormous obstacles in founding each one of her convents. The process was never anything but a beleaguering uphill battle requiring political, business, and negotiation finesse; unwavering stamina and courage; and, above all, obedience to God's will in the face of what often seemed like insurmountable obstacles. When the bells rang to announce the first Mass at San Jose, for instance, the townspeople rioted, closing their shops and storming the convent in an attempt to terrify the nuns into fleeing.

Church officials doubted Teresa's divine visions, insisting instead that she was possessed by the devil. And the Inquisition itself came knocking more than once at Teresa's convents, demanding to inspect documents and threatening excommunication and imprisonment. In 1576 she was forced to "retire" to St. Joseph's convent in Toledo, and it was only after three years and several pleading letters to King Philip II of Spain that the investigation of her and other reformers was finally dropped.

Despite the overwhelming obstacles, Teresa went on to found sixteen convents across Spain before the end of her life, all of them in the Discalced (which literally means "barefoot") Carmelite order and adhering to the four principles she established: a required vow of poverty and a renunciation of property, no social or class distinctions, enclosure (cut off from all contact with the outside world), and obedience.

Writing in Peace

When she wasn't traveling by stagecoach across the Spanish countryside to visit one of her convents, or negotiating with funders or church leaders for permission to found another, Teresa often confined herself to the quiet of her cell to write. Her superiors required that she keep an account of her spiritual journey. Much of what we know today about her visions, prayer life, and business dealings comes from her own autobiography, the *Vida*, which she wrote, edited, and updated over a period of several years. While both the *Vida* and the *Foundations*, a book about the establishment of her convents, are largely practical, Teresa's later work and the one contemporary Christians most commonly associate with her, *The Interior Castle*, was a labor of love.

Teresa considered *The Interior Castle* the result of divine intervention. The nuns who witnessed her writing it noted later at her canonization hearings that she often wrote with her eyes not on the page but raised heavenward. In the midst of her hectic life, Teresa relished this time alone with God and pined for more of it. "I never have peace and quiet for writing, and have to work in snatches," she wrote. "I wish I had more time, because when the Lord inspires me, everything gets said much more easily and in a much better way. Then it is like doing a piece of embroidery with the pattern right in front of you."[7]

Practice and Perseverance

Numerous essays and biographies about Teresa of Ávila attest to her rich and fruitful legacy as a heroine of the Christian faith. More than four hundred years after her death, she continues to be lauded as a relentless and courageous reformer, saint, writer, theologian, and mystic. Yet beyond the convents she founded and the words she wrote is perhaps an even greater legacy and an example for modern-day Christians.

As it turns out, Teresa of Ávila was not much different from us. Wooed by worldly pursuits and conflicted over what direction her life should take, she turned to God in desperation and slowly learned to listen to and obey him. She struggled with some of the same temptations and sins we struggle with today and was frustrated with what she saw as her flaws and shortcomings. Yet she persevered in prayer, despite the fact that it initially did not come easily to her. Through practice and persistence Teresa learned to connect with God on a progressively deeper level, and when she finally heard his voice amid the cacophony of other distractions, she heeded him. God, in turn, transformed Teresa of Ávila from a woman distracted by the world to a woman who changed it.[8]

8

Anne Askew

More Than a Martyr

(1521–1546)

The woman who stood shivering next to the rack in the dank, cold cell was given one last chance to recant. Name the others who believe as you do, she was told, and you will walk away unharmed. Refusing to utter a word, she was stripped to her cotton shift and forced to climb onto the rectangular wooden frame, where her wrists and ankles were bound with ropes and fastened to the rollers.

The woman was quiet at first as the Lord Chancellor Thomas Wriothesley and Sir Richard Rich, a member of King Henry VIII's council, slowly began to crank the ratchet. But as tension increased on the ropes, a loud popping noise echoed throughout the chamber, the sound of cartilage and ligaments snapping as her limbs were pulled in opposite directions. First moaning and then screaming, the woman finally fainted from the pain, her body pulled so violently that it was stretched taut, suspended five inches over the rack itself. By the time the torture was halted, her shoulders and hips had been pulled from their sockets, her knees and elbows dislocated, her muscles stretched beyond repair. She was now permanently disabled, and still she had not uttered a single name.

Her torturers ordered her removed from the rack and carried back to her prison cell. Seventeen days later, on July 16, 1546, Anne Askew, age twenty-five, was burned at the stake as a heretic.

A Gentlewoman Turned Rebel

Born the daughter of a knighted member of Parliament and a high sheriff of Lincolnshire, Anne Askew could have slipped easily and un-noticeably into a life of leisure and wealth. Although almost nothing is known about her childhood, one can surmise from her in-depth knowledge of Scripture and her writing ability that Anne was most likely well educated and affluent. As English professor Elaine Beilin notes, Anne Askew "could have lived a prosperous, conventional life as a gentlewoman in Lincolnshire, England. Instead, she broke the law and defied the rules of her society."[1]

Anne's tendency toward rebellion began early, when, at the age of fifteen, she was forced to marry her deceased sister Martha's fiancé, Thomas Kyme, but refused to adopt his surname. It's thought that the couple had two children, although that fact has not been adequately substantiated. According to John Bale, who edited and published Anne Askew's *Examinations* shortly after her death, her conversion from Catholicism to Protestantism and her ongoing conflicts with the priests in Lincolnshire led Kyme to "vyolentlye" drive her "oute of hys howse."[2] Eventually, according to Bale, Anne sought a divorce in London, and although the divorce was not granted, she remained in the city, proselytizing against the Catholic doctrine and distributing tracts in favor of the Protestant Reformation. By the time of her first arrest on the charge of heresy in 1545, Anne had gained a signifi-cant following. In fact, King Henry VIII's own wife, Katherine Parr, a Reformer herself, was one of Anne's sympathizers and was rumored to have sent her clothes and other supplies while she was in prison.

Only a Sign

It may seem odd that King Henry VIII was so vehemently opposed to Protestant reformers like Anne Askew, especially considering that he himself was a Protestant. After all, he split with the Roman Catholic Church in 1534 and founded the Church of England. Yet he did so primarily to annul his marriage to Catherine of Aragon, who had borne him only a single daughter, so he could marry his mistress, Anne Boleyn, a member of Queen Catherine's entourage. Four wives later (Jane Seymour, Anne of Cleves, Catherine Howard, and Katherine Parr), and despite serving as head of the Church of England, Henry VIII remained a Catholic at heart and a believer in Catholicism's core theological teachings. He was intolerant of Protestant Reformers, including the increasingly popular Anne Askew.

By the late 1530s the Reformation had heralded the redistribution of church lands and the printing and distribution of 8,500 English Bibles for every parish church. However, the passage of the Act of Six Articles in 1539 halted the Reformation until 1547, when Henry VIII died and his son, Edward VI, succeeded to the throne. Under the Act of Six Articles, anyone who published, preached, taught, argued, or held any opinion against the Catholic doctrine of transubstantiation would be deemed and judged a heretic and would suffer the "paynes of death by way of burninge."[3] Only two witnesses were required to accuse a suspect, and all local officials were ordered to enforce the act. "Transubstantiation, the doctrine that at every Mass the whole substance of the consecrated elements of bread and wine converts into the real body and blood of Christ, became the most controversial theological issue of the day," Beilin acknowledges.[4] And it was this issue, in particular, that doomed Anne to death.

When Anne asserted in her Second Examination that the bread is "onlye sygne or sacrament" and "but a remembrance of hys death, or a sacrament of thankes gevynge for it,"[5] she committed blatant heresy according to the Act of Six Articles. Furthermore, her insistence on Scripture as the ultimate authority was problematic as well. During her First Examination, for instance, she reiterated to her interrogators that "scripture doth teache me" and "I believe as the scripture infourmeth me."[6] She angered her prosecutors when she challenged them to find any dishonesty in her, claiming that there were many who claimed to read and know Scripture but who did not live out Jesus' teachings as well as she did.

Anne made frequent mention of her gender throughout her Examinations, and, as Beilin points out, she used silence, her own questions, and irony as tools to defend herself. Her male interrogators, who included the bishop of London and other powerful state and church officials, charged that Anne blatantly disregarded Saint Paul's proclamation that women should remain silent in the churches (see 1 Cor. 14:34). Not only did Anne vehemently defend her right to discuss Scripture, noting, "I knew Paules meanyge so well as he, which is, i. Corinthiorum xiiii. that a woman ought not to speake *in the congregacyon* by the waye of teachyne,"[7] she also retaliated with this ironic barb when she was asked to expound on those verses in the courtroom: "I answered, that it was agaynst saynt Paules lernynge, that I beynge a woman, shuld interprete the scriptures, specyallye where so many wyse lerned men were."[8]

In spite of her aptitude in the courtroom—or perhaps in part because of it—Anne was convicted of heresy. She accepted the judgment quietly, without drama. Refusing to see a priest for confession, she resolutely stated her innocence and her beliefs in writing after the trial, just a few days after she was tortured on the rack. She emphatically denied the charge of heresy and declared that she would confess her sins not to a priest but to God directly, fully confident that she would be forgiven.

Today Anne Askew is considered a Protestant martyr, best known as the only woman on record to have been both tortured in the Tower of London and burned at the stake. In fact, a 1998 episode of the Learning Channel's *Tales from the Tower* focused almost exclusively on those aspects of her character, highlighting her gruesome racking and burning at the expense of the bigger picture. "Askew's *Examinations* has been fragmented and fished for the parts needed to shape the reinvention of Anne Askew as required for hagiography, ballad, sermon, novel—or television episode," Beilin observes.[9]

The truth is, there's much more to Anne Askew than her macabre demise. To overlook her contributions as a writer, an eloquent speaker, and a woman of faith in favor of the dramatic, grisly details of her death does her a grave disservice. Anne Askew wrote and spoke eloquently and convincingly about her convictions, and more importantly, she lived out those convictions until her dying day. While we twenty-first-century women need not fear death at the stake for proclaiming our faith, we would do well to ask ourselves a simple question: Would we be willing to declare our faith with even an iota of the courage and conviction of Anne Askew?

9

Anne Hutchinson

The Perseverance of a Puritan Preacher

(1591–1643)

The judges filed silently into the crowded meetinghouse on a chilly Tuesday in 1637 and sat knee to knee on wooden benches at the front of the hall. They were followed by eight somber, black-robed ministers who would serve as witnesses in the trial. The last judge to enter the hall, Massachusetts Bay Colony Governor John Winthrop, sat primly in the cushioned chair before the benches, and with a sharp rap of his gavel on the desk, he quieted the unruly crowd as he called the defendant forward.

Dressed in a long black cloak, a white linen smock laid over her black dress and petticoat, and a white coif covering her neatly plaited hair, the forty-six-year-old mother stood alone, without an attorney or an advisor. In the early stages of pregnancy with her sixteenth child, she might have been any other Puritan woman in seventeenth-century New England. But despite her pious, maternal appearance,

Anne Hutchinson was considered by many on that dank November day to be an imminent danger to the Massachusetts Bay Colony: a witch, an instrument of Satan, and a heretic. And forty male judges were poised to put her back in her place.

A Puritan Preacher Is Born (Who Just So Happens to Be a Woman)

Anne Hutchinson was born Anne Marbury in Alford, Lincolnshire, England, in 1591, the daughter of Francis Marbury and Bridget Dryden. An Anglican pastor with strong Puritan leanings, Francis was imprisoned for two years and placed under house arrest for his outspoken criticism of what he considered the clergy's lack of suitable education. During his years of house arrest, Francis taught his children, including his daughters, despite the fact that education was almost exclusively offered only to boys and men during that time. Although he died suddenly at the age of fifty-five, Francis Marbury left an indelible mark on his nineteen-year-old daughter, Anne. She would carry on her father's questioning nature, his contempt for authority, his deep faith, and his desire to share that faith with others.

The year after her father's death, Anne married childhood friend William Hutchinson, and not long after, the couple heard the young Puritan minister John Cotton preach for the first time. Captivated by Cotton's dynamic preaching, Anne and William routinely traveled six uncomfortable hours on horseback to hear him in person. Anne was particularly drawn to Cotton's theology of absolute grace, which would serve as the foundation for her own teachings years later in Massachusetts. The problem, of course, was that Cotton was much too radical for the Church of England, and after many complaints against his nonconformist preaching, he was forced to flee to New England.

Anne was devastated, and from that moment on, she pursued one goal with fervor: to follow her minister and mentor to Boston. No matter that she had a husband and eleven children, ages eight months to nineteen years old. No matter that it would require an arduous, two-month journey of more than three thousand miles across a tumultuous sea to settle in a new and unfamiliar land. Anne was determined.

One year later, in 1634, Anne, William, ten of their children, and William's elderly mother, Susanna, set sail from England aboard the *Griffin*, the same ship that had carried Cotton and the Hutchinsons' eldest son to Boston the year before. As Winnifred King Rugg said in her biography *Unafraid*, "Always Anne led and William followed."[1]

From Midwife to Preacher

Anne launched a midwife practice soon after arriving in Massachusetts, but that role quickly blossomed into one of spiritual advisor. Soon she was hosting gatherings of women in her home for Bible studies, and it wasn't long before word reached the husbands, who began to attend Anne's meetings too. This behavior was definitively un-Puritan, but that didn't stop Anne. Not only did she discuss and elaborate on Cotton's sermons, but she also began to offer her own views on religion, arguing that an "intuition of the Spirit," rather than good works, was the only valid evidence that one was chosen by God for eternal salvation.

Anne's Puritan theology had its foundation in the basic tenets of Calvinism, which maintained that salvation is God's free gift, a gift that humans cannot attain through rituals or good works. But in advocating the practice of reading the Bible in the vernacular, meditating on Scripture alone and with others, and, in some cases, experiencing the revelation of God's Word through the Holy Spirit, Anne took Puritanism to the extreme. Her theology suggested that one could receive the word of God directly from the Holy Spirit, an idea that the colonial leaders found not only threatening but also heretical. The Puritan leaders saw Anne leading her followers away from the church, toward an existence in which the church and ministers would no longer be needed, when believers would commune with and be moved directly by the Holy Spirit. "You have stepped out of your place," said Reverend Hugh Peter of Salem, and "have rather been a husband than a wife; and a preacher than a hearer; and a magistrate than a subject."[2]

So there Anne stood, in a frigid Cambridge church, before forty judges and a room packed with both antagonists and supporters. Yet John Winthrop was hard-pressed to specify a charge. As biographer Eve LaPlante notes in *American Jezebel*, both Anne and Winthrop "knew she had done nothing criminal. As a woman, she had no publicly sanctioned role. Her actions were invisible."[3] In fact, Anne's first-ever recorded words are contained in the first sentence she spoke in court: "I am called here to answer to you, but I hear no things laid to my charge."[4]

In the end, Winthrop accused Anne of publicly criticizing local ministers in comparing them unfavorably with Cotton and suggesting that they were not "sealed with the spirit of grace." But even after insisting that the eight ministers testify against her, he could not prove his case. It actually looked like Anne might escape with only minor charges against her; that is, until she made a bold—and some would say gravely unwise—move: she began to lecture the men right there in the meetinghouse courtroom. It was as if she couldn't help herself; once Anne began to preach, she couldn't stop. For several minutes she detailed exactly how and when she heard directly from God, not only through Cotton and her brother-in-law, the minister John Wheelwright, but also from God himself in what she called "immediate revelation."

"How do you know it was the Spirit?" an incredulous voice shouted from the benches. "By the voice of his own spirit to my soul," Anne answered, calmly sealing her fate.[5] As she went on to cite how the Holy Spirit was revealed to her through verses in Isaiah and Daniel, Anne gathered steam, concluding her testimonial with this emphatic declaration:

Therefore, take heed how you proceed against me, for you have no power over my body. Neither can you do me harm, for I am in the hands of the eternal Jehovah my Savior. I am at his appointment. The bounds of my habitation are cast in Heaven. No further do I esteem of any moral man than creatures in his hand. I fear none but the great Jehovah, which hath foretold me of these things. And I do verily believe that he will deliver me out of your hands. I know that for this you go about to do to me, God will ruin you and your posterity and this whole state![6]

The men were exuberant, especially Winthrop, who knew he had finally uncovered a charge that would hold against her: Anne had claimed a direct revelation from God, which was considered heresy. Most Protestants at the time viewed ministers as necessary interpreters of God's Word and believed that no man, and certainly no woman, could claim that direct connection and communion. "This has been the ground of all these tumults and troubles. This is the thing that has been the root of all the mischief," Winthrop exclaimed, pointing at Anne triumphantly.[7]

At that, judge Thomas Dudley pronounced, "I am fully persuaded that Mistress Hutchinson is deluded by the Devil, because the Spirit of God speaks truth in all his servants."[8] More than thirty judges agreed, and Anne Hutchinson, in what came to be known as the Antinomian Controversy, was deemed "a woman not fit for society" and banished from Massachusetts. In a subsequent church trial led by her beloved minister John Cotton, who accused her not only of lying but also of licentious behavior, she was also excommunicated from the Puritan church.

Moving and the Massacre

Shortly after her move to Rhode Island with her family, Anne, who had been ill throughout her pregnancy, went into labor and delivered not an infant but a mass of tissue. Her late miscarriage was fodder for much gossip in Boston, and Cotton even sermonized on her misfortune, connecting the circumstances of her "unnatural birth" with her heretical ideas.

Anne, however, did not let tragedy subdue her for long and was soon hosting Scripture meetings and preaching to groups of men and women in her Rhode Island home. However, with rumors circulating that Massachusetts would absorb the Rhode Island colony, she was forced to move again. Shortly after the unexpected death of her husband in 1641, the widowed Anne, now fifty years old, moved her family 130 miles away to the Dutch settlement of New Amsterdam (what is now northern Bronx, New York). She was eager for a fresh start, especially for her youngest children, and was relieved to find that she and her extended family were the only English settlers in the newly formed Dutch colony.

The Hutchinsons and the Dutch families lived side by side but culturally distanced from one another. They didn't speak the same language or share the same customs, and while Anne's neighbors viewed her as harmless—they were not threatened by her religious convictions—they considered her ways bizarre, especially her refusal to keep guns in her house. Anne had always been supportive of Native Americans and wasn't worried. As it turned out, her nonchalance toward her Siwanoy Indian neighbors was a grave error.

On a clear-skied autumn day in September 1643, Anne's Dutch neighbors frantically warned her of a coming attack, begging her to flee from the house with her family. Insisting that she had good relations with the natives, she refused to arm herself. Not long after, a band of Siwanoy warriors invaded the Hutchinson property and seized and scalped sixteen people, including Anne, seven of her children, her son-in-law, and several servants. They then dragged the bodies into the house along with the cattle and set it on fire. There was only one survivor of the massacre: Anne's nine-year-old daughter, Susanna, who had been picking blueberries away from the house. She lived with the tribe for about eight years, adopted by the chief, Wampage, who changed his name to "Ann-Hoeck," after his most famous victim.

Back in Boston, Anne's detractors proclaimed the massacre the work of God's hand. "The Lord heard our groans to heaven, and freed us from this great and sore affliction," wrote the Reverend Thomas Weld from London. Winthrop deemed the church "sweetly repaired" by the death of Hutchinson, whom he named "this American Jezebel," after the infamous Old Testament pagan queen.[9]

Civil Liberty, Religious Toleration

Imagine for a moment how isolated and abandoned Anne must have felt when she was betrayed by some of her closest confidants, including her own friend and spiritual mentor, John Cotton. Imagine how crushed she was when she heard how Cotton railed against her in his sermons. Imagine the fear and isolation she felt after she was banished from Massachusetts and excommunicated from her church. Yet even after she was publicly shamed, convicted of heresy, forced to flee her home, and mocked in the midst of suffering and grief, she stayed steadfast in her faith and convictions, convinced that she had the right and the authority as a believer to communicate directly with God.

Today a bronze statue of Anne Hutchinson, her eyes lifted toward heaven, her arm encircling a young girl, stands in front of the Massachusetts State House in Boston. "Courageous exponent of civil liberty and religious toleration," reads the inscription on the marble pediment. A number of other memorials in Rhode Island and New York, as well as the Hutchinson River and Hutchinson River Parkway in New York, are named in her honor and testify to her legacy and contributions. Yet the most telling testimony of Anne's legacy isn't inscribed on a memorial or echoed in the name of a busy highway or a meandering river. It's in the example of her steadfast conviction, her determination, and her unwavering faith in God. Anne Hutchinson sacrificed her own life for the right of religious freedom, a right most of us take for granted today.

10

Anne Bradstreet

Colonial Kindred Spirit

$(1612-1672)$

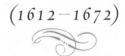

One hundred passengers pressed against the rails of the *Arbella* to catch their first sight of the New World. As they breathed in the sweet scent that breezed from the shore, they glimpsed a pigeon soaring over the ship's deck, the first sign in sixty-two days that life existed beyond the roiling waves. Three days later, on June 12, 1630, the sea-weary travelers disembarked to survey their new home: Salem plantation, three thousand miles from their native England. Anne Bradstreet, seventeen years old and newly married, was one of many who stepped foot on the foreign shore. As she stood in the mud amid her family's crates and trunks, her heart sank at the desolate sight.

It's easy to understand her dismay. Anne's life in Northampton, England, had been one of comfort and leisure. Her father, Thomas Dudley, had been employed as a steward to the Earl of Lincoln; her mother, Dorothy, was a woman of noble birth. As a young girl, Anne had lived in a large, comfortable home, complete with numerous servants to handle most of the domestic chores. She had enjoyed afternoon tea, whiled away the hours browsing her father's personal library full of hundreds of books, and occupied herself with a bustling social life.

Compare that cultured existence to what Anne glimpsed as she stepped from the *Arbella* onto the shore of the New World. The primitive settlement consisted of about forty crude dwellings, only a third of which resembled actual houses. They were constructed of roughly hewn oak frames and pine boards. They had thatched roofs, oil-paper windows, and wattle-and-daub chimneys made from woven strips of wood bound with a sticky mixture of dirt, sand, dung, and straw. And these were the upscale homes. The rest were cave-like dugouts burrowed into hillsides or "English wigwams," tent-like structures made with pliant branches and covered with boughs.

Life for the colonial settlers was fraught with discomfort, sickness, and death. Summers seared hot, while winters were frigid and damp. Few of the colonists were as fortunate as Anne and her family, who did not lose any immediate family members. Hundreds of settlers died of illness, scurvy, and starvation during the first year, and hundreds more retreated to England, disheartened by the crippling illnesses, grinding homesickness, and unrelenting hunger and cold.

Because Salem village was overcrowded and provisions were in short supply, some of the newly arrived colonists, including Anne, her husband, Simon, and her parents and siblings, relocated to Charlestown, near the mouth of the Charles River. However, Charlestown was quickly deemed unsuitable, and Anne, her family, and a group of other colonists eventually moved to Newtown, a few miles up the Charles River. There, in her second year in Newtown, Anne fell gravely ill with a "lingering sickness like consumption," which, she later wrote in her private memoirs, she believed to be "a correction I saw the Lord sent to humble and try me and do me Good: and it was not altogether ineffectual."[1] When she recovered, Anne wrote what's now considered one of her earliest poems, entitled "Upon a Fit of Sickness":

> Twice ten years old not fully told
>   since nature gave me breath,
> My race is run, my thread spun,
>   lo, here is fatal death.
> All men must die, and so must I;
>   this cannot be revoked.
> For Adam's sake this word God spake
>   when he so high provoked.
> Yet live I shall, this life's but small,
>   in place of highest bliss,
> Where I shall have all I can crave,
>   no life is like to this.
> For what's this but care and strife
>   since first we came from womb?
> Our strength doth waste, our time doth haste,
>   and then we go to th' tomb.
> O bubble blast, how long can'st last?
>   that always art a breaking,
> No sooner blown, but dead and gone,
>   ev'n as a word that's speaking.
> O whilst I live this grace me give,
>   I doing good may be,
> Then death's arrest I shall count best,
>   because it's Thy decree;
> Bestow much cost there's nothing lost,
>   to make salvation sure,
> O great's the gain, though got with pain,
>   comes by profession pure.
> The race is run, the field is won,
>   the victory's mine I see;
> Forever known, thou envious foe,
>   the foil belongs to thee.[2]

Stepping-Stone Poetry

These early attempts at verse are not considered her best work. Described as "technically amateurish" and "remarkably impersonal even by Puritan standards,"[3] the poetry was less an expression of Anne's day-to-day experiences in the settlement than, as poet Adrienne Rich points out, "a last compulsive effort to stay in contact with the history, traditions, and values of her former world." Yet these early poems are a beginning, "a psychological stepping-stone to the later poems which have kept her alive for us."[4]

As biographer Elizabeth Wade White notes, "Only a conscious and ardent desire to become a poet, combined with a strong sense of spiritual dedication, could give the necessary courage for such an act to a Puritan woman of 1636."[5] It was no small feat for a Puritan woman like Anne—a wife and mother of eight children, living in the wilderness of the New World—to find the time and creative energy to compose poetry. Likewise, the fact that her brother-in-law and later her readers were supportive of her work is a testament to its importance. The Puritans were a serious and self-disciplined people who viewed every action in light of its value in God's eyes. Clearly they deemed Anne's work as both creatively and spiritually valuable.

Anne's first volume of poetry, *The Tenth Muse*, was published without her knowledge by her brother-in-law, who took the manuscript with him and had it printed when he returned to England in 1650. She had intended the poems only for her family's eyes, and she was not only shocked by their appearance in print but also horrified by the fact that many of them were unedited drafts. At the same time, though, the positive reception of her work gave Anne the confidence to continue writing and to find her true voice. The titles of her later poems, all of which were published after her death, reveal a distinct change not only in form but also in subject matter. No longer wedded to a formulaic style or to imitating the contemporary or classical poets, Anne ventured boldly into her own experiences to write more personally about the events of her own life: the departure of her eldest son, Samuel, to England; the loss of her home to a devastating fire; the fear of childbirth; the death of a grandchild.

These private poems are also more confessional than her public work, often revealing what she considered her flaws and spiritual shortcomings. For instance, from her private journals we know that Anne struggled to overcome the lure of worldly temptations, and she accepted her recurring illnesses, fevers, and fainting spells as God's way of reforming her and redirecting her spiritual course. In a 1657 journal entry Anne writes about her physical suffering, noting, "I trust it is out of His abundant love to my straying soul which in prosperity is too much in love with the world."[6]

We also glimpse this tension between worldly temptation and godliness in one of her most famous poems, "Upon the Burning of Our House," in which she writes, "I blest His name that gave and took, That laid my good now in the dust," followed by the admission that she casts her "sorrowing eyes" on the ruin to gaze upon the trunk, the chest, and the store she counted best, "my pleasant things in ashes lie." For several lines Anne pines over all the treasures lost and the memories that will no longer be made before finally chiding herself for her shallow materialism, concluding:

> And did thy wealth on earth abide?
> Didst fix they hope on mold'ring dust. . . .
> The world no longer let me love,
> My hope and treasure lies above.[7]

Clearly Anne used both poetry and journaling to exercise her creativity and wrestle with her spirituality.

Public Versus Private Anne

Her stated intention for writing was "to declare the truth, not to set forth myself, but the glory of God." Yet her writing, especially the poems and personal letters published after her death—material that she never intended for the public eye—also reveals a deeper struggle.

Only three of the eighteen poems she released to "publick view" are specific statements of her religious faith, and as White notes, all three are by-the-book examples of Puritan belief. But it was in her private memoirs, which she wrote to be shared posthumously with her children—so they would know "what was your living mother's mind"[8]—that Anne divulged her deepest spiritual musings, including her doubts and questions.

"I have often been perplexed that I have not found that constant joy in my pilgrimage and refreshing which I supposed most of the servants of God have," she confessed to her children. She admitted that she made a concerted effort to maintain her faith, yet at the same time she wrestled with accepting the existence of God and the truth of the Scriptures. "Many times hath Satan troubled me concerning the verity of the Scriptures, many times by atheism how I could know whether there was a God," she confessed. "I have argued thus with myself. That there is a God, I see. If ever this God hath revealed himself, it must be in His word, and this must be it or none."[9]

Likewise Anne struggled with her religious denomination, wondering aloud whether the "Popish religion" (Catholicism) might in fact be the "right" one. The Catholics have the same God, the same Jesus, and the same Scriptures, she observed, but they interpret it all a bit differently. Then again, she decided, their "vain fooleries," "lying miracles," and "cruel persecutions of the saints"[10] were enough to turn her back toward Protestantism.

By the conclusion of the confessional letter to her children, Anne reported that she had largely overcome her spiritual conflicts. "I have not known what to think," she wrote, "but then I have remembered the works of Christ that so it must be . . . and I can now say, 'Return, O my Soul, to thy rest, upon this rock Christ Jesus will I build my faith.'"[11] Despite the letter's positive conclusion, though, Anne's admissions would have been considered blasphemous by many of her fellow Puritans, including her father, who was, as White notes, a "staunch condemner of anything that suggested a 'toleration.'"[12]

The fact that Anne laid out her struggles so honestly in this heartfelt letter to her children is a testament to her search for truth, as well as her conviction that her faith—as well as her children's, should they struggle in the same way—would prevail over doubt. It's clear that Anne endeavored to offer her children solace and hope on their own faith journey and was willing to risk being deemed a heretic, should it come to that, in order to speak truthfully about the fact that faith did not always come easily to her.

Anne Bradstreet lived four hundred years before us, and she faced trials and hardships we will never live or understand. Yet she is also a real, relatable woman who walked through many of the same spiritual questions we grapple with four centuries later. As she poured her heart into the pages of her journal in poetry and prose, we see ourselves—our own questions, our own doubts, our own hopes—reflected in her authentic words. And just as she offered her sage and honest advice to her children, so that they "may gain some spiritual advantage by [her] experience,"[13] we too can find comfort and hope, as well as a kindred spirit, in Anne Bradstreet.

11

Margaret Fell

"I Shall Stand for God and Truth"

(1614–1702)

Rumors flew as the traveling preacher made his way over the craggy landscape toward Swarthmoor in northern England. Margaret Fell, mistress of Swarthmoor Hall, was eager to meet the man who was said to have founded a brand-new religion. Two days later, as George Fox stood on a pew in the parish church and preached, Margaret rose to her feet in amazement. Then, as Fox rebuked those who understood the Scriptures only for themselves, without the illumination of the Spirit of Christ, she sank back into the pew, crying bitterly. "This opened me so, that it cut me to the heart; and I saw clearly that we were all wrong," Margaret wrote later. "I cried in my spirit to the Lord, 'We are all thieves; we are all thieves; we have taken the Scriptures in words, and know nothing of them ourselves.'"[1]

That pivotal moment in the church pew was the beginning of a half-century of work for the Quaker Fellowship—work that would bring Margaret Fell to the royal court of King Charles II, as well as to the prison dungeons of Lancaster Gaol.

A People of Peace

Before she committed herself to the Quaker movement, Margaret needed to address an urgent domestic concern. Her husband, Judge Thomas Fell, had been traveling during Fox's visit, and as he made his way home from London, he was intersected by the parish rector and several neighborhood friends, who warned him that his wife and children had been bewitched by a traveling preacher during his absence. Startled and angered by this disturbing accusation, Fell hurried home to Swarthmoor Hall to confront his wife. That night during dinner, with all seven children silently gathered around the table, Margaret described her conversion experience to her husband.

After Fell spoke with Fox himself, he was somewhat appeased, but not enough to abandon the Anglican Church. Instead, he allowed his wife to convert to Quakerism and to host the meetings in his home, although he would not attend. Two days later, the first Meeting of Friends took place at Swarthmoor Hall, a tradition that continued for nearly forty years.

Margaret was instrumental to the successful spread of Quakerism in its early years, despite the fact that she was tied to her home and family. In dozens of letters, essays, and pamphlets, some composed only a few months after her conversion, she illustrated clearly and convincingly the fundamental Quaker belief in the Light of Christ, which came to be known simply as the Inner Light. Quakers repudiated the sacraments, ordained clergy, and any outward form of religion, believing that they hindered the divine Inner Light. They believed that the work of the Holy Spirit in the faithful had even greater authority than Scripture itself, and during meetings, they would often sit in silence, waiting to speak until moved by the Holy Spirit. They also did not feel the same oppressive weight of sin in their lives as their spiritual cousins, the Puritans. While they knew that sin existed, of course, they focused more on the presence of the divine light and, as Fox stated it, "that of God in every man."[2] Fox preached that a state of "perfection" through Christ's indwelling Spirit was possible for every believer.

Margaret also wrote about the issue of Quaker persecution, which was rampant in seventeenth-century England under the rule of both Oliver Cromwell and King Charles II. Thousands of Quakers were imprisoned for their refusal to take any oath whatsoever, which they viewed as directly opposed to Christ's express prohibition in the Gospel of Matthew:

> But I say, do not make any vows! Do not say, "By heaven!" because heaven is God's throne. And do not say, "By the earth!" because the earth is his footstool. And do not say, "By Jerusalem!" for Jerusalem is the city of the great King. Do not even say, "By my head!" for you can't turn one hair white or black. Just say a simple, "Yes, I will," or "No, I won't." Anything beyond this is from the evil one. (Matt. 5:33–37)

In May of 1660 Margaret traveled with her oldest daughter to London to appeal to King Charles II for the release of Quaker prisoners, including Fox, who had been arrested at Swarthmoor Hall and incarcerated in Lancaster Castle. Initially she appealed to the king and his brothers, the dukes of York and Gloucester, via letters, in which she explained in detail why the Quakers refused to take oaths. She also wrote a paper entitled "A Declaration and an Information from Us the People of God Called Quakers," which was delivered to the king. It was the first document to proclaim the Quakers' belief in peace and their refusal to use weapons for any purpose:

> We are a people that follow after those things that make for peace, love and unity; it is our desire that others' feet may walk in the same, and [we] do deny and bear our testimony against all strife and wars and contentions. . . . Our weapons are not carnal but spiritual. . . . And so we desire, and also expect to have the liberty of our consciences and just rights and outward liberties, as other people of the nation.[3]

Margaret also met with King Charles II in person, often as frequently as three times in one week, relentlessly urging him to release the prisoners and making the case for the Quaker principles again and again. Finally, four months after her arrival in London, George Fox and several other prisoners were released.

"King of My Conscience"

The respite did not last long. While Margaret was still in London, a proclamation was passed prohibiting Quaker meetings and resulting in the imprisonment of more than four thousand Quakers over the span of a few weeks. Margaret's second oldest child, Bridget, who was left in charge of the management of Swarthmoor and the younger siblings, wrote to her mother that forty-three Swarthmoor Friends had been arrested without warrant—some from their homes, others from the market or their workplaces. In some counties, not a single male Friend was left free.

Convinced that it was the Lord's will for her to stay in London and petition for the release of the prisoners, Margaret soldiered on, faithfully penning letters to Charles II, the royal family, and his council. Finally, more than twenty letters and numerous in-person visits later, the king and his council released imprisoned Quakers and restored their liberty. Margaret finally returned to Swarthmoor, fifteen months after she'd left it in Bridget's hands.

In 1663, Margaret, now the widowed mother of seven children, was arrested and brought to trial for holding Quaker meetings in her home. Four of her daughters stood in the courtroom, watching anxiously as the judge held out the Bible to their mother. Each time he asked her to take an oath, Margaret refused, finally acknowledging before the judge and the jury, "If you ask me never so often, I answer you that the reason why I cannot take it is because Christ hath commanded me not to swear at all; I owe my allegiance and obedience to him."[4] Exasperated, one of the justices called out, "Mistress Fell, you may with a good conscience (if you cannot take the oath) put in security, that you will have not more Meetings at your house."[5]

When she adamantly refused to cease holding the Quaker Meetings in her home, the clerk held the Bible out to her a final time, urging her to remove her glove and place her hand on the cover. "I never took an oath in my life. I have spent my days thus far, and I never took an oath," she replied. "I own allegiance to the King, as he is the King of England, but Christ Jesus is King of my conscience."[6]

The courtroom grew quiet, and with her daughters watching from the benches behind her, the judge read Margaret's sentence: life imprisonment and complete forfeiture of her property. She was terrified, not only for what awaited her behind bars but also for her children, who would now be without either parent. Yet she remained steady and hopeful in God, despite her dire circumstances. "Although I am out of the King's Protection, yet I am not out of the protection of the Almighty God," Margaret declared, before the judge ordered her removed from the courtroom.[7]

"For the Sake and Service of the Lord"

Margaret was imprisoned in Lancaster Castle for four years, from 1664 to 1668. Her small cell was exposed to England's dank, rainy weather, and conditions were atrocious, but Margaret didn't waste the ample time available to her. While in prison she continued to appeal to King Charles II, employing increasingly sharp admonitions to remind him of his broken promises. She also wrote several tracts in defense of Quaker principles, as well as four books, including her most famous, *Women's Speaking Justified*, in which she defended the right of women to serve as public preachers. Garnering from Scripture the example of twenty-four biblical women to support her argument, she maintained that women who were in the Spirit could speak just as men did, for it was the Spirit, not the woman herself, who was speaking.

Just over a year after she was released from prison, Margaret married George Fox, eleven years after her first husband's death. Much of their marriage was spent apart, as Fox spent most of his time preaching and converting in London, while Margaret focused on familial responsibilities and growing the Quaker Meetings at Swarthmoor. She entered into the union with her eyes wide open, aware that marriage to a traveling preacher would not be easy:

> Though the Lord had provided a habitation for him, yet he was not willing to stay at it, because it was so remote and far from London where his service most lay. And my concern for God and his holy eternal truth was then in the north, where God had placed and set me; and likewise for the ordering and governing of my children and family; so that we were willing both of us to live apart for some years upon God's account and his truth's service, and to deny ourselves of that comfort which we might have had in being together, for the sake and service of the Lord and his truth.[8]

In fact, the couple was apart so often, Margaret saw her husband only once in the six months preceding his death in 1691. She received the news of Fox's death by letter from London. "A prince had fallen today in Israel," wrote fellow Quaker and longtime friend William Penn.[9]

Distance wasn't the only difficulty associated with Margaret's second marriage. Her only son, George, had deeply opposed the union. He was adamantly against Quakerism and resented George Fox for converting his mother. He had suffered bitterly during her long imprisonment in Lancaster, and his hostility increased after he married and became a father himself—so much, in fact, that he was instrumental in his mother's second imprisonment in Lancaster Castle. George accused his mother of breaking the Conventicle Act of 1664, which forbade religious meetings comprised of five or more people outside the auspices of the Church of England. As the result of her only son's vicious accusations, Margaret spent 1670 to 1671 imprisoned once again.

For God and Truth Till the End

In her eighty-eight years, Margaret Fell never put herself, nor anyone else, before her God. Not a single person ever swayed her from her service and loyalty to the Lord—not a judge nor a jury; not the king nor his council; not even her own children, who watched their mother led to prison twice for her refusal to compromise her beliefs. Still writing just five months before her death in 1702, Margaret renewed her commitment to the Religious Society of Friends and to God. "I give this my testimony, while I breathe upon the earth," she wrote, "that I shall stand for God and Truth."[10] From the moment she rose to her feet in church until the moment she breathed her last, Margaret Fell remained faithful to the tenets of Quakerism. She had indeed stood strong and resiliently "for God and Truth."

12

Susanna Wesley

More Than the Mother of Methodism

(1669 – 1742)

Susanna Wesley stepped down from the coach and stood in the yard, absorbing the village and landscape around her. She spotted the tiny church across the field where her husband, Samuel, would preach on Sundays. She observed a handful of rustic village homes; the flat, wind-beaten land; the scraggly reeds springing from muddy ditches and a few ravaged trees bent in the distance. A thick mist had settled over the barren fields. Susanna then turned and crossed the threshold of the rectory, the modest home where she would bear nineteen children, raise ten of them to maturity, and spend the next thirty-nine years of her life.

Country Life and Problem Parishioners

Susanna Wesley's new life as the wife of a pastor in rural Epworth, England, was a far cry from her upbringing in London. Born the youngest of twenty-five children, she was educated at home, and although she never attended college or even boarding school, she was raised a gentlewoman, with many of her lessons supplemented by the intellectual atmosphere encouraged by her father, a prominent London pastor. Dr. Annesley frequently entertained theological scholars in his home, and one such scholar was Samuel Wesley, whom Susanna married in 1689 at age nineteen.

Life in rural Epworth was difficult for the Wesleys. A rigid, moralistic pastor with a penchant for fiery rhetoric, Samuel did not connect well with his uneducated parishioners, who viewed him with suspicion as an outsider. Indeed, the city-born and city-bred Samuel was an inept farmer who also proved himself incapable of managing his land and finances, a task Susanna eventually oversaw in addition to running the household and homeschooling their children.

Relations between Samuel and his parishioners deteriorated over the years, and the villagers often retaliated against the Wesley family, going so far as to burn their crops, damage the rectory, and abuse their livestock. They also despised Samuel's royalist sympathies. The situation came to a climax during the local elections in 1705, when Samuel promised to vote for a particular candidate and then publicly repudiated his commitment, infuriating the men of Epworth. While he was out of town casting his vote, the villagers harassed Susanna, who just days prior had given birth, by shouting and firing pistols beneath her bedroom windows. The night ended in tragedy when the nurse, who had been caring for the newborn infant, accidentally smothered the baby when she rolled over during her sleep. The hysterical nurse burst into the rectory in the early morning and placed the dead infant in Susanna's arms.

Not long after that tragic incident, an enraged parishioner demanded that the broke Samuel immediately pay the debt he owed to him. When Samuel was unable to produce the funds, he was arrested and imprisoned in Lincoln Castle for three months, leaving Susanna with a total of ten shillings on which to subsist. However, even after Samuel claimed arson as the cause of the 1709 fire that burned the rectory to the ground—a fire that nearly killed their young son John, who had been trapped on the second floor—he never sought to move to another parish, stubbornly arguing, "Tis like a coward to desert my post because the enemy fire thick upon me."[1]

In addition to their problems with the parishioners, Susanna and Samuel didn't always get along well themselves. "Theirs was the union of two very strong characters," biographer Rebecca Lamar Harmon notes. "Samuel's quick-tempered pronouncements were met by the calm, well-reasoned opinions of Susanna, who on her side had difficulty in changing once she had made up her mind."[2] When her son John was an adult, Susanna once candidly admitted to him that she and Samuel "rarely agreed on a particular matter,"[3] including their politics.

Both Susanna and Samuel believed in the divine right of kings, but they disagreed over who, in fact, was entitled to that divine right. Samuel enthusiastically supported William of Orange and Mary when they supplanted the Stuarts in 1688. However, Susanna considered William of Orange a usurper and refused to utter "Amen" to her husband's dinnertime prayer for him. The two stubbornly dug in their heels on the issue, until finally Samuel declared, "Sukey, if that be the case, we must part, for if we have two Kings, we must have two beds."[4] For her part, Susanna asserted that she "would apologize if she was wrong, but she felt to do so for expediency would only be a lie and thus a sin."[5]

Samuel kept his word and Susanna kept hers, she believing that because William and Mary were usurpers, the divine right belonged to the Stuarts alone. "Since I'm willing to let him quietly enjoy his opinions, he ought not to deprive me of my little liberty of conscience," she wrote to a friend.[6] The two refused to compromise, and as a result, Samuel moved to London for five months, until the death of King William and Anne's accession to the throne prompted him to return home.

Despite their disagreements and stubbornness, Susanna and Samuel loved and respected one another, and Susanna was devoted to her husband in spite of his failings. "He is not fit for worldly business," she admitted in a letter to her eldest son, Samuel. But she added,

"Where he lives, I will live, and where he dies, I will die and there I will be buried. God do so unto me and more also if aught but death part him and me."[7]

Renewing and Saving a Soul

Not only did Susanna oversee a busy household, manage the family's land, and participate in the parish duties expected of a minister's wife, she also single-handedly educated her large family. In order to homeschool so many children effectively, she established a systematic method from which she rarely strayed. As the children grew older, they learned not only reading, writing, arithmetic, and the classics but also how to recite the Lord's Prayer, memorize Scripture, honor the Sabbath, and mind their manners. "There was no such thing as loud playing or talking allowed of," she explained, "but everyone was kept close to business for the six hours of school. . . . Rising out of their places, or going out of the room, was not permitted except for good cause; and running into the yard, garden, or street, without leave, was always esteemed a capital offence."[8]

Susanna firmly believed in the importance of a thorough education for the girls as well as the boys, and she had very specific opinions on how that education should be executed. For instance, she believed that girls should be taught to read before they were instructed in their household work, "for the putting children to learn sewing before they can read properly is the very reason why so few women can read fit to be heard, and never to be well understood."[9]

Although she was strict with her students, Susanna was an infinitely patient and gifted teacher. "I wonder at your patience," her husband exclaimed one day, after observing her repeat again and again the same instructions to the same child. "You have told that child twenty times the same thing."

"If I had satisfied myself by mentioning it only nineteen times, I should have lost all my labor," she calmly replied. "It was the twentieth time that crowned it."[10] Susanna deemed the education of her children a valuable necessity and her most important responsibility as a mother. Even more, she considered it her personal ministry. She believed not only their intelligence and their future livelihood but their very souls were at stake. On the subject of subduing the self-will of her children, Susanna was adamant:

> Heaven or hell depends on this alone, so that the parent who studies to subdue [self-will] in his child works together with God in the renewing and saving a soul. The parent who indulges it does the Devil's work; makes religion impracticable, salvation unattainable, and does all that in him lies to damn his child body and soul forever.[11]

Despite her commitment to her children's education, there were occasions in which Susanna felt unsatisfied with her contribution to society. At one point, after her daughter Emilia read aloud to her about a Danish missionary, Susanna decided her own contributions to the betterment of society were lacking. As a result, she vowed to change her situation in the only place she could: her own home. Realizing that her children might be deficient in individual attention, she established a rotating schedule of evening "conferences," during which she met with each child to discuss whatever was on his or her mind, from spiritual questions to more ordinary concerns.

Content to Fill a Little Space

During Samuel's long absences to London, Susanna hosted evening worship services in her kitchen, a fact that displeased her husband. It made no matter to him that her kitchen services attracted more participants than the substitute preacher's Sunday morning services—Samuel simply couldn't condone her actions. Susanna held her ground and was firm in her reply. "As to its looking particular [unseemly], I grant that it does," she acknowledged in her letter, "but so does almost everything that is serious, or that may anyway advance the glory of God or the salvation of souls, if it be performed out of a pulpit, or in the way of common conversation."[12] Determined and stubborn as ever, Susanna continued with her kitchen services. She referred to her kitchen congregation as "our Society," and conducted them in much the same way as the Methodist Societies later formed by her famous preacher son, John Wesley.

Susanna also played an important and influential role when John was first considering the ministry. While Samuel desired that his son pursue further higher education, Susanna disagreed, urging John to become ordained as soon as possible. "I think the sooner you are a deacon the better," she wrote to John, referring to higher education in her letter as "trifling studies."[13] John followed his mother's advice and was ordained a deacon by the bishop of Oxford in 1725, a decision that would dictate the course of his life.

After Samuel died in 1735 and Susanna went to live with John at what was called the Foundry, the Methodist headquarters in London, she was not initially convinced by the teachings of the Methodist movement. But the more she talked with her sons John and Charles about their newfound religious experiences, and the more she witnessed firsthand their remarkable accomplishments, the more enthusiastic she became of Methodism. Soon Susanna was teaching classes to women at the Foundry herself and participating in the open-air tent meetings that differed so dramatically from the stately rituals of the Church of England in which she'd participated all of her life. She also helped to convince John of the benefit of lay preachers, who helped to spread Methodism around England and beyond.

"I am content to fill a little space if God be glorified," Susanna once wrote.[14] It's true, if we were to consider her contributions by contemporary, worldly measures of success, she would not rate highly. Susanna Wesley never preached a single sermon. She never published a book or founded a church or led a mission. In fact, we would not know Susanna Wesley today were it not for her two most famous sons, John and Charles. Why then, you might ask, should she be considered a heroine of the Christian faith?

Susanna's disciplined educational and child-rearing regimen shaped her children, particularly her sons, into upstanding citizens and important spiritual leaders. And her unwavering commitment to her role as God's collaborator in the work of saving souls confirmed her as a critical spiritual influence in her children's lives.

Yet Susanna Wesley is much more than the mother of John and Charles Wesley. She's much more than the "mother of Methodism," as historians have deemed her. Susanna Wesley serves as *our* spiritual mentor as well, a woman to emulate in our own modern-day lives. Through her quiet but steadfast example, Susanna demonstrated that spiritual development begins not in church and not in Sunday school but at home—around the kitchen table and within ordinary, everyday life. She reminds us that the work of parenting is more than potty training, lessons in table manners, and managing sports schedules. It is the sacred work of renewing and saving souls.

13

Hannah More

Setting the Stage for Sunday School

$(1745-1833)$

She stood in the back of the church, her lace veil shielding her tears, a bouquet wilting in her hands. The guests shifted in the pews, murmuring to one another and turning to glance over their shoulders at the bride waiting nervously at the end of the aisle. After stalling for what seemed like hours, the bride's family finally told the guests to go home. Clearly the groom was not going to show up. Again.

Hannah More was jilted at the church altar not once but three times—each time by the same suitor, a man by the name of William Turner. After the third no-show, a humiliated and heartbroken Hannah fled to the English countryside to recover, vowing she would never consider marriage again. There was, however, a silver lining in the disaster. The fickle groom compensated Hannah for her distress with a lifetime annuity of two hundred pounds, enough to ensure her financial independence. At the time, Hannah likely could not have imagined or foreseen the impact this love loss would have on her life, not only as a famous English playwright, but also as a Christian writer, an evangelist, and a philanthropist.

A Fame Turned Sour

Unlike most fathers of the time, Jacob More believed in the education of women and thus taught his five daughters, including his fourth-born, Hannah, a wide variety of subjects, from the basics of reading and writing to the more traditionally masculine pursuits of Latin and mathematics. Hannah wrote her first plays at boarding school—pastoral dramas with a moral lesson that were performed by the young ladies and later sold to other schools around England. After completing her own studies, she taught at the boarding school, which had been started by her older sisters, for several years before eventually moving to London. There she met the eminent actor-manager David Garrick, who played a critical role in her rise as a successful playwright.

One of Hannah's first plays, *The Inflexible Captive*, opened to great acclaim at the Theatre Royal in Bath in 1775. Yet Hannah was not satisfied. Not only did she consider Garrick's influence and promotion of her work as the sole reason for her success, she was also uncomfortable with the praise and flattery that accompanied her rising fame. Feeling that she needed to prove herself as a legitimate author, she turned her attention to poetry. Two weeks later, she completed *Sir Eldred of the Bower*, a ballad set in medieval England, and submitted it for publication along with *The Bleeding Rock*, a poem about her failed relationship with Turner. Both were well received (although *The Bleeding Rock* less so, perhaps because the poem was too personal for London literati).

Her confidence in her own literary abilities restored, Hannah returned to writing plays, and in 1777, Covent Garden, the largest patented theater in London, produced her best-known play. *Percy* was considered both a commercial and a literary success. It generated a substantial profit and catapulted Hannah into lasting fame—a fame, however, that would soon sour.

In 1779, two major incidents impacted both Hannah's reputation and her self-identity. First, her longtime friend and mentor David Garrick died. And second, her most recent play, *The Fatal Falsehood*, was an abysmal failure. In addition, Hannah was accused of plagiarizing *The Fatal Falsehood*—charges that were ultimately proven false but damaged Hannah's reputation nonetheless. As biographer Charles Howard Ford observed, "1779 was a nadir in her life, but it also marked a turning point. . . . From a famous literary lady with a didactic streak, she became the personification of the godly laywoman."[1] After her literary demise in 1779, Hannah More never again wrote for the London stage.

"Too Good a Christian for an Author"

Hannah felt conflicted about her role as a famous playwright and a woman of society. Even in the midst of her success, she balked against the pressure to conform to trends. While the Garricks coached her on the necessity of socializing with the aristocrats in order to further her career, she inwardly mocked what she considered high-society silliness. Hannah especially despised the ridiculous fashion fads, and it galled her to imitate them when she ventured out in public. In the 1770s, London women wore their hair elaborately piled high atop their heads, often adorned with hats, feathers, flowers, and even fresh fruit. The hairstyles towered so high, in fact, that women were often forced to duck through doorways. Hannah acquiesced to the current styles, yet privately complained in a letter to her sisters that "nothing can be conceived so absurd, extravagant, and fantastical, as the present mode of dressing the head."[2] She also resisted traveling and visiting on Sundays, which she considered a breach of the Sabbath commandment, although the Garricks insisted that she make exceptions in order to mingle with the highly influential noblemen and their wives.

While every one of Hannah's plays and poems centered on a moral, Christian theme, she considered herself a hypocrite because her daily reality did not mirror the fictional lives she created. As she struggled to balance her inner integrity and values with the worldly expectations of society, Hannah increasingly felt that she came up short. As her publisher told her, "she was 'too good a Christian for an author.'"[3] Despite her Christian subject matter, Hannah gradually began to realize that the theater was an ineffective vehicle for conveying godliness.

It's not entirely surprising, then, that Garrick's death, combined with the failed play, the plagiarism scandal, and an increasing discomfort with her role in high society, propelled Hannah to withdraw completely from the public. She fled London and sequestered herself with Garrick's widow at her homes in Adelphi and Hampton. The two grieved quietly together, receiving very few visitors and settling into a peaceful routine of reading and contemplation.

During the winter of 1780, Hannah attended several sermons by the Reverend John Newton, a former slave-ship captain turned abolitionist and Anglican clergyman, and author of the hymn "Amazing Grace." Inspired by Newton's message that Christians should actively participate in the world in order to improve it, Hannah ended her self-imposed seclusion and reentered London society, "now bent on wielding her pen in the moral and ethical instruction of grandees and their families."[4]

Once again immersed into elite social circles, Hannah was now on a twofold mission: first, to educate the aristocrats in the basics of Scripture, and second, to inspire them to act on their faith. The elite class's scriptural ignorance astonished Hannah, and as a result, she wrote *Sacred Dramas*, a series of skits that dramatized Scripture in dialogue form, to be read rather than performed. This was a risky move. Just recently the prominent English writer Samuel Johnson had vehemently criticized a male contemporary for publishing something similar, noting that "all amplification [of Scripture] is frivolous and vain."[5] But Hannah persisted, feeling strongly that society's elite desperately needed a clear introduction to the Bible.

Reaction to *Sacred Dramas* was surprisingly favorable. The Quaker philanthropist Jonas Hanway was prepared to criticize the skits for "taking an undue liberty with the Scriptures,"[6] but instead, as soon as he finished reading them himself, he bought more copies to donate to a nearby boarding school. Likewise, Bishop of London Robert Lowth, poet Anna Barbauld, and educator Sarah Trimmer all praised Hannah's creative approach. Yet, as Ford noted, most of those who praised *Sacred Dramas* were already converted. Hannah had failed to reach her targeted audience: the biblically ignorant elite.

"The Mainspring of the Machine"

Hannah believed that in order to have true reform, change needed to start at the top with the upper class and then seep down to influence the lower classes. Yet as biographer Mary Alden Hopkins points out, while Hannah was indeed a critic, she was a mild one. "Her words did not bite like Swift's or lash like Pope's. No one writhed under her scorn."[7] She focused instead on domestic reforms, criticizing the fact that elite women often visited the hairdresser on Sundays, the Sabbath. She was pleased to learn that the queen, after reading her 1788 book *Thoughts on the Importance of the Manners of the Great to General Society*, stopped summoning an outside hairdresser on the Sabbath and had her tresses arranged by one of her own attendants instead.

Yet Hannah's criticism wasn't always subtle. Her long poem *The Slave Trade* was praised as an important contribution to the abolitionist cause. The poem launched her as a champion of the anti-slavery movement, and she joined like-minded friends, including John Newton and William Wilberforce, in the cause. Wilberforce was a particularly significant influence in Hannah's life. They first met in Bath in 1786, and he became a regular visitor to her cottage at Cowslip Green and later to her house about a mile away at Barley Wood, where Hannah lived with her four sisters. Knowing Hannah's propensity for an active faith, Wilberforce announced during a visit with her in 1787 that "something had to be done for Cheddar."[8]

"We found more than 2,000 people in the parish, almost all very poor," wrote Hannah about the village of Cheddar. "We went to every house in the place, and found every house a scene of the greatest vice and ignorance. We saw but one Bible in all the parish, and that was used to prop a flower-pot. No clergyman had resided in it for forty years. One rode over from Wells to preach once each Sunday. No sick were visited, and children were often buried without any funeral service."[9]

The idea of a Sunday school emerged from that visit. While Hannah appreciated the financial support of Wilberforce and other male benefactors, she also made it clear from the outset that she and her sister Martha would found the school and directly oversee it. Wilberforce endorsed the sisters' plans, comparing them to Spencer's lady-knights battling numerous ogres and referring to them as "the mainspring of the machine."[10]

In October 1789, Hannah and her sister Martha opened their first Sunday school in a barn in Cheddar, despite the local farmers' declaration that "religion would be the ruin of agriculture."[11] The object of the classes was to teach children Scripture and shape them into honest, virtuous citizens. It didn't take long for the sisters to realize that the children's parents negatively influenced any progress they made on Sunday, so as a result, they launched Sunday school classes for adults as well, particularly for women. They taught the mothers Scripture, as well as skills like spinning, weaving, knitting, sewing, and cooking, and also encouraged the women to participate in what they called "benefit societies." Each week the women deposited a small sum, as little as a penny, into the community coffer, which made funds available for sick members and even grants to cover maternity leave.

Within ten years of establishing the first Sunday school in Cheddar, Hannah and Martha founded more than a dozen such schools in neighboring villages across the countryside. The sisters annually donated more than two hundred Bibles, Common Prayer Books, and Testaments to these schools, as well as hundreds of Hannah's "Cheap Repository Tracts," a series of moral tales and ballads written to counter the bawdy chapbooks sold by peddlers to the uneducated around the countryside. As Mary Alden Hopkins noted, "The English

Sunday School plan in which the Mores play so early and important a part attained an importance unforeseen by its originators. . . . It is no exaggeration to say that the More sisters helped raise the standards of living, of techniques, of ethics and of grace, in generations then unborn."[12]

"Action Is the Life of Virtue"

It's clear from her early success as a playwright that Hannah More could have carved out a comfortable life for herself as a member of upper-class London society. Yet it's also obvious that something about that life of materialism, wealth, and decadence didn't feel right to Hannah—it lacked satisfaction on a deeper, more spiritual level. "Action is the life of virtue, and the world is the theatre of action," she once wrote.[13] While she yearned to make her mark on the world, Hannah was interested in a particular kind of influence—not simply as a famous playwright who wrote about virtue and godliness but as a woman who actually lived it. What Hannah More didn't realize was that her life of virtue would have such a lasting impact more than two centuries after her death.

14

Phillis Wheatley

'Twas Mercy

$(1753-1784)$

The slender teenager stood before eighteen of the most prominent, powerful, and respected men in colonial Boston—among
them Massachusetts governor Thomas Hutchinson, Lieutenant
Governor Andrew Oliver, statesman John Hancock, and Reverend
Charles Chauncy. Altogether the esteemed group was comprised
of seven ordained ministers, three poets, six government officials,
and several key figures in the battle for independence. They were
gathered for one reason: to determine whether the shy, young girl
was, as she claimed, the legitimate author of the twenty-eight poems
she clutched in her hands. The men in the room, along with most of
Boston's literate public, doubted the girl's literary authenticity. After
all, as an African slave, she was considered intellectually inferior and
incapable of writing such high-caliber poetry.

As she stood poised before the tribunal, the girl prepared herself
to endure an oral examination that would not only determine the

course of her own life and work but also impact an entire race. As Henry Louis Gates Jr. noted, "The stakes . . . were as high as they could get for an oral exam. She [was] on trial and so [was] her race."[1] Furthermore, as Gates noted, the "jury" wasn't exactly an association for the advancement of colored people. Not only were the eighteen men assembled arguably the most highly educated and powerful men in Boston at the time, but the majority owned slaves. One even worked as a slave dealer.

No transcript of the exchange between the tribunal and the poet exists, so we can't know for sure the nature of the examination or the questions that were asked that day. But we do know this: at the examination's conclusion, Phillis Wheatley walked out with a certificate of authentication signed by all eighteen examiners, an attestation that was included in the prologue of her first published book:

> We whose Names are under-written, do assure the World, that the Poems specified in the following Page, were (as we verily believe) written by Phillis, a young Negro Girl, who was but a few Years since, brought an uncultivated Barbarian from Africa, and has ever since been, and now is, under the Disadvantage of serving as a slave in a Family in this Town. She has been examined by some of the best Judges and is thought qualified to write them.[2]

The book, published in England in 1773 (despite the attestation, Boston publishers still refused to consider it) and entitled *Poems of Various Subjects, Religious and Moral*, is considered the first book of poetry written in English by a person of African descent.

A Poet Is Born

Phillis Wheatley was one of six million enslaved Africans to arrive in the Americas between 1700 and 1808. She landed in Boston on July 11, 1761, aboard the *Phillis*, the vessel after which she was renamed by her owners, Boston merchant and tailor John Wheatley and his wife, Susanna. Because she wrote so little about her native Africa, almost nothing is known about her life prior to her arrival in Boston, including her birth name or her exact birthplace. Historians surmise that she was born in either Senegal or Gambia.

Likewise we know little about her Middle Passage aboard the *Phillis*. As biographer Vincent Carretta points out, "Perhaps her experience was understandably so traumatic that she was never able or willing to reimagine it."[3] All we know is that of the ninety-six enslaved Africans who crossed the Atlantic on the *Phillis*, only seventy-five survived to be sold in Boston, a mortality rate of nearly 25 percent during the journey. A child of seven years old, Phillis disembarked from the ship thin, sickly, and naked, missing her middle two top teeth. It's said Susanna Wheatley chose her from the more robust, healthy females exhibited because of "the humble and modest demeanor and the interesting features of the little stranger."[4]

Phillis was treated by her master and mistress like a member of the Wheatley family rather than a typical slave in eighteenth-century colonial Boston. She was spared the hours of washing, ironing, cooking, baking, sewing, and knitting that the majority of female house slaves endured. Instead, she was educated not only in rudimentary reading and writing and the basic tenets of Christianity but also in the classics. Just four years after her arrival in Boston, Phillis was adequately literate in English to compose a letter to a Presbyterian minister and write a short elegy on the death of a neighbor. She was allowed access to a dictionary and was given a place to write, where she studied her favorite authors, including Alexander Pope and Homer and Ovid in translation. As Carretta observes, "The education Phillis Wheatley received . . . would have been very impressive for a white man of high social standing at the time."[5]

"The Most Reviled Poem in African-American Literature"

As an ardent Congregationalist, Susanna Wheatley felt obligated to introduce Phillis to Christianity, and she dealt with her slave's spiritual education as conscientiously as she did that of her own two children. Phillis was baptized in 1771 and subsequently came to believe that

God's providence included the enslavement of Africans, a view that infuriated African Americans in the twentieth century, particularly during the 1960s and '70s.

"Let us rejoice in and adore the wonders of God's infinite Love in bringing us from a land Semblant of darkness itself, and there the divine light of revelation (being obscur'd) is as darkness," Phillis wrote to her friend and fellow native African Obour Tanner in 1772. "Here the knowledge of the true God and eternal life are made manifest; But there, profound ignorance overshadows the Land. . . . Many of our fellow creatures are pass'd by, when the bowels of divine love expanded toward us. May this goodness & long Suffering of God lead us to unfeign'd repentance."[6]

Phillis's best-known poem, "On Being Brought from Africa to America," was written when she was fourteen years old and has been called "the most reviled poem in African-American literature."[7] The eight-line poem follows the argument she made in the letter to Tanner—namely, that it was God's mercy that brought her as a slave from Africa to America, subsequently allowing her the opportunity to know Jesus:

> 'Twas mercy brought me from my pagan land,
> Taught my benighted soul to understand
> That there's a God, that there's a Saviour too:
> Once I redemption neither sought nor knew,
> Some view our sable race with scornful eye,
> "Their colour is a diabolic die."
> Remember, Christians, Negros, black as Cain,
> May be refin'd, and join th' angelic train.[8]

Modern critics have vilified Phillis for rejecting her African heritage and condoning slavery. She has been criticized for being nothing but a clever imitator of the eighteenth-century poet Alexander Pope, as well as for being "too white," having "a white mind," and playing the role of an "early Boston Aunt Jemima."[9] While we can understand how this particular poem's verses are problematic, given what seems to be her justification of the slave trade, as Carretta notes, the poem is theologically consistent with Phillis's religious convictions. "Like anyone with faith in an omnipotent, omniscient and benevolent God," Carretta observes, "Wheatley believes that the evil of enslavement that caused her exodus from Africa has to serve an ultimately positive purpose that may as yet be unknowable to humankind."[10] Phillis perceived her personal enslavement to be the ironic catalyst for her introduction to and union with God.

This connection between her enslavement and her embrace of Christianity is not, however, proof that Phillis condoned slavery or diminished it as less than the horrific evil it was. Many of Phillis's other poems and letters express a bitter opposition to the slave trade, a fact that's been overlooked by many contemporary scholars. In a 1774 letter to her friend Samson Occom—a letter that was subsequently reprinted in eleven New England newspapers—Phillis stated her boldest antislavery protest, condemning those who regularly boasted of Christian charity yet held slaves at the same time:

> In every human Breast, God has implanted a Principle, which we call Love of Freedom; it is impatient of oppression, and pants for Deliverance . . . and I will assert that the same principle lives in us . . . This I desire not for their Hurt, but to convince them of the strange Absurdity of their Conduct whose Words and Actions are so diametrically opposite.[11]

Clearly she was not afraid to criticize the blatant double standard that existed among Christian slaveholders, including her own master and mistress.

From Extraordinary to Obscure

When it became obvious that Susanna Wheatley would not be able to convince a Boston printer to publish Phillis's first book despite the signed attestation, Susanna secured the support of London's Countess of Huntingdon and began to pursue a British publisher. In 1773 Phillis sailed with the Wheatleys' son, Nathaniel, to London to meet her patron. By then, having published dozens of poems in American and London newspapers, she was an international celebrity. As her ship set sail from Boston, newspapers reported her every move. The *Boston News-Letter* declared on May 3 that the "extraordinary Negro Poet" was about to depart.[12]

Phillis left London after just six short weeks, without having met Countess Huntingdon. She and Nathaniel were called home to attend to a terminally ill Susanna, who languished for nearly a year before dying in March of 1774. Her mistress lived to see Phillis's landmark book in print. *Poems on Various Subjects, Religious and Moral* was published in London in 1773 by Archibald Bell, an obscure printer of religious books. The volume was widely reviewed by English and Scottish newspapers and magazines, at least two of which noted the hypocrisy of the Wheatleys, who went to enormous lengths to tout the talents of their slave poet but did nothing to free her from enslavement. "We are very much concerned," wrote a reviewer, "to find that this ingenious young woman is yet a slave."[13] Shortly after her return, after being enslaved for twelve years, Phillis was emancipated by the Wheatleys.

Susanna and John Wheatley may have treated Phillis as a virtual member of the family when she was young, but it's clear that her legal status as a slave made her far from such. When John died in 1778, his last will and testament bequeathed the bulk of his estate to his son, Nathaniel, and the remainder of it to his daughter, Mary. Phillis's name was not mentioned. Despite the fact that she was invited into the company of such notable figures as George Washington and Benjamin Franklin, circumstances grew increasingly difficult for Phillis after her emancipation, and she struggled to earn a living off her published writing. The prominent leaders who had supported her writing years earlier either had died or, by the start of the Revolutionary War in 1776, had fled Boston or been forced to fend for themselves.

A few days after the death of her former master, Phillis accepted the marriage proposal of John Peters, a black grocer in Boston—a decision, Carretta notes, "no doubt prompted at least in part by her desire for some degree of social and economic security."[14] Not a lot is known about this period of Phillis's life, except that it was the beginning of the end. The couple struggled financially. John was imprisoned for debt, and their two children died in infancy. Still writing and still in search of a publisher for her second volume of poetry, Phillis placed her last advertisement for a book publisher in the September 1784 issue of *Boston Magazine*. Two months later, her husband still imprisoned, Phillis died alone at the age of thirty-one, poverty-stricken, destitute, and in relative obscurity. Some historians suggest that a third infant child died a few hours later.

Unshaken

Phillis Wheatley's life as a Christian seems overshadowed by her historic contributions as an African American poet. But think for a moment about her thirty-one years. Wrenched from her home and family at seven years old, she endured inconceivable atrocities on the long voyage from Africa to America, arriving naked, half alive, alone, and terrified, to be sold like an animal to strangers in a land where she couldn't speak a word of the language and knew not a soul. She served as a slave, was considered nothing more than a piece of property, and was forced to defend her intelligence before a group of white men who defined her as an "uncultivated barbarian." Yet in spite of the profound suffering and humiliation she endured, Phillis Wheatley praised God as good—a God of kindness, mercy, and love. Given similar circumstances, how many Christians would stand as firmly as she did, with their trust in God's benevolence unshaken?[15]

15

Elizabeth Fry

Quaker Prison Reformer

$(1780-1845)$

I t took a moment for her eyes to adjust to the dimness, but when they did, she was astonished by what she saw. Nearly three hundred women were packed into two rooms, most of them in tattered rags, their hair matted, faces streaked with grime. Some were attempting to cook in the cramped quarters, while others hunched over buckets of dirty water, trying to do their washing. Many sprawled motionless on the filthy straw. As the stench of unwashed bodies filled the frigid air, the woman struggled to resist the urge to hold a handkerchief over her nose. Babies screamed, and as she stood there surveying the scene, she watched as two prisoners stripped off the clothes from a dead infant to clothe a baby still living.

Elizabeth Fry left London's Newgate Prison that day, went home, bathed, and changed into fresh clothing. The next day she returned, this time with armloads of flannel baby clothes, blankets, and clean, thick straw. She and a friend distributed the supplies, comforted the mothers, and helped to dress the babies in warm flannel. Her lifelong ministry as a prison reformer had begun.

Transformation

Elizabeth wasn't an obvious candidate for such grueling work. She was considered "delicate" as a child, and illness, anxiety, and depression plagued her from youth through her old age. She suffered from nervousness, stomach upset, and relentless toothaches, symptoms that isolated her from both her peers and her siblings, who also found her socially awkward and withdrawn. After her mother's death when Elizabeth was thirteen, the young girl's self-isolation intensified, and "her dark moods hung like thunder-clouds over the house and created an oppressive atmosphere."[1]

Elizabeth also struggled spiritually. She was inclined toward religion yet constantly battled what she considered worldly temptations and was torn between duty and pleasure. When she allowed herself to enjoy such pleasures as dancing and socializing, she was quick to reprimand herself in her journal for succumbing to such frivolity.

On the other hand, Elizabeth also struggled against periods of skepticism. "My mind is so much inclined to scepticism and enthusiasm that if I argue and doubt I shall be a total sceptic," she wrote in her journal. "If on the contrary, I give way to it and, as it were, wait for religion I may be led away."[2]

In the midst of this quandary, Elizabeth met the American Quaker William Savery when he arrived in England to preach at a Meeting of Friends. As she sat in the front row and listened to Savery advocate for peace, Elizabeth was transfixed. Not only did Savery spark a new and exciting religious fervor in her, she was also attracted to him, even though he was married. "I always feel quite a palpitation at my heart at the sound of his voice," she admitted in her journal. Elizabeth realized that religion and her feelings for Savery were dangerously connected. "I shall always love religion through him but must always love it away from him," she wrote before leaving London for her hometown of Earlham.[3]

Elizabeth's father and siblings were alarmed by her sudden piousness. It was obvious she had been transformed. She resisted luxuries, refused to shop for a new silk gown with her sisters, read the Bible constantly, abstained from dancing and singing, and began to attend Meetings twice on Sunday in the tradition of the Plain Quakers. Yet she was torn, not wanting to alienate her family by adopting the bonnet and "thee" and "thou" language of the Quakers she admired. Although she succumbed to her family's pressure and gave in to dancing and parties from time to time, for the most part Elizabeth stayed firm in her aspirations to adopt the Plain Quaker life. "Even acting right will sometimes bring dissensions in a family," she reassured herself in her journal.[4] She finally convinced her family that her Quakerism was no passing whim. By the time she met her future husband, banker and Quaker Joseph Fry, whom she married in 1800, Elizabeth was a Plain Quaker in heart, speech, and dress.

Restlessness . . . and Release

Elizabeth did not adapt well to married life. For starters, she found the Fry family coarse, narrow-minded, and not nearly religious enough for her. Also, she was irritated by her husband's lack of business finesse, his constant humming, his interest in chess and nonreligious reading material, and his inclination to spend money frivolously. She was bored, restless, and agitated; frustrated by her inability to manage the servants; and exhausted from hosting frequent dinner parties and house guests.

Motherhood did nothing to ease her dissatisfaction. After nearly every birth, Elizabeth suffered from postpartum depression that often lasted for months. She was an anxious mother who fretted over every ailment. By the time Elizabeth was twenty-four, she had three children under the age of five and questioned whether she would ever have a role beyond that of wife and mother. "It does appear to me as if I might become the careworn and oppressed mother," she wrote in her journal.[5] Later, on her eighth wedding anniversary, she reflected, "Various trials of faith and patience have been permitted me; my course has been very different from what I expected, and instead of being, as I had hoped, a useful instrument in the Church militant, here I am a careworn wife and mother, outwardly nearly devoted to the things of this life!"[6]

Her father's death in 1809, however, changed the course of Elizabeth's life. Although she had regularly attended Quaker Meetings up to this point, Elizabeth had never testified publicly. The few times she had felt inclined to speak at a Meeting, she was so overcome with anxiety that her body trembled uncontrollably and she feared she would faint. Her father's death released her from his lifelong disapproval of her religious choices and psychologically freed her to speak. She felt, she wrote, "like a bottle that has been corked up and pressed down and now there is an opening inside, there is much to run out." As she wrote the day her father was buried, "I think this will make way for me in some things that have been long on my mind."[7] Shortly after her father's funeral, Elizabeth began to speak at Meetings, a practice she continued for the rest of her life.

Mother, Minister, Prison Reformer, and More

In 1811, one month after giving birth to her seventh child, Elizabeth was formally acknowledged as a minister by the Society of Friends. While her brothers John and Daniel disapproved of her public speaking and her sisters criticized her for neglecting her family, her husband supported her, taking on more and more of the household responsibilities while Elizabeth traveled farther from home. When Stephen Grellet, a French aristocrat who had settled in America and converted to the Society of Friends, visited London's Newgate Prison in 1813 and surveyed the appalling conditions, he immediately summoned Elizabeth, who was known by then for her compassion for the city's poor. By 1817 she had firmly established herself as London's foremost prison reformer.

Not only did Elizabeth advocate for better prison conditions, including more space and adequate clothing and food, she also persuaded the authorities to allow her to launch an education program for the imprisoned women and their children. And since the male authorities refused to help her run the school, she organized the Association for the Improvement of the Female Prisoners at Newgate. This committee of twelve Quaker women alternated daily visits to the prison to run the program, which included an introduction to the Scriptures and a work-for-pay initiative that enabled the prisoners to earn a few shillings a week for their needlework. Elizabeth also enlisted the inmates' unanimous consent when it came to instituting the program's twelve rules, which included appointing a supervising matron; assigning specific work tasks; allotting a period in the morning and evening for reading Scripture; and forbidding all begging, cursing, gaming, card playing, quarrelling, immoral conversation, and improper reading material such as novels and plays. Each rule was voted on separately by a show of hands—a cooperative practice that was unheard of at the time. These rules were later adapted for use in prisons across Europe.

As her work in the prisons progressed, Elizabeth grew increasingly opposed to the death penalty. At the time, criminals could be executed for more than two hundred offenses, including stealing something as small as a pair of stockings or passing a forged bank note. Elizabeth personally but unsuccessfully campaigned for Charlotte Newman and Mary Ann James, who were hanged for forgery. A year later, she and her brother John advocated for the life of one of her favorite prisoners, Harriet Skelton, a maid who was later executed for passing forged bank notes. Elizabeth considered capital punishment an evil practice that produced evil results, a declaration she made to the House of Commons Committee on London Prisons. The committee listened to her testimony, but it didn't change their minds.

Elizabeth's successful prison reform made her famous across Britain and beyond, but it also provoked the ire of her critics. Village gossipers and the national media alike suggested that the Frys had sent six of their nine children off to relatives so that Elizabeth would be free to pursue her prison work. And while it was true that several of the Fry children lived away from home for a few months, it was because the family was suffering financially. That said, Elizabeth never made excuses for herself when it came to her choices. She believed prison reform was her divine calling, and she allowed nothing—not her own health, her family, or public opinion—to stand in the way.

In 1827 Elizabeth published a small book entitled *Observations on the Visiting, Superintendence and Government of Female Prisoners*, in which she advocated for the role of women in society. "No person will deny the importance attached to the character and conduct of a woman in all her domestic and social relations, when she is filling the station of a daughter, sister, a wife, a mother or a mistress of a family," she wrote. "But it is a dangerous error to suppose that the duties of females end here."[8] Elizabeth suggested that women could make a profound impact in ministering not only to female prisoners but also to those in hospitals, asylums, and workhouses. There was much more work to be done, Elizabeth acknowledged, so why not encourage those with so much compassion for their own gender to be useful? It was a radical proposal, and one that suggests Elizabeth may have viewed her work as a personal necessity as well as a divine calling.

Forging Ahead with Reform

The Fry family suffered a major setback in 1828 when they were forced to declare their business, Frys Bank, bankrupt. Rumors flew, and Elizabeth herself was accused of withdrawing money from her husband's bank to fund the Newgate Association and other charities. While waiting for the bailiffs to arrive to take an inventory of the property, Elizabeth took note of her surroundings, stunned that she no longer owned anything, including the house itself. Yet at the end of the day, despite the fact that her home, land, and furniture were all confiscated, she thanked God for his blessings. The following Sunday, she stood in the Meeting and testified that she loved and trusted God in times of adversity as well as prosperity.

Although her siblings generously gave the Frys a substantial amount of money, they were forced to fold their bank entirely and relinquish their still-viable tea- and coffee-importing business to Elizabeth's brothers, with Joseph staying on as a salaried employee. They also moved from their rambling country house to a suburban home in West Ham, offered to them by Elizabeth's brother Samuel. Worse than the financial ruin, though, was the public disgrace. Six months after declaring bankruptcy, Joseph Fry was formally disowned by the Religious Society of Friends. Elizabeth, though still allowed to attend Meetings and participate in the Yearly Meeting, was acutely aware of her diminished position. Still, she was a minister, a calling she would not abandon. Not long after the financial debacle, she ignored the warnings of her siblings, who insisted it was improper for her to continue her religious work, and departed for Stamford alone via stagecoach to visit yet another prison.

After her death from a stroke in 1845, Elizabeth's daughters scoured forty-four volumes of her journals to remove all traces of their mother's struggles and weaknesses. She was canonized by biographers and viewed by many as a saint. Yet while the original, unedited versions of these journals and the biographical portraits produced in more recent years divulge Elizabeth's flaws, they also reveal a more complex, real, relatable woman. It's in the spotlight of these very weaknesses and character flaws that we see and relate to the true Elizabeth Fry. She struggled her entire life with anxiety and depression. She wrestled with her faith as well as with her role as a wife and mother, and she suffered the criticism of many who disagreed with everything from her prison reforms to her parenting. Yet she persevered, courageously defying societal expectations, weathering sharp and often vicious criticism, and forging ahead, determined to fulfill what she believed was her God-given calling. Sometimes, as in the case of Elizabeth Fry, God calls us to step out of our comfort zones. The choice is ours to answer yes.

16

Jarena Lee

The Power to Speak

$(1783 - ?)$

The young woman leapt to her feet before she even realized what she was doing. Standing at her place in the pews, she interrupted the bishop's sermon on Jonah and began to preach on the text herself. As the bishop stood speechless in the pulpit, the church members turned to gape at the woman preaching from the pews. When she was finished, she collapsed into her seat, mortified by her own outburst and terrified that she would be immediately expelled from the church. Instead, to her surprise, the bishop turned to the bewildered congregation and claimed that Jarena Lee was called by the Lord to be a preacher.

The Lord's Handmaiden

Aside from the few details she provides in her own autobiography, not much is known about Jarena Lee's childhood. We know that she was born to free parents in Cape May, New Jersey, and was sent at the age of seven to work as a maid about sixty miles from her home. We know that she didn't see her parents again for fourteen years, and that Jarena saw her family only four times in her entire life. We don't know Jarena's maiden name, the names of her parents or siblings, or how she learned to read and write.

Despite the fact that her parents were irreligious, "wholly ignorant of the knowledge of God,"[1] Jarena's faith was strong. Her first order of business when she moved to Philadelphia at the age of twenty-one was to find a church. She tried a number of different denominations, but when she discovered the African Methodist Episcopal Church led by Reverend Richard Allen, Jarena felt immediately, as she put it, that "this is the people to which my heart unites." Three months from the first service she attended at the Philadelphia A.M.E. Church, her "soul was gloriously converted to God."[2]

Despite her joy at finding a faith community, Jarena struggled with such severe depression that she was tempted on more than one occasion to commit suicide. Convinced that she would never find happiness and contentment, she prayed relentlessly for relief. Finally, after four years of desperate wandering in the wilderness of despair, Jarena felt that she was not only converted but also sanctified by God, a fact that she believed led to her full recovery from depression.

As an African American woman in pre–Civil War times, Jarena Lee ventured boldly into uncharted territory when she felt the call to preach. When she first recognized the call, no one was more surprised than Jarena herself. In fact, when she heard the clear voice directing her to preach the gospel, her first response was an emphatic no. "No one will believe me!" she replied aloud to the command. Initially Reverend Allen was hesitant as well, informing a relieved Jarena that the Methodist theology did not support women preachers. He encouraged her to hold prayer meetings and to exhort, but he drew the line at preaching. "This I was glad to hear," wrote Jarena, "because it removed the fear of the cross."[3] Accepting Allen's verdict, Jarena was content to marry Pastor Joseph Lee and move with him to Snow Hill, a small town outside of Philadelphia.

Still, as much as she wanted to, Jarena couldn't shake the feeling that she was called to preach. The more she pondered this strange directive from God, the more she began to see it not only as possible but as inevitable. "For as unseemly as it may appear now-a-days for a woman to preach," she wrote, "it should be remembered that nothing is impossible with God. And why should it be thought impossible, heterodox, or improper, for a woman to preach, seeing the Saviour died for the woman as well as the man."[4]

After her husband died only six years into their marriage, Jarena returned to Philadelphia and her church home with her two young children. Shortly after her return, Allen, who was now bishop of the African Episcopal Methodists of America, gently rebuffed Jarena's plea to preach a second time. This time, though, Jarena was not to be deterred. Sensing a loss of momentum in Allen's sermon on Jonah, she sprang to her feet "as by an altogether supernatural impulse"[5] and began to preach to the shocked congregation. At the conclusion of her sermon, even Bishop Allen had to admit that her calling was legitimate.

The following Sunday, after begging God to allow her to preach anywhere but in church, Jarena knocked on a neighbor's door and asked if she could lead a prayer meeting in the woman's living room. That day she preached to a congregation of five. Six months later, leaving her young son in the hands of a neighbor, she traveled thirty miles with her infant to another Methodist church, where she preached for a week. There, "by the instrumentality of a poor coloured woman, the Lord poured forth his spirit among the people," Jarena wrote. "The Lord gave his handmaiden power to speak for his great name, for he arrested the hearts of the people, and caused a shaking amongst the multitude, for God was in the midst."[6]

Life on the Road

Jarena worked as an unordained itinerant preacher for more than thirty years, traveling ceaselessly, sometimes walking twenty miles at a time to preach at two churches in one day. In a single year she traveled more than two thousand miles and delivered 178 sermons. We don't know what happened to her young son or her infant, who are mentioned only once in her autobiography. Her ministry was her entire existence, and she sacrificed everything, including her family, for it.

Because she could not earn an official living as a preacher, Jarena was dependent on the charity and hospitality of others. Occasionally she received a freewill offering collected from a service, but more often she did not know the source of her next meal or where she might find a roof over her head. Life for an itinerant preacher in the early nineteenth century was exceedingly difficult, and for Jarena, it was further complicated by the fact that she was a woman and an African American. As Anna Carter Florence notes, nineteenth-century ladies did not, as a rule, leave their domestic sphere and travel alone. To do so was uncouth as well as dangerous. Says Florence, "African American women traveling in the North faced the perpetual threat of male assaults to both body and character."[7] Further complicating matters, Jarena traveled into slave territory as a missionary, a gravely dangerous endeavor considering that any black person, even a free black person, who crossed the Mason-Dixon Line could be legally enslaved, regardless of his or her free status in other states. But as Florence also notes, "God calls whom God will. If the preacher is a black woman in antebellum Philadelphia in the year 1811, a woman whom no one will believe and for whom living out the call will be unimaginably difficult, so be it: God does not call preachers to be believed. God calls preachers to preach."[8]

If Jarena was ever afraid, she did not let on in her autobiography. She was focused entirely on one goal, regardless of the enormous risks and sacrifices involved. Against all odds, Jarena preached. "My tongue was cut loose, the stammerer spoke freely," she wrote. "The love of God, and of his service, burned with a vehement flame within me—his name was glorified among the people."[9]

"My Ardour Abates Not a Whit"

Writing her autobiography was a natural extension of what Jarena understood as her life's work. Entitled *The Life and Religious Experi-*

ence of Jarena Lee, a Coloured Lady, Giving an Account of Her Call to Preach the Gospel, the book was published by Jarena at her own expense in 1836. Today the book is considered the first spiritual autobiography ever written by an African American woman. In the book's conclusion, Jarena clarified exactly why her story needed to be told and publicized. "But for the satisfaction of such as may follow after me," she stated, "I have recorded how the Lord called me to his work, and how he has kept me from falling from grace, as I feared I should."[10] The book sold so well in its first printing that Jarena financed a second printing in 1839 and then petitioned the African Methodist Episcopal Church to publish the autobiography as part of its official inventory. However, while the book committee accepted Bishop Allen's autobiography for publication, they rejected *The Life and Religious Experience of Jarena Lee*, citing the manuscript as indecipherable and in need of explanation.

As Florence notes, "The rejection of Lee's book, of course, had nothing to do with writing style, and she knew it."[11] After all, this was a woman who had spent three decades as an itinerant preacher, a woman who had preached thousands of sermons, certainly more than most men. While it was unlikely that the manuscript was in need of further explanation, it was quite likely that the church was not prepared to support such a radical endeavor.

Stung by the rejection, Jarena revised the manuscript on her own, this time including seventy additional pages specifying her preaching duties, as well as details concerning which congregations had either supported or rejected her ministry as a female preacher. The 1849 edition of Jarena's book sparked an immediate backlash in the denomination. "Clergy who had once encouraged Lee in her struggle for recognition now rejected both her book and her ministry," Florence observes, "making it clear that women preachers, especially those who dared to criticize men in pulpits and in print, would no longer be tolerated in the A.M.E. Church."[12] As a result, in 1852 the denomination declared its official ruling: women were not allowed to preach.

Just three years after the last printing of her autobiography, women were effectively removed from any formal leadership in the A.M.E.

Church, and Jarena herself disappeared from historical records. We don't know if she continued to preach in her remaining years, nor do we know the year or the circumstances of her death.

What we do know is this: Jarena Lee believed the Lord had given her, "his handmaiden," the power to speak in honor of his great name, and she demonstrated her determination to fulfill that calling, regardless of great personal expense. She may have lost her reputation, her profession, her status, and her loved ones, but Jarena never lost her faith. "In all things he has proved himself a God of truth to me," she wrote in the closing paragraph of her autobiography, "and in his service I am now as much determined to spend and be spent, as at the very first. My ardour for the progress of his cause abates not a whit."[13] Although the history books cannot prove it, Jarena Lee undoubtedly spent the rest of her life serving God, and her legacy as a preacher and a heroine of the faith continues to serve and inspire us today.

17

Ann Hasseltine Judson

Bringing the Knowledge of Truth to Burma

(1789–1826)

G o then, and do all in your power to enlighten their minds, and bring them to the knowledge of the truth," the reverend advised the young girl sitting before him in the pew. "Teach them that they have immortal souls."[1] It was a tall order for a girl of twenty-three, married in her parents' dining room only hours before. But the young lady, still dressed in her wedding finery, met the preacher's stern gaze with a firm gaze of her own, refusing to shrink from his command. Ann Hasseltine Judson was about to become America's first female missionary, and she was ready.

Born in Bradford, Massachusetts, in 1789, the same year the young United States began its government under the Constitution, Ann Hasseltine didn't always entertain such lofty spiritual ambitions. As a teenager, she enjoyed parties and dancing more than piety and prayer. But Ann's priorities changed dramatically after she read Hannah

More's *Strictures on Female Education.* Try though she might, Ann could not get More's teachings out of her head, particularly this adage: "She that liveth in pleasure is dead while she liveth."[2] Although her friends continued to pursue frivolity and fun, Ann took More's adage to heart and turned inward, spending more and more of her time praying and reading books like John Bunyan's *Pilgrim's Progress.*

Ann's life changed forever the day a young man named Adoniram Judson came to dine with the Hasseltines. The two fell in love almost immediately, and not long after, Adoniram wrote to Ann's parents, asking for her hand in marriage. John and Rebecca Hasseltine were appalled. After all, Adoniram was about to embark on what many in the small community considered a preposterous idea. He planned to sail to Burma, where he would spend the rest of his life as a missionary. Her parents realized that if Ann accepted Adoniram's marriage proposal, they would likely never see their daughter again.

Adoniram and Ann were married on February 5, 1812. The following morning before dawn the two crept out of her parents' house while the family slept and departed via horse and carriage through the thick snow toward Salem. Goodbyes were painful, Adoniram convinced Ann; this way was for the best. Deacon Hasseltine apparently disagreed. Less than a mile from home, Ann's father, a cloak thrown hastily over his nightshirt, caught up with the two runaways on horseback and demanded they return home to say a proper good-bye.

A few hours later, tearful farewells finally behind them, Adoniram and Ann made their way to Salem, where they boarded the *Caravan.* The ship sailed on February 9, 1812, and finally anchored in the Bay of Bengal three months later. Despite the fact that the new missionaries met unexpected resistance from both the Indian government and the East India Company, who feared the Gospels could stir a revolutionary reaction in the natives, Adoniram and Ann persevered. They initially spent several months in the Isle of France (now the Republic of Mauritius), five thousand miles southwest of India, and then finally secured passage on a ship to Burma. En route, as the ship heaved on the roiling waves, Ann lay on the deck beneath a thin canvas tarp and gave birth. The baby was stillborn and was buried at sea. A few days later Adoniram carried a weak and grieving Ann to the rail as they neared shore so she could glimpse the land she would call home.

Nearly eighteen months after they had departed from Massachusetts, the Judsons watched together as the creaking *Georgiana* sailed into the entrance of the Rangoon River. From the swampy banks, a handful of Burmese stared awestruck at the foreigners as the ship crept upstream. Rangoon itself was a tiny town, comprised of nothing more than a motley collection of teak and bamboo houses. Along the crowded, muddy streets, priests with shaven heads and saffron-colored robes jostled destitute lepers and naked children smoking cigars. A cacophony of voices all yelling in an incomprehensible language created an intolerable din as Ann and Adoniram surveyed the place they would make their home. It was, Ann recalled later, the unhappiest day of her life.

Baptizing the Burmese

The couple was forced to adapt to life in Rangoon quickly and was soon accustomed to the oppressive heat, the sight of elephants parading regally in funeral processions, and the foreign flavors of curry and plantains. Because she communicated with servants and merchants on a daily basis, Ann learned Burmese much more quickly than her husband, who spent every morning practicing the language with a teacher.

Their mission work, on the other hand, was another story. "Your religion is good for you, ours for us," the Burmese repeated time and time again.[3] Still, the Judsons persevered. Adoniram constructed a zayat, a small bamboo building with a thatched roof where Buddhist lay preachers traditionally offered instruction. From the front steps he shouted, "Ho! Everyone that thirsteth for knowledge," over and over until a small crowd of fifteen curious adults had gathered for the first service.[4] Each Sunday more and more Burmese were drawn to the zayat, until finally, after six years of the Judsons' continuous praying, a timber merchant named Maung Nau rose before the congregation of thirty and proclaimed his belief in Jesus. A few weeks later, a substantial crowd gathered as Nau was immersed in a pond a few steps from the zayat and baptized beneath the gaze of a Buddhist statue.

When he wasn't preaching from the steps of the zayat, Adoniram worked on translating the Bible into Burmese, beginning with the Gospel of Matthew. After another American missionary arrived in Rangoon with a printing press, they printed what they called "holy books," including the Gospel of Matthew, the story of Adam and Eve, the Ten Commandments, and a catechism Ann had written for the small group of Burmese children she taught every day in the mission house.

Ann also held Sunday meetings for Burmese women in her home. Although they listened politely as she discussed Christianity, most had no desire to give up their Buddhist faith. One woman confessed she'd rather spend eternity in hell with her own family and ancestors than in heaven with a lot of people she didn't know. Finally, though, Ann's persistence was rewarded. In June of 1820, a young Burmese woman awakened Ann and Adoniram in the middle of the night. Mah Men-lay had participated in Ann's Sunday meetings for several months and had decided she was ready to be baptized. In the darkness, with Ann holding the lantern, Adoniram baptized the first Burmese woman into the Christian faith and the tenth member of the Burmese Christian church.

Affliction and Mercy

While victories were few, hardships were ever-present. When her eight-month-old son died in 1816, Ann, though wracked by grief, willed herself to focus on the grace of God. "Eight months we enjoyed the precious little gift, in which time he had so completely entwined himself around his parents' hearts, that his existence seemed necessary to their own," she wrote to her parents. "But God has taught us by afflictions what we would not learn by mercies—that our hearts are His exclusive property, and whatever rival intrudes, He will tear it away. . . . We do not feel a disposition to murmur, or to inquire of our Sovereign why He has done this. . . . Oh, may it not be in vain that He has done this."[5]

Although Ann eventually grew to love Burma, the oppressive climate proved detrimental to her fragile health. Suffering from a severe liver ailment, she was forced to leave her adopted home in 1822 and return to America, a journey she never anticipated she would make when she left New England ten years earlier. While she regained her health, she wrote a history of the Burmese mission, a book that was widely read in America and awakened many to the conditions of the Burmese women and the importance of female missionaries working among them.

After more than a year apart from her husband, Ann returned to Burma. Shortly after, war broke out between Britain and Burma, and on June 8, 1824, more than a dozen Burmese burst through the front door of the mission house and interrupted the Judsons at dinnertime. During a few panicked, chaotic moments, Adoniram's arms were lashed tight with a cord and he was dragged from the house, paraded through the streets of Rangoon, and thrown into Let-may-yoon, the death prison. The Burmese assumed that Adoniram, an American missionary, was working as a spy for the British.

Pregnant with her third child, Ann moved into a shack outside the prison and lobbied unsuccessfully for months for Adoniram's release. When she wasn't petitioning government officials, she provided food and clothing for her husband and hauled an earthenware chamber pot to and from his cell. When the couple was allowed to meet privately for a few moments, Adoniram begged her to dig up his manuscript of the New Testament, which he had buried in the garden. Ann sewed the book into a pillow, and although Adoniram didn't dare read it in his cell, resting his head on it each night comforted him.

On January 26, 1825, Ann gave birth to a baby girl. The baby was small and sickly, and Ann was so weak after the birth that she was unable to walk to the prison to introduce Adoniram to his new daughter until nearly three weeks had passed. Finally, after more than seventeen months in prison and nearly a year after his daughter was born, Adoniram was released near the end of the Anglo-Burmese War. Ann had suffered from dysentery and spotted fever during her husband's last weeks in prison, and by the time he was freed, she was near death. When Adoniram first glimpsed her prone figure on the bed in their home, he didn't recognize the gaunt, lifeless body as Ann's. Her black curls had been shorn, and a dirty cotton cap covered her bare scalp. When he cradled her limp body to his chest, her eyelids barely flickered open.

Although she was not expected to live, Ann recovered enough to travel with her infant daughter to Amherst, a British-occupied city in lower Burma that was thought to be the best option for her fragile health. Immediately after arriving she began to oversee the construction of a new mission and school. But as it turned out, her health had been irreparably weakened. On October 26, 1826, Ann died at the age of thirty-six as she waited for her husband to return from a trip. After Adoniram received the news of Ann's death via a black-sealed letter, he wrote to her mother back in America, noting that according to those who had been at her deathbed, Ann had borne her sufferings with meekness, patience, magnanimity, and Christian fortitude. "Much she saw and suffered of the evil of this evil world; and eminently was she qualified to relish and enjoy the pure and holy rest into which she has entered," he wrote. "True, she has been torn from her husband's bleeding heart, and from her darling babe; but infinite wisdom and love have presided, as ever, in this most afflicting dispensation. Faith decides that it is all right; and the decision of faith, eternity will soon confirm."[6] The Judsons' daughter died six months after Ann.

In spite of the dire hardships she endured, Ann never lost faith in her mission or her God. "The consolation of religion, in these trying circumstances, were neither few nor small!" she wrote to her brother while Adoniram was imprisoned. "It taught me to look beyond this world, to that rest . . . where Jesus reigns and oppression never enters."[7] Nor did she regret her decision to dedicate her life to missionary work in Burma, despite the fact that the visible results of her work were so few. Though she departed from America's shores with a romanticized, idealized vision of mission work, she quickly adjusted to the hard reality of life in a dangerous, foreign environment. After ten long years in Rangoon, Ann and her husband had managed to convert only eighteen Burmese, yet nothing in her letters or journals indicates that she or Adoniram despaired. Ann believed that eighteen converted Christians, although an incremental start, were enough to carry the mission forward. And she was right. By the time Adoniram died in 1850, sixty-three churches had been established in Burma, with 163 missionaries and native preachers leading more than eight thousand converted Burmese.

Although Ann served only fourteen years in Burma, she lived the words her preacher had spoken on her wedding day—and then some. She brought the knowledge of truth to Burma and has since inspired thousands more around the globe.

18

Mary Lyon

A Thousand Streams

(1797–1849)

When Mary Lyon stood before her class and paraphrased the verse she knew by heart—"My father and mother forsook me, but the LORD took me up"[1]—she wasn't simply repeating memorized lines from Psalm 27. She spoke from personal experience. After her father died, Mary's mother remarried and moved several towns away with her younger children, leaving Mary behind on the family's one-hundred-acre farm in Buckland, Massachusetts, to manage her older brother's household. She cooked on the open hearth; baked bread; spun and dyed wool; wove coverlets; sewed clothes and embroidered linens; preserved fruits and vegetables; churned butter; made cheese, jam, soap, and candles; cured meat; washed clothes; and swept floors—all for the wage of one silver dollar a week. Thirteen-year-old Mary was left virtually on her own to fend for herself.

Women's Education Advocate, Servant of God

Even worse, perhaps, than the loneliness and separation from her family was the fact that Mary's heavy domestic responsibilities forced her to abandon what brought her the most joy: school. Fortunately, her brother's marriage liberated Mary from her domestic roles, and in 1814, at age seventeen, she was offered her first teaching job at a one-room schoolhouse in Buckland. No formal training was required—Mary's reputation as a stellar student years earlier was enough to qualify her for the job.

She was paid 75 cents plus board per week, far less than the standard ten to twelve dollars a month a male teacher received in the same role. As was the custom of the day, Mary "boarded round," meaning she lived an equal number of days in each pupil's home, which in this case required that she move every five days. Mary didn't find teaching easy or enjoyable, despite her own zeal for learning. She struggled with disciplining her students, especially on rainy days when the unruly older boys were temporarily released from their work in the fields and returned to her classroom. During that long first term she resolved more than once that she would never teach again after her contract was up.

By the time the next term rolled around, however, Mary had changed her mind. Not only did she continue to teach, she also decided, against her family's wishes, to pursue her own higher education. Her stepfather, who still controlled Mary's finances, finally agreed to let her use her father's inheritance to enroll at Byfield Seminary, north of Boston. But he was so incensed he charged Mary by the mile for the use of his horse to make the three-day journey to the school.

At Byfield, Mary was particularly inspired by headmaster Reverend Joseph Emerson, whose religious convictions composed the foundation of his instruction. It was under Emerson's tutelage that Mary's vision of Christian-centered higher education for women first began to take shape. "Mary Lyon . . . kindled at the possibility of dedicating her life to the service of God in a way that made continuing demands on her power to learn and to reflect, as well as on her eagerness to serve," observes biographer Elizabeth Alden Green.[2] Mary became known as an advocate for the education of women as her reputation as a gifted teacher continued to spread far beyond Buckland. First and foremost, she yearned to serve God, and she viewed her work as an educator in light of her calling.

The Vision Takes Root

Mary took a dramatic step in her career in 1834 when she left Ipswich Female Seminary, where she had worked as a teacher and principal with her close friend, Ipswich founder Zilpah Polly Grant, to focus her efforts entirely on raising money to fund a new institution of higher learning for women. It was not the best time to ask people for donations—the United States was in a severe economic depression—but Mary was relentless. She had neither the financial backing of a church nor a single wealthy patron to support her. Instead, she wrote hundreds of personal fund-raising letters, crafted newspaper articles and advertisements outlining her vision, and visited schools as far away as Detroit to research curriculum and administrative practices. She also single-handedly persuaded prominent men to fund her enterprise and created a board of trustees comprised of what she called "benevolent gentlemen." Mary did not underestimate the power of these male benefactors. The plans, she wrote to Zilpah, "should not seem to originate with us, but with benevolent gentlemen," acknowledging that "many good men will fear the effect on society of so much female influence, and what they will call female greatness."[3]

In an 1836 article published in the *Boston Recorder*, Mary made a vigorous bid for support from the church, which had long funded colleges for men:

> Who can survey the ground for the last 20 years, and count up the thousands, and tens of thousands of dollars, which have been generously raised in behalf of these institutions, and not be filled with

gratitude to Him. . . . But while we thus rejoice in what had been done, we cannot but inquire with painful emotions, why has not the hand of public beneficence been equally extended towards the higher institutions of the other sex?[4]

Despite her impassioned pleas, Mary did not get the support of the church. However, she did raise more than fifteen thousand dollars in three years, much of it the result of her tireless door-to-door solicitation throughout the western Massachusetts hill towns and beyond. "She spread out the whole subject, talking so fast that her hearers could hardly put in a word, anticipating every objection before it was uttered, and finally appealing to their individual humanity and benevolence," observed a friend who accompanied Mary on many of her home visits. "She uttered no falsehood; she poured out truth; she offered arguments to make out her case; and, last and best of all, she carried the will of nearly every person with whom she labored."[5]

While there were a handful of large donations of one thousand dollars or more, most contributions were modest, five or ten dollars of hard-earned money at a time. Fund-raising was painfully slow, but when she despaired, which was not often, Mary put her trust in God. "When all human help and human wisdom fail," she wrote to Zilpah in 1835, "and all knowledge of future events, as connected with present causes, and present actions, seems entirely cut off, how sweet it is to go to One, who knows all from the beginning to the end—to One who can direct our very thoughts, and who can take us individually by the hand, and lead us in a plain path."[6]

Mary also mapped out the vision for her school during these years, a vision like none other. While most women's educational institutions of the time were available only to the affluent, Mary intended her school to be affordable and accessible to women of modest means. She devoted her mission not to the higher or poorer classes, she explained in a letter to Zilpah, but to the middle class, which she described as "the main springs, and the main wheels, which are to move the world."[7] Mary felt a kinship with the middle class. It

135

was, after all, the class to which she as a farmer's daughter belonged and the one she felt called to support. She planned to keep tuition costs low—sixty dollars per year—by instituting a unique policy that would require the students to perform all the domestic chores, from washing, ironing, cleaning, and food preparation to dish washing, gardening, and maintaining the fires.

A Work of Solemn Consecration

On November 8, 1837, eighty young women, some of whom had traveled three days by horse and carriage to reach South Hadley, Massachusetts, walked through the doors of the nearly finished Mount Holyoke Female Seminary to begin their pursuit of higher education. The new students were instructed to bring their own bedding, two spoons, an atlas, a dictionary, and a Bible. Furniture was sparse due to funding constraints, and construction crews scurried to complete the finishing touches on the building as the women arrived. At the time, there were 120 colleges for men in the United States. Mount Holyoke was the first institution of higher education for women, although it was not officially decreed a college by the Massachusetts state legislature until 1888.

Mary insisted the school not be named in her honor, so it took the name of a nearby mountain peak. Its motto was from Psalm 144: "That our daughters may be as cornerstones, polished after the similitude of a palace."[8] From her earliest dreams of the school, Mary had always considered its creation the holy work of the Lord. "How often have I endeavored to consecrate all the parts, all the interests, which God has given me in this contemplated institution, most sacredly and solemnly to his service," she wrote to Zilpah in 1835, "and how often have I endeavored to pray, that every one, who had any thing to do in building up this institution, may never call aught his own. O that every one, who puts a finger to the work, by giving the smallest contribution of time—of money—or of influence, might feel that this is a work of solemn consecration—a work to be reviewed by the light of eternity."[9]

Once its doors were open, Mary ensured that Mount Holyoke provided a sound spiritual foundation for its students as well. Each dormitory room was equipped with two tiny, private alcoves so roommates could have a quiet personal space for devotions and prayer. Virtually every student enrolled at Mount Holyoke during Mary's lifetime attended two Sunday services at the village church and studied and recited passages from Scripture on the weekends. They also joined social prayer circles based on how they had classified themselves upon entrance: as a church member, as having no hope of salvation, or as somewhere in between. The students and teachers prayed regularly for missionaries, and the first Monday in January was dedicated to praying for the conversion of the world. Mary and her teachers prayed for the conversion of each student, and twice a day, half-hour periods were set aside for private prayer and meditation.

Despite her emphasis on a strong spiritual foundation, Mary struggled with a sense of inadequacy as a religious advisor. She often asked friends to pray that God would direct and inspire her in religious instruction, and she frequently felt lost and overwhelmed by her role. Yet clearly the Mount Holyoke students were impacted by Mary's spiritual leadership, both in and out of the classroom. The class notes taken by student Eliza Hubbell, who attended Mount Holyoke from 1840 to 1844, reveal a glimpse of Mary's teachings. "Religion is fitted to make us better in every situation in life," Eliza's notes read. "Our common duties will be more perfectly discharged if we are under the control of the Holy Spirit's influence. She did not wish us to be like soap stone, which crumbles as it is rubbed, but like gold, which shines brighter, the more it is used."[10]

Mary Lyon was not a women's rights activist in the same way her contemporaries such as Lucretia Mott and Elizabeth Cady Stanton were. She did not campaign for the right for women to vote, and there is no indication that she attended or even referred to the famous 1848 women's rights convention in Seneca Falls. Yet her advice to her students spoke volumes about her unwavering confidence in women's abilities. "Be willing to do anything and anywhere," she urged the young women. "Be not hasty to decide that you have no physical or mental strength and no faith or hope."[11]

As Elizabeth Alden Green notes, Mary Lyon didn't waste time trying to prove that the intellectual ability of the sexes was equal; she took it for granted. Instead, she emphasized how her female students should use their intelligence and abilities—not for pleasure and not for themselves, but to carry out God's work in the world. "Every one we see seems to desire something of honor, ease, pleasure or improvement that will make something more of himself," she acknowledged. "We ought to turn the current of feeling towards others and it will branch out into a thousand streams. How much happier you would be to live in a thousand beside yourself, rather than to live in yourself alone."[12]

Today more women than men are enrolled in colleges and universities across the United States, a reality that would have seemed unimaginable to most nineteenth-century Americans—with the exception of Mary Lyon. The woman who had urged her students, "Go where no one else will go—do what no one else will do,"[13] did exactly that in the fifty-two years of her life. In 1837, eighty young women made history when they crossed the threshold of a single brick building. Today, over 175 years later, 2,200 women from forty-eight states and nearly seventy countries enroll annually to study at Mount Holyoke, which has become one of the most prestigious colleges in America. Mary Lyon's God-given vision flowed into eighty young women. Nearly two hundred years later, it has branched into a thousand streams.

19

Sojourner Truth

Declaring the Truth to the People

(1797–1883)

There was no church available to her, no congregation with whom to worship. As a slave, Isabella Van Wagenen was forced to make do, so she turned to the place most accessible to her: the outdoors. She wove an arbor out of willow brush on an island where two small streams converged near her master's farm. It was here, beneath the tangle of branches and beside a gentle waterfall, that Isabella worshiped God, talking with him "as familiarly as if he had been a creature like herself."[1] She related all her troubles and suffering to God in minute detail, pausing from time to time to inquire, "Do you think that's right, God?" and begging to be delivered from evil. At her makeshift altar beneath the willow arbor, Isabella bargained with God, promising to live a life of purity and self-sacrifice for others if he would release her from the burdens of slavery. In late fall of 1826, she heard an answer to her prayers. God instructed her to take her infant and flee her master's farm, leaving her husband and her other four children behind.

"His Love Flowed as from a Fountain"

Born a Dutch-speaking slave in rural Ulster County, New York, Isabella Van Wagenen was sold several times before landing at the farm of John and Sally Dumont. Both her master and mistress physically and sexually abused Isabella during the sixteen years she lived with them. When she finally escaped with her infant daughter, Isabella walked five miles to the home of an antislavery couple, who took her in and paid John Dumont twenty-five dollars to cover the remainder of her contract (she was to be released under general emancipation on August 4, 1827). A month before her official emancipation, though, Isabella's determination wavered. She decided to return to Dumont's farm, but just as she was about to step into his carriage, she was struck with a vision from God:

> God revealed himself to her, with all the suddenness of a flash of lightning, showing her, "in the twinkling of an eye, that he was all over"—that he pervaded the universe—"and that there was no place where God was not." . . . All her unfulfilled promises arose before her, like a vexed sea whose waves run mountains high; and her soul, which seemed but one mass of lies, shrunk back aghast from the "awful look" of Him whom she had formerly talked to, as if he had been a being like herself.[2]

When Isabella recovered from this vision, she found that Dumont had departed without her.

"Oh God, I did not know you were so big," she exclaimed aloud, and then walked back into her neighbor's home to resume her life there. In the months that followed, Isabella began to feel the presence of a friend who "appeared to stand between herself and an insulted Deity," like "an umbrella had been interposed between her scorching head and a burning sun."[3]

"Who are you?" she repeatedly inquired of this comforting presence, until finally, "after bending both soul and body with the intensity of this desire, till breath and strength seemed failing . . . an answer came to her, saying, distinctly, 'It is Jesus.'"[4] Isabella had heard of Jesus, but until this point she had always considered him merely an important man, like Washington or Lafayette. Now she realized exactly who Jesus was and how much he loved her. His love, she said, "flowed as from a fountain."[5]

Not long after her baptism in the Holy Spirit, as she later referred to this experience, Isabella moved to New York City, where she became an itinerant preacher with the Methodist Perfectionists, a community that broke from the traditional Methodist Church to pursue a more radical practice of simple living through the Holy Spirit. In the city she also fell under the spell of street corner preacher Robert Matthews, who called himself "the Prophet Matthias" and operated "the Kingdom of Matthias," which we would now consider a cult. Isabella willingly gave him money from her savings and served as his housekeeper. Her narrative reports that she was physically abused by Matthias and hints that his wife may have sexually abused her as well. Although she freed herself from Matthias's grip in 1835 when he was accused of murder, her experience with "the Kingdom" suggests that Isabella, although on her way to self-confidence and independence, still yearned for structure and family and grappled with her place in the world.

"Ain't I a Woman?"

On June 1, 1843, God renamed Isabella "Sojourner," "because I was to travel up an' down the land, showin' the people their sins, a' bein' a sign unto them." She then asked God for a last name, "'cause everybody else had two names; and the Lord gave me Truth, because I was to declare the truth to the people."[6] Sojourner Truth left her home at dawn that day, on Pentecost, and crossed the bridge to Long Island with the rising sun warm on her back. Recalling the fate of Lot's wife, she refused to look over her shoulder until she felt sure the wicked city was too far behind her to be visible.

141

Sojourner preached at camp meetings around New England until the onset of cold weather. Then she made her way to Northampton, Massachusetts, where she joined a utopian commune called the Northampton Association of Education and Industry. The association offered Sojourner an opening into the abolitionist and suffragist movements. She gave her first antislavery speech in Northampton in the fall of 1844, and in May 1845 she spoke to the annual meeting of the American Anti-Slavery Society in New York City. Sojourner stayed in Northampton even after the commune dissolved, and it was there that she dictated her *Narrative of Sojourner Truth*, which was self-published and printed on credit in 1850. She charged twenty-five cents per copy and acted as her own distributor and bookseller, using the earnings to repay the printer and pay off the three-hundred-dollar mortgage on her newly purchased house.

Sojourner's most famous speech was made in 1851 at the Ohio Women's Rights Convention in Akron. The Stone Church was stifling on that late May day, packed with men and women who had come to listen to the antislavery feminist speakers. Sojourner captivated the audience with both her intimidating physical presence and her words. At nearly six feet tall, she was a statuesque figure with a deep, booming voice. She was also a skilled orator who used humor to soften her scathing critiques. "Her manner of speaking undercut the intensity of her language," explains biographer Nell Irvin Painter. "To capture and hold her audience, she communicated her meaning on several different levels at once, accompanying sharp comments with non-verbal messages: winks and smiles provoking the 'laughter' so often reported. . . . The humor was shrewd, for it allowed her to get away with sharp criticism, but it permitted some of her hearers to ignore her meaning."[7]

The speech, which has come to be known as "Ain't I a Woman?," is both history and legend, in part because of a newspaper article published in the New York *Independent* twelve years after the Akron conference. The article's author, Frances Dana Gage, exaggerated and embellished Sojourner's original performance. In fact, there is some question of whether Sojourner even uttered the rhetorical question

"Ain't I a woman?" a single time, never mind the four times included in Gage's article. Marius Robinson, who served as secretary of the convention, printed Sojourner's address in full shortly after she made it, and while the speech was a rousing declaration of women's rights, it did not include the phrase that has come to symbolize Sojourner Truth.

By 1858 Sojourner was famous enough to convene a series of her own meetings in Indiana, one of which prompted an incident that further increased her fame. During the meeting a group of proslavery men challenged Sojourner's authenticity as a woman, claiming her to be a man in disguise. The charge polarized the audience, with the proslavery advocates insisting that Sojourner step into a private room to show her breasts to a select group of women, thus proving her gender. Sojourner took the suggestion one grand step further. As she quietly disrobed before the entire packed hall, she responded with a verbal attack that shamed her critics. "In vindication of her truthfulness, she told them that she would show her breast to the whole congregation," reported the Boston *Liberator*, "that it was not to her shame that she uncovered her breast before them, but to their shame."[8] As Painter notes, "Truth had turned the challenge upside down. Her skillful remaking employed the all-too-common exhibition of an undressed black body, with its resonance of the slave auction that undressed women for sale. What had been intended as degradation became a triumph of embodied rhetoric."[9]

Sojourner's fame also brought its share of harassment, threats, and prejudice. At one point, when told the building she was scheduled to preach in would be burned, she responded, "Then I will speak to the ashes."[10] But her quick wit and determination didn't always protect her. After being physically assaulted and injured by one particularly violent mob, Sojourner was forced to walk with a cane for the rest of her life.

A Lifetime of Advocacy

Sojourner put her reputation to work during the Civil War by helping to recruit black troops for the Union Army, including her grandson, who enlisted in the 54th Massachusetts Regiment. When she met President Abraham Lincoln, whom she described as kind and cordial, she spoke to him with her usual honesty and humor. "I told him that I had never heard of him before he was talked of for president," she explained in her *Narrative*. "He smilingly replied, 'I had heard of you many times before that.'"[11]

Sojourner continued to rally for change even after Lincoln's Emancipation Proclamation. In 1865, she advocated for the desegregation of streetcars in Washington, DC, by riding in cars designated for whites, an act that resulted in the dislocation of her arm by an angry conductor. Later in her life she argued for the right of former slaves to own land. She passionately supported the movement to secure land grants from the federal government but was ultimately unable to sway Congress.

Although she is remembered as one of the foremost leaders of the abolition movement and an early advocate of women's rights, during her later years Sojourner broadened her interests to include prison reform, property rights, and universal suffrage. Abolition was one of the few causes Sojourner saw realized in her lifetime. The constitutional amendment barring suffrage discrimination based on sex, on the other hand, wasn't ratified until 1920, nearly four decades after her death.

Sojourner Truth died before dawn on November 26, 1883. She claimed to have been at least 105 years old, but in reality she was closer to eighty-six. Regardless of her age, she believed strongly that it is a person's accomplishments rather than their chronological age that determine whether a life should be considered long or short. "Some have been on earth scores of years, yet die in infancy," she said in her *Narrative*.[12] From her bed she uttered her last words, "Be a follower of the Lord Jesus," to a Grand Rapids, Michigan, newspaper reporter two days before she died.[13] According to her own measures and her impressive list of accomplishments, Sojourner Truth lived long, yet as her last words attest, she placed one accomplishment far above all the rest. She was a follower of her Lord Jesus indeed.[14]

20

Phoebe Palmer

Trials to Triumphs

$(1807-1874)$

She sat still in the dim nursery, her son wrapped in a blanket in her arms. She didn't sing a lullaby or rock the infant. She didn't smooth the delicate wisps of hair or stroke his soft cheek. She simply stared straight ahead in quiet shock. Her seven-week-old infant was dead, her second child to die in two years. She was childless once again.

"I will not attempt to describe the pressure of the last crushing trial," she wrote a few weeks later. "Surely I needed it, or it would not have been given. . . . After my loved ones were snatched away, I saw that I had concentrated my time and attentions far too exclusively, to the neglect of the religious activities demanded. Though painfully learned, yet I trust the lesson has been fully apprehended. From henceforth, Jesus must and shall have the uppermost seat in my heart."[1] Phoebe Palmer truly believed that the death of her children (five years later she would lose a third child in a tragic nursery fire) was the result of her inattention to God, and she responded by zealously throwing herself into her personal pursuit of Jesus.

A Proneness to Reason

Although she was raised by devout Methodist parents, faith as defined by the Methodist Church did not come easily to Phoebe. According to Methodism's founder, John Wesley, two points were particularly critical in the church's orthodoxy: first, complete assurance of one's salvation, and second, what was called Christian perfection. Wesley believed that the true Christian should experience a discernible conversion moment as tangible assurance of one's salvation. This conversion experience and assurance of salvation would subsequently lead to a level of spirituality in which one was able to live without habitual sin, in a state governed by pure love. Wesley termed this sinless state "Christian Perfection," but he also referred to it by a number of different expressions, including perfect love, entire sanctification, full salvation, and perfect holiness, after which the holiness movement was named.

Phoebe was deeply troubled by the fact that she had not experienced an authentic conversion moment. Methodist conversion was typically defined as an emotional experience, and Phoebe was a logical, rational woman rather than an emotional one. She yearned to feel God in her heart and soul as others did, and as they implied she should, but she simply didn't. While she was sincerely devoted to God, she felt like an utter failure because she didn't seem to be as outwardly or inwardly moved by his love as others were. She longed to live in the ancient biblical days, when one's relationship with God seemed more objective and pragmatic. "Had I lived in that day, how gladly I would have parted with everything . . . and have purchased the best possible offering," she wrote, referring to the Old Testament practice of animal sacrifice. "All I would have to do, would be to lay it upon the altar and know that it was accepted."[2]

Without the assurance of salvation Phoebe was stymied, spinning her spiritual wheels and unable to proceed on to the next steps toward Christian perfection. She wrote about herself in the third person in her book, *The Way of Holiness*, saying, "Not unfrequently, she felt like weeping because she could not weep."[3]

Finally Phoebe experienced a spiritual breakthrough under the guidance of her sister, Sarah, with whom Phoebe and her husband, Walter, lived in New York City. After wrestling for several years with both her inability to pinpoint a specific conversion moment and her "proneness to reason," as she put it, Phoebe embraced what she called "the act of believing" as adequate assurance of her salvation. "I now see that the error of my religious life has been a desire for signs and wonders," she wrote. "Like Naaman, I have wanted some great thing, unwilling to rely unwaveringly on the still small voice of the Spirit, speaking through the naked Word."[4] Phoebe concluded that belief itself, plain and simple, was grounds for assurance. She decided to rely on the Bible, which she believed to be the Word of God to man, as well as on faith, which she defined as "taking God at his word and relying unwaveringly upon his truth."[5]

Out of the Ordinary Sphere

Sarah also introduced Phoebe to the concept of the Tuesday Meetings. Initially Sarah led these weekly women's prayer meetings in their home, but when she and her husband moved, Phoebe reluctantly took the reins. The meetings quickly grew from a women's prayer group and Bible study to a coed vehicle for promoting and studying the principles of holiness—that is, sanctification—an integral part of Methodism.

The Tuesday Meetings were unusual for several reasons. Not only did they attract members of both genders, they were also nondenominational. By the mid-1860s, Baptists, Congregationalists, Dutch Reformed, German Reformed, Presbyterians, Episcopalians, and Quakers joined the Methodists in the meetings. Phoebe maintained that Christian perfection was a leading doctrine of the Bible rather than a doctrine particular to any denomination. All were welcome to attend, so long as they were there as a witness to holiness, as a sincere seeker of holiness, or as a genuinely interested observer and at least open to the teaching.

The meetings also emphasized the participation of laypersons. Although ministers attended, they did not dominate or even lead the meetings, and at least in the early days, neither did Phoebe herself. Rather, firsthand accounts of personal religious experiences and testimonies composed the greatest portion of the meetings. Any person present was encouraged to offer a testimony, read or recite a memorized Bible verse or passage, lead the group in a hymn or prayer, or request a prayer from others present. The inclusiveness and relaxed atmosphere of the meetings was particularly conducive to the active participation of women. "If recorded testimonies are to be taken as an accurate indicator of female participation, fully as many women as men would be heard from at a typical gathering," biographer Harold Raser observes. "Proclaiming the credo 'whether male or female, all are one in Christ Jesus,' the Tuesday Meeting seems to have quite successfully acted this out in its own structure."[6]

The egalitarian nature of the Tuesday Meetings paved the way for Phoebe to grow into her role as a preacher and leading revivalist. Technically, Phoebe agreed with critics who, based on Paul's first letter to the Corinthians, claimed that women should not preach. But as the invitations for her to speak at larger and larger gatherings came rolling in, she responded willingly, believing that God had specifically called her to stand before his people and proclaim his truth. "It is the order of God," she said, "that women may occasionally be brought out of the ordinary sphere of action and occupy in either church or state positions of high responsibility."[7]

Over time, the informal Tuesday Meetings segued into larger events held not only in homes around New York, New England, Canada, and later in England but also in halls and churches. As Phoebe's fame increased, she began to lead the Methodist camp meetings, which were originally developed on the frontier and then eventually established in permanent campgrounds in cities. During these summer camp meetings, Phoebe led and encouraged hundreds of believers at a time to declare their sanctification during the altar testimony.

Whether or not she defined herself as such, Phoebe was, in these camp meetings and in the churches and halls where she frequently spoke, a preacher in every sense of the word. She appealed to men and women alike, and her talents lay in the fact that she was an accessible, deliberate, direct, and intensely earnest speaker. Her addresses "mingled simplicity, earnestness and power," noted one British newspaper. Another described her as "clear, pointed and scriptural" and "addressed more to the understanding than to the feelings of her audience."[8] Clearly the rational, levelheaded approach to faith that had so frustrated Phoebe earlier in her spiritual journey now proved to be one of her greatest assets.

A Fixed Heart

Beginning around 1841, Phoebe's mission to fulfill her calling led her farther away from home and for longer and longer periods. For the first twenty years of her revivalist career, she traveled without her husband, Walter, and her children, and while this was personally difficult for her, Phoebe was resolute in what she considered the proper order of her priorities. After the death of her third child, in the midst of grief and despair, Phoebe came to understand that God intended a purpose for her suffering. "My darling is in heaven doing angel service," she wrote in her journal. "And now I have resolved that the service, or in other words, the time I would have devoted to her, shall be spent in work for Jesus. And if diligent and self-sacrificing in carrying out my resolve, the death of this child may result in the spiritual life of many. . . . And now my whole being says, with a strength of purpose beyond anything before attained, 'My heart is fixed, O, God, my heart is fixed!'"[9]

To put her work ahead of her family was nothing short of radical for this time period. But Phoebe did not waver in her commitment to God as her first priority. "By endeavoring to make all things subservient to the duties of religion, showing manifestly before my family that I seek *first* the Kingdom of God and its righteousness, God honors the intention and adds needful sustainments," she wrote in her journal in 1857.[10]

In addition to her vigorous preaching duties, Phoebe was also a prolific writer, a social activist in the temperance movement, and an advocate for the urban poor. During the 1840s, as she was launching her revivalist mission, Phoebe also published three books: *The Way of Holiness, Entire Devotion to God*, and *Faith and Its Effects*. In addition, she served as editor of the newspaper *The Guide to Holiness*, which she and Walter purchased in the 1860s. The couple built the subscription list of *The Guide*, as it was later called, from a floundering ten thousand to nearly forty thousand readers, and Phoebe effectively used it as a national platform from which to expound on her evangelistic travels and the holiness movement in general.

As a founding director of America's first inner-city mission—New York City's Five Points Mission—Phoebe was an active advocate for the urban poor. Despite resistance, she raised the necessary funds to build a chapel, schoolrooms, and a residence facility to house twenty needy families at a time, free of charge. The initiative later expanded to include a day school, the Five Points House of Industry, which employed more than five hundred people, and a number of social welfare programs. Between 1840 and 1850 she also made regular visits to women imprisoned at the infamous Tombs prison, noting in her journal that many of the women were probably hearing religious truth for the first time and listened with more attention than was generally witnessed in actual houses of worship.

Phoebe Palmer suffered the loss and grief every parent dreads—not once but, unimaginably, three times in her early years of motherhood. It's clear from the anguished words poured into her journal that she suffered these trials deeply. Yet it's equally clear that these profound losses spurred in her an unrelenting mission to fulfill what she understood as her calling. In some of Phoebe's last letters and journal entries, written only months before she died, we see evidence that Phoebe remained confident in God's goodness and grace, despite the immeasurable losses she endured. "Now, we know that all things work together for good, to them that love God," she wrote to a friend in 1874.[11] Shortly before she died, Phoebe reiterated this conviction, attributing her life's work to Jesus and noting, "My trials have been triumphs. Every new conflict has furnished an occasion for a new victory."[12] Phoebe Palmer had paved the way to perfect holiness for thousands, a mission that helped her to triumph over personal tragedy.

21

Harriet Beecher Stowe

She Wrote for Freedom, She Wrote for Hope

(1811–1896)

She sat in a sturdy wooden chair pulled close to the bed, and as one languid hour passed into the next, she gazed at her young son's face, flushed and sweaty with fever. As he tossed and moaned, slipping in and out of consciousness, she draped cool cloths over his forehead, praying fervently that he would recover. He did not. Harriet Beecher Stowe's young son died of cholera while she watched helplessly at his bedside. "It was at *his* dying bed, and at *his* grave," Harriet later wrote about Charley, "that I learnt what a poor slave mother may feel when her child is torn away from her."[1]

Educated as a Man, Restless as a Woman

Harriet Beecher was born the seventh of thirteen children in Litchfield, Connecticut. After her mother died when Harriet was just five years old, her father, Lyman Beecher, remarried and sent Harriet to live at the Hartford Female Seminary under the direction of her older sister Catharine, who had founded the elite school in 1823 with another sister, Mary.

As the daughter of a prominent Calvinist preacher, Harriet was expected to give her life to Christ, and she did so at the age of thirteen. Her father's greatest worry was the state of his children's unconverted souls, and he frequently bemoaned the fact that he was able to lead successful revivals for hundreds yet struggled to bring his own children to Christ. Under this heavy weight, several of the Beecher children were spiritually paralyzed well into adulthood, which only intensified Lyman's anxiety. Harriet, on the other hand, quietly acknowledged to her father one morning after listening to one of his Sunday sermons that she had officially converted. She was a Christian, and she was at peace.

Harriet was a precocious student, and by the time she left the seminary in 1827 at age sixteen, she was proficient in Latin, Greek, French, Italian, mathematics, geography, history, rhetoric and oratory, the natural and mechanical sciences, and music. In other words, Harriet was one of the few women in nineteenth-century New England to benefit from an education equivalent to that of a young man.

She left Hartford with her stellar education to join her father and stepmother in Boston. But Harriet's options were limited. She could marry and raise children. She could pursue missionary work. Or, like her sister Catharine, Harriet could become a teacher. Frustrated and unable to make a decision about the next step in her life, Harriet succumbed to depression. "I don't know as I am fit for anything, and I have thought that I could wish to die young and let the remembrance of me and my faults perish in the grave, rather than live, as I fear I do, a trouble to everyone," she wrote to Catharine.[2] She complained of feeling "so useless, so weak, so destitute of all energy,"[3] yet unable to sleep at night, weeping and worrying until midnight. Catharine recognized her sister's turmoil and immediately wrote to their father, insisting that Harriet return to help her run the Hartford Female Seminary in place of Mary, who was suffering from anxiety and consumption.

The job distracted Harriet and soothed her troubled spirit, and along the way she discovered a passion for teaching composition and rhetoric. She stayed at the seminary until 1832, when Lyman accepted a position at Lane Seminary in Cincinnati and the Beechers moved west. Although she initially resisted the move, Ohio eventually proved to be fertile ground for Harriet.

"You Must Be a Literary Woman"

During her first two years in Cincinnati, Harriet once again succumbed to restlessness and indecision. She was torn between what she assumed was her expected role—a schoolteacher at Catharine's newly launched Western Female Institute—and her passion: writing. Harriet had already experienced some literary success with the publication of her first book, *Primary Geography for Children*, a textbook that earned her 187 dollars, about 15 percent of her father's annual salary and almost as much as Catharine earned in a year of running her school. But writing was still very much a radical career choice for women at the time, and Harriet wasn't convinced she should take the risk.

Parlor literature allowed Harriet to segue into the literary life. Like parlor music, parlor literature was a centuries-old pastime. Typical activities included singing, piano playing, and dramatic readings of essays and poems. The advent of literary clubs provided a more formal audience for this domestic literature, with men and women gathering in home parlors to read verses, ballads, and sketches they had written, which often contained humorous references to local people and events and were frequently satirical in nature. Harriet Beecher's literary career was formally launched in the Semi-Colon Club, a Cincinnati literary society that attracted transplanted New Englanders. Harriet, with her background in composition and her love of letter writing, was skilled at creating the light, humorous, accessible tone that made parlor literature so appealing. One of her most memorable character sketches, "Uncle Lot," was based on her grandfather, a cantankerous New England farmer. When Harriet submitted the popular sketch to a competition sponsored by *Western Monthly* magazine, she won fifty dollars and a boost in her confidence.

"Parlor literature afforded Harriet Beecher an advantage she never lost: an intimate relationship to her audience," observes biographer Joan Hedrick. "When *Uncle Tom's Cabin* burst on the national scene in 1851, the intimate narrative voice of that book, its appeal to domestic institutions and reader emotions, had had a long foreground in Harriet Beecher's apprenticeship in parlor literature."[4]

Not only did Harriet find her literary voice in the parlor, she found her husband there as well. Harriet had met both Calvin Stowe and his wife, Eliza, in the Semi-Colon Club. Two years after Eliza died of cholera, Harriet and Calvin, who worked with her father as a theology professor at Lane Seminary, were married. Although Harriet seemed to abhor the idea of marriage (just a half hour before the ceremony, she wrote to her sister Georgiana that she had been "dreading and dreading the time" when she would "cease to be Hatty Beecher and change to nobody knows who"[5]), Calvin proved to be one of her most enthusiastic advocates and an unwavering supporter of her writing career.

When Harriet doubted her role as a writer, Calvin buoyed her confidence. "Our children are just coming to the age when everything depends on my efforts," Harriet wrote to Calvin from Boston in 1842, where she was meeting with a publisher. "They need a mother's whole attention. Can I lawfully divide my attention by literary efforts?"[6]

"You must be a *literary woman*. It is so written in the book of fate," Calvin answered. "Make all your calculations accordingly, get a good stock of health, brush up your mind, drop the E out of your name, which only encumbers it and stops the flow and euphony, and write yourself only and always, *Harriet Beecher Stowe*, which is a name euphonous [sic], flowing, and full of meaning; and my word for it, your husband will lift up his head in the gate, and your children will rise up and call you blessed."[7] The matter was settled. Harriet would write. Her husband had baptized the former Mrs. H. E. Beecher Stowe into the name that would go down in literary, abolitionist, and American history: Harriet Beecher Stowe.

"Must We Forever Keep Calm and Smile?"

Gayle Kimball observes that one of the greatest challenges in Harriet's life was her desire and struggle to believe that she was saved as a Christian. Although she accepted Jesus and claimed her faith as a young child, the feeling of peace she'd initially experienced didn't last long. By the time she was a young adult, Harriet consistently grappled with her perception of the punishing God of her childhood and the gentler God she wanted to trust and love. Her brother George's suicide in 1843 further shook her "like an earthquake," and she prayed fervently "that Christ would 'make his abode' within her soul."[8] Her spiritual struggles are reflected in much of her writing, including *Uncle Tom's Cabin*. While the passage of the Fugitive Slave Law in 1850 enraged Harriet and was certainly a catalyst behind *Uncle Tom's Cabin*, several biographers have suggested that Harriet also had personal reasons to write such a response to slavery. When her beloved son Charley died of cholera in 1847, Stowe admitted that "much that is in that book . . . had its root in the awful scenes and bitter sorrows of that summer."[9]

As the number of kidnappings and forced reenslavements increased daily as a result of the Fugitive Slave Law, Harriet, now living in Brunswick, Maine, became increasingly frustrated with the negligence of the press and the public. "Must we forever keep calm and smile and smile when every sentiment of manliness and humanity is kicked and rolled in the dust and lies trampled and bleeding and make it a merit to be exceedingly cool?" she wrote to her brother, the minister Henry Ward Beecher.[10]

Finally, she took the matter into her own hands. In March 1851 she wrote to her editor, "Up to this year I have always felt that I had no particular call to meddle with this subject, and I dreaded to expose even my own mind to the full force of its exciting power. But I feel now that the time is come when even a woman or a child who can speak a word for freedom and humanity is bound to speak."[11] She proposed a serial that would run in three or four segments. Harriet had no idea that the story would sprawl into a novel that would run in weekly installments in the abolitionist journal the *National Era* from June 5, 1851, to April 1, 1852. It was published in book form in March 1852, and less than a year later, *Uncle Tom's Cabin* had sold an unprecedented three hundred thousand copies.

God "Knows All about Mothers' Hearts"

One can't argue that Harriet Beecher Stowe's greatest contribution was that of an abolitionist writer. It's said that President Lincoln himself, upon meeting the diminutive Harriet, exclaimed, "So you're the little woman who wrote the book that started this great war!" Yet her novels are appealing and powerful not only for their political impact but for their ability to reach the reader on a personal, intimate level as well. Underlying her statements and questions about human rights and freedom are deeper, more personal questions about truth, faith, hope, love, suffering, and salvation.

In 1857 Harriet's son Henry, a student at Dartmouth, drowned while swimming with friends in the Connecticut River. In her grief, Harriet not only revisited her younger son Charley's death, she also returned to the questions of salvation that had plagued her earlier in life. Harriet fretted that Henry had died unsaved, and her letters to Catharine reveal a desperate search for evidence that would prove her son did not plummet to hell because he hadn't formally given himself to Christ. Her novel *The Minister's Wooing*, written in the year following Henry's death, was Harriet's answer to her theological wrestling.

In the book the character of Mrs. Marvyn is unable to reconcile herself to her son's death at sea and his everlasting damnation, and it is only the consoling words of Candace, the Marvyns' former slave, that finally offer her comfort. God "knows all about mothers' hearts; He wont break yours," Candace assures the bereft mother.[12] Thus

Harriet was finally able to transform her own image of God from that of a distant and punishing Creator to a kind, forgiving, loving God based on her own understanding of a mother's love. "He who made me capable of such an absorbing unselfish devotion as I feel for my children so that I could willingly sacrifice my eternal salvation for theirs," she later wrote to her sister, "he certainly did not make me capable of more disinterestedness than he has himself—He invented mother's hearts—& he certainly has the pattern in his own."[13]

The questions Harriet wrestled with so courageously and transparently in her fiction undoubtedly offered countless grieving parents and troubled Christians an alternative to the stern, impersonal God they were accustomed to. Her solution to the question of salvation wasn't complicated theology; it was simply love, as demonstrated by Christ himself and his own self-sacrifice. Harriet Beecher Stowe's prolific writing is a powerful statement about basic human rights, justice, and freedom that made an indelible impact on American history. But on a more personal level, her novels are also an intimate walk through suffering and grief—a walk each one of us, in one way or another, recognizes and understands. Her search for answers is a familiar one, and her quest—one that ultimately ends in love—gives us hope and courage as we walk similar paths.

22

Florence Nightingale

Called to the Crimea and Beyond

(1820 – 1910)

Awoman wearing black boots, a black wool gown, and a white bonnet walked slowly down the dim hallway, appraising the dismal scene. Men lay side by side on the hospital floor, their ragged clothing soiled with excrement, dried mud, and blood. In addition to their battle wounds, they suffered from cholera and dysentery and were crawling from head to toe with vermin. Medicine and basic medical supplies were virtually nonexistent, and even food was scarce. Some of the patients were served raw meat and little else. The conditions were the worst she had ever seen.

Never in the Army's history had such unrestricted access to a military hospital been granted to a woman. Florence Nightingale and her thirty-eight nurses made history as they stepped across the threshold of this rudimentary hospital on the edge of the Black Sea. But they couldn't be preoccupied with such distractions. More work waited than they could possibly manage, and every day hundreds more injured and dying British soldiers were taken ashore and transported up the steep slope to a hospital sorely unequipped to treat them.

He Called Her to His Service

From the start, Florence Nightingale was certain her life's calling was to help suffering people. By the time she was a teenager, Florence was regularly visiting the village's ill and needy. She recorded prescriptions and remedies in a notebook constructed out of scrap paper and old letters. She also included observations related to the illnesses of family members, noting, for instance, how many teeth "Pop" had pulled at the dentist and the status of Uncle Octavius's lower back pain. When the influenza epidemic swept through southern England in 1837, Florence was the only member of the household, aside from her grandmother and the cook, who did not fall ill. For a month she tirelessly nursed her family members and others, concluding, when the worst of the flu had subsided, "I have killed no patients, though I have cured few."[1]

While Florence took a rational approach to faith, she also consistently sought personal union with God. As a child, Florence once conducted an experiment to determine if her prayers were being answered. She recorded what she prayed for, as well as what she considered an appropriate amount of time for the prayer to be answered, but was disappointed to find that when she looked for the results of divine intervention, she couldn't find much evidence for it. On the other hand, she often found the presence of God in nature and in the acts of goodwill she witnessed in the people around her. While Florence remained a nominal Anglican, she ceased attending church regularly by the time she was in her thirties. She was influenced by a wide range of philosophies and theologies, including the medieval Roman Catholic mystics, Lutheranism, the teachings of John Wesley, and the social progress and public-service elements of Unitarianism.

Because she was so rational minded and leery of the supernatural, Florence always carefully analyzed each call she heard from God to discern whether it was an inward revelation or a mystical or hallucinatory sensation. Not long after the flu epidemic, on February 7, 1837, a date noted in her personal calendar, Florence heard a call from God. The voice did not specify exactly what form her service would take, but it was clear enough to convince Florence that she should not dismiss it.

Called to the Crimea

Despite her obvious passion for and skills at nursing, Florence's parents had no intention of allowing their daughter to pursue such a career. It was unthinkable that Florence, a wealthy, upper-class, educated gentlewoman, would consider an occupation so closely connected to domestic service. Upon hearing of their daughter's plan to train at the Salisbury Infirmary, William and Fanny Nightingale dismissed it as selfish foolishness. Furthermore, they reasoned, Florence was expected to marry, and as an attractive young lady, she had plenty of suitors from whom to choose. One, the politician and poet Richard Monckton Milnes, courted her for nine years before she ultimately rejected him to pursue her calling.

For a while, Florence accepted her parents' wish and bitterly acquiesced to the life of a gentlewoman. Her dreams crushed, she fell into a deep depression. "God has something for me to do for Him or He would have let me die some time ago," she wrote. "I hope to do it by living, then my eyes would have indeed seen His salvation, but now I am dust and nothing, worse than nothing, a curse to myself and to others."[2] As it turned out, Florence simply could not abandon what she understood as her God-given calling. "O God, Thou puttest into my heart this great desire to devote myself to the sick and sorrowful," she wrote in her diary while traveling in Egypt. "I offer it to Thee. Do with it what is for Thy service."[3]

After unsuccessfully pleading with her father one more time to change his mind, she began to research hospitals in private and secretly settled on the Institution of Nursing Sisters, which had been founded by the prison reformer Elizabeth Fry at Kaiserswerth, Germany, in 1840. Although her stay at Kaiserswerth was brief, Florence observed the work of each ward in the hospital, as well as the spartan living conditions of the deaconesses. She later summarized her findings in a thirty-two-page pamphlet, "The Institution of Kaiserswerth on the Rhine, for the Practical Training of Deaconesses." When Florence returned to London in 1853, she accepted a job as superintendent at the Institute for the Care of Sick Gentlewomen. Noting that his daughter would not be deterred, William Nightingale offered her an annual income that generously augmented her salary.

In late 1854, Florence received a letter that changed her life. Her good friend Sidney Herbert, Britain's secretary of war, asked her to organize a corps of nurses to tend to the sick and wounded soldiers in the Crimea. This was a dramatic and desperate step by the British government. Up to this point no female nurses had been stationed at hospitals in the war, not only on account of their gender, but also as a result of their poor reputation. Many nurses lacked real caretaking skills, were inclined to drunkenness, and spent more time cavorting with the patients in the wards after dark than they did actually caring for them. However, as thousands of wounded, ill, and dying soldiers poured into understaffed hospitals, England had no choice but to call in female nurses. Within weeks of receiving Herbert's letter, Florence accepted the position of superintendent of nurses in the English general military hospitals in Turkey. She assembled a team of thirty-eight nurses from a variety of religious orders and sailed with them to the Crimea, disembarking in Scutari on the morning of November 4, 1854.

Because of their tenuous position, the nurses initially were not allowed to care for any of the soldiers in the ward unless granted explicit permission by the medical officer in charge. Florence adhered to the military regulations with scrupulous attention. Neither she nor any of her nurses even entered a ward or fetched so much as a bedpan unless specifically requested to do so. However, it didn't take long, with five hundred gravely ill and wounded men arriving at a time, for the surgeons and medical officers to abandon the protocol. Soon Florence and her nurses were working twenty-hour shifts, soaking off the filthy, bloody bandages from wounds that had been dressed on the battlefield ten days earlier, assisting with amputations, and administering what basic care they could with so few supplies. "We are steeped up to our necks in blood," Florence wrote.[4]

When she wasn't involved in triage, Florence tackled the appalling conditions in the hospital, which was rife with rats, lice, and other vermin. She embarked on a vigorous campaign to wash the men, feed them nutritious food, and provide clean clothes and bedding. She obtained boilers from the Army engineers and transformed a small house near the hospital into a laundry. She bypassed official government procedures and convinced Herbert to send supplies directly from London. And after her appeal was published in *The Times*, she received hundreds of pieces of linen and thousands of pounds in donations. She also planned for, organized, and paid out of her own pocket for two hundred Turkish carpenters to refloor a section of the Barrack Hospital that had been damaged by a fire.

Despite Florence's herculean efforts, the death toll skyrocketed to 42 percent over the winter of 1855, not from war wounds, but from illnesses like dysentery and cholera. When the British government finally sent the Sanitary Commission to investigate the hospital in March of 1855, it was discovered that the building sat on a cesspool, with its sewers clogged with the carcasses of rotting animals. A decomposing horse blocked a large pipe that carried water into the hospital. Likewise, raw sewage was found to be seeping into the hospital's water supply. The sanitation team cleared the hospital's ventilation system, repaired windows so they could be opened, refloored the corridors, whitewashed walls, and reengineered the flow of sewage into the sea. By June of 1855, the mortality rate at the hospital swiftly declined to 2 percent. At the time, credit for the turnaround was given to the sanitation overhaul, although more recently historians have noted that the improvement was more likely due to the arrival of warmer weather and an overall reduction in overcrowding at the hospital.

Beyond the Lady with the Lamp

Florence has been both criticized and canonized for her role in the Crimean War. As biographer Gillian Gill notes, "In the nineteenth century too much credit for that drop [in mortality] was probably given to Florence Nightingale in person. In the twentieth century she was certainly given too little."[5] The fact is, while Florence initially believed the death rates at her hospital were due to poor nutrition, a lack of supplies, and the overworking of soldiers, after she returned to Britain and began to collect evidence for the Royal Commission on the Health of the Army, she came to believe that most of the soldiers died as a result of poor sanitary conditions. This knowledge profoundly influenced her later career, when, though largely bedridden by a chronic illness, she advised the British government on military hospital reform, advocated for sanitation improvements in Britain and India, founded a nurses' training school at St. Thomas's Hospital in London, and wrote *Notes on Nursing*, which was used as a cornerstone of nursing curriculum for decades.

To highlight only the romanticized, mythologized version of Florence Nightingale as the "lady with the lamp" is to do a disservice to some of her most significant and lasting contributions in nursing, military hospital reform, and hospital sanitization. Yes, she toiled at the bedside of thousands of injured and dying men and walked miles of dim corridors with an oil lamp burning brightly in her hands. But her work following the war, conducted largely from the confines of her own bed, was equal to if not more important than her wartime service for its impact on the overall history of health care. When Florence offered her skills and passion, her "great desire to devote [herself] to the sick and sorrowful" to God that day during her vacation in Egypt, she could have never imagined the outcome. God used Florence Nightingale's great desire and devotion beyond her wildest expectations.[6]

23

Harriet Tubman

"I Was Free; They Should Be Free"

(1820–1913)

They walked for six hours in darkness, stumbling over roots and stones, branches lashing their faces, their bare feet torn and bleeding from prickly sweet-gum burrs. When the first faint streaks of dawn lit the horizon, the group of twenty-five fugitives hunkered down in a remote swamp to wait out the day until they could travel again under cover of darkness. Morale was low. Deprived of food, wet, uncomfortable, and exhausted, the group prepared to leave the swamp as dusk fell.

Suddenly one man stood up and declared it was too much: he had decided to take his chances and return to the plantation. A stout woman turned to face him, insisting that his return would compromise the entire party. When he refused to continue with the group, she stepped close to him, pulled a revolver from the folds of her dress, and aimed it at his head, hissing, "Move or die!" The man complied, and less than a week later she led him across the border into Canada, a free man.

It was almost unheard of for a former slave to return to the South once he or she had escaped into freedom. But Harriet Tubman was the exception. After she fled from Maryland to Philadelphia in the fall of 1849, she returned to her home state approximately thirteen times on exceedingly dangerous secret missions to liberate family and friends. As an Underground Railroad conductor, Tubman led seventy slaves to freedom and gave instructions to fifty more who traveled to freedom on their own. Her extraordinary courage and determination earned her the name Moses, after the biblical leader who led the enslaved Israelites out of Egypt to freedom.

Escape and Rebirth

Like most slaves, Harriet Tubman—who was born Araminta "Minty" Ross—never knew her birth date. As the abolitionist and runaway slave Frederick Douglass noted, slaves knew as much about their age "as horses know of theirs," and the closest they estimated an actual birthday was whether it was near "planting-time, harvest-time, cherry-time, spring-time or fall-time."[1] We do know that Harriet was the fifth of nine children and was born in either late February or early March 1822, on the plantation of Anthony Thompson in Dorchester County, Maryland.

When she was six or seven years old, Araminta was hired out, first at a nearby farm as a housekeeper and then at another farm as a nanny to a sickly infant. Her mistress kept a whip beneath her pillow, and if Araminta stopped rocking the baby's cradle during the night, or if her mistress was awakened by the infant's cries, the young nanny was beaten across the chest, neck, and shoulders, often numerous times in a single night.

As a young teenager, Araminta was hired out as a field hand on a neighboring plantation, and it was around this time that she received a near-fatal blow, intended for another slave, to her head, which resulted in frequent seizures and periods of narcolepsy for the rest of her life.

Araminta's severe head injury coincided with a period of increased religious fervor. She was known to burst into raucous and excited hymn singing and praise, and she often spoke about hearing the voice of God and experiencing vivid dreams and visions that foretold the future.

While slaves were not permitted to attend religious services led by African American preachers, they were often encouraged or forced to attend the white congregations with their master's family. Araminta and her family attended Methodist services (their master's son was an ordained Methodist minister), but her family was also likely influenced by Episcopal, Baptist, and Catholic teachings and probably attended camp meetings held by itinerant white ministers as well. While contemporary scholars aren't sure how and where Araminta came to memorize Scripture, we do know through her own words that faith was a very personal experience for her.

"When invited to join in prayers with a white master's family, 'she preferred to stay on the landing, and pray for herself.' Praying for strength to make her 'able to fight,' Tubman's pleadings became her own private rebellion," writes biographer Clifford Kate Larson. "Later Tubman would come to believe that her repeated attempts to retrieve enslaved blacks from the South were a holy crusade."[2]

In 1849, now married to John Tubman, a free black man, Araminta launched a prayer vigil for the soul of her new master, Edward Brodess, begging God for his conversion to Christianity so he would come to see the cruelty of slavery and repent. Soon, though, she heard a rumor that Brodess planned to sell her and her brothers, so she switched strategies and began to pray for her master's death: "I changed my prayer, and I said, 'Lord, if you ain't never going to change that man's heart, kill him, Lord, and take him out of the way, where he won't do no more mischief.'"[3]

When Brodess suddenly died not long after, Araminta felt terribly guilty about her prayers, but she also realized that rather than assuage her worries, her master's death only exacerbated her suffering. Fearing she would be sold by Brodess's widow to pay off debt, and despite her husband's pleas for her to stay, Araminta fled the planation with her two brothers in September 1849. When her brothers got cold feet and returned to the plantation, Araminta forged ahead alone, through Maryland, along the treacherous byways of Delaware, and into the free state of Pennsylvania. "When I found I had crossed that line," Tubman later recalled, "I looked at my hands to see if I was the same person. There was such a glory over everything; the sun came like gold through the trees, and over the fields, and I felt like I was in Heaven."[4]

Araminta Tubman was indeed a new person, at least in name. As was common for fugitive slaves, she changed her name once she crossed into freedom. She was reborn as Harriet Tubman, a name that would be carried through American history.

Spoken Direct to Her Soul

It didn't take Harriet long to realize that freedom didn't necessarily guarantee happiness. She missed her family and worried about them constantly. She wasn't content knowing her loved ones were still enslaved, so she immediately began to strategize how to rescue them. "I was a stranger in a strange land; and my home, after all, was down in Maryland; because my father, my mother, my brothers and sisters and friends were there. But I was free, and *they* should be free."[5] She found work as a maid and cook in various hotels and for families in Philadelphia, where she had settled, and hoarded her earnings, communicating with family members via an extensive network of fugitives, free blacks, and abolitionists all along the eastern seaboard.

Receiving word that her niece Kessiah and Kessiah's two children were going to be auctioned off in Baltimore, Harriet masterminded their escape with the help of Kessiah's free husband. Following the success of that rescue, she returned to Baltimore just two months later to lead her brother Moses and two other men to freedom. Harriet continued rescue operations from her base in Philadelphia even after the Fugitive Slave Law was passed in 1850. Southern slaveholders were now pursuing their runaway slaves more aggressively, making Philadelphia and every northern American city unsafe for fugitives.

Most of Harriet's family moved to Canada in the fall and winter of 1851, but Harriet stayed put, unable to rest until she'd rescued all of her enslaved family members.

Harriet was extraordinarily clever with her rescue strategies. Knowing newspapers were not printed on Sundays, she carefully planned departures for Saturday evenings, thus runaway slave advertisements would not be published until Monday, giving her a head start on slave owners and officials. She traveled at night, as was common, but she preferred planning her escapes for the winter months, when the nights were long and people were less likely to be outdoors. She often disguised herself as an elderly woman or a man and frequently sang spirituals encoded with secret messages. If danger was imminent, Harriet would sing a particular spiritual to warn the party, and when the danger cleared, she changed the words or the tempo of the song to alert them that it was safe to move on.

Her fearlessness was legendary, but according to Harriet, it was her faith that fueled her and provided protective intuition. "When danger is near, it appears like my heart goes flutter, flutter," she said.[6] Others testified to the presence of the divine at work. "Harriet seems to have a special angel to guard her on her journey of mercy . . . and confidence [that] God will preserve her from harm in all her perilous journeys," said Underground Railroad comrade Thomas Garrett. "I never met with any person of any color who had more confidence in the voice of God, as spoken direct to her soul," he added.[7]

Nurse, Scout, and Spy

By 1860 Harriet had led dozens of slaves to freedom, including her elderly parents, whom she guided on a dangerous mission to Canada. But her work was not done. When the Civil War broke out in 1861, she realized a new role awaited her: first as a nurse serving the Union Army and later as a scout and spy, utilizing her knowledge of covert travel and her survival skills. Her reconnaissance helped Colonel James Montgomery capture Jacksonville, Florida, in 1863, and later that year, Harriet also played an integral role in the famed

Combahee River Raid. On June 2, 1863, she guided three steamboats past Confederate torpedo mines to designated spots on the South Carolina shore, where hundreds of slaves waited under cover. As the steamboats sounded their whistles, more than seven hundred slaves scrambled aboard to freedom.

This raid made Harriet the first woman to lead an armed assault during the Civil War. And while several white women famously served during and after the war as spies or smugglers, fewer than a handful of black women can be credibly called Civil War spies. "Tubman's gift was, again and again, to make her appearance when the enemy least suspected, working behind the scenes," writes biographer Catherine Clinton. "Federal commanders came to depend on her, but kept her name out of official military documents. Her missions were clandestine operations, and as a black and a woman she became doubly invisible."[8]

Preparing a Place

Despite her years of military service, Harriet never received regular compensation and for decades was denied a government pension. As a result, she constantly struggled with debt, even in her later years after she had remarried. Finally, after much discussion and disagreement, Congress awarded her a pension of twenty dollars per month in 1899—more than thirty years after the conclusion of the Civil War, as Harriet herself was approaching age eighty.

In the last years of her life, Harriet was active in the women's suffrage movement, working alongside leaders like Susan B. Anthony and Emily Howland. She also opened up her home in Auburn, New York, to the poor and needy, particularly African American elderly and disabled people who were not eligible for social services assistance, which was still largely available only to whites at the time. Because so few homes for the aged admitted black residents, Harriet decided to fund one herself, and in 1903 she donated a parcel of land she owned to the African Methodist Episcopal Zion Church in Auburn, with the stipulation that it should be used for a home for "aged and indigent colored people."[9] Although nearly penniless when she originally won the bid for the land at a public auction, Harriet wasn't concerned about her lack of funds. When asked how she was going to pay for the land, she responded, "I'm going home to tell the Lord Jesus all about it."[10]

On March 10, 1913, Harriet died in a room in the Harriet Tubman Home, the residence for the elderly she had founded years prior. Shortly before she took her last breaths, she quoted verses from John 14 to those gathered at her bedside: "I go to prepare a place for you, that where I am you also may be"[11]—fitting final words for a woman who had prepared a place of freedom, comfort, and security for so many in her lifetime.[12]

24

Antoinette Brown Blackwell

"Why Should I Not Pray?"

(1825–1921)

Although the room was full to capacity, not a single whisper could be heard in the hush of quiet anticipation. The clacking of a woman's shoes across the floor echoed through the large space as she walked to the lectern. Standing behind the podium, she paused a moment and then, looking directly into the audience, launched into her temperance speech, her voice ringing with authority. Seconds later, her words were lost in an uproar as the men in the room leapt to their feet, bellowing in protest, shouting, and pounding the floor with their canes. After the organizer of the convention brought the room to order, the delegates voted, passing a resolution that forbade women to speak on the issue. While women's work behind the scenes on behalf of the temperance movement was appreciated, that afternoon the men in the room concluded "the public platform of discussion is not the appropriate sphere of women."[1]

Undeterred, the following afternoon the same woman attempted to address the meeting a second time, and again she was barred from speaking. Yet as she left the room amid the hissing and shouts of the audience, she felt a surging confidence that would not be quelled: "There were angry men confronting me and I caught the flashing of defiant eyes, but above me and within me, there was a spirit stronger than them all."[2]

Less than one week later, she stood before an audience once again, this time at the front of a small Congregational church in South Butler, New York. On that day, September 15, 1853, Antoinette Brown was ordained as the first woman minister in America.

Pushing Boundaries

Antoinette recalled an incident in which, as a very young girl, she felt compelled to pray aloud during a family prayer gathering. Later, when her brother William asked what had prompted her spontaneous prayer, she answered matter-of-factly, "Because I think I am a Christian, and why should I not pray?"[3] Antoinette's family accepted her answer and encouraged her to speak and pray whenever she was moved by the Spirit at family gatherings and informal prayer meetings at their local Congregational church. Not long after, just before she turned nine, Antoinette decided to answer an altar call. The minister, flustered by her youth, didn't interrogate her as he usually did the adults, so Antoinette took the opportunity to make her own statement of her Christian faith. The church voted unanimously to receive her into membership.

Antoinette was a precocious child. Well-schooled in mathematics, composition, rhetoric, and French, she completed her secondary education by age fifteen. The following spring she was asked to teach the youngest children in a small district school a few towns over from her parents' house. She was paid $1.50 a week plus board. She sent most of her earnings to her parents, with the exception of a few coins each week, which she saved to purchase writing paper for her personal compositions.

With precious few jobs available to women in the 1840s, Antoinette was well aware that teaching could become her lifelong occupation. But by the time she had reached her late teens, she had set her sights on another ambition altogether: she yearned to become a minister, despite the fact that at the time, women were never considered for ordination. Three years after she made this monumental decision, Antoinette had saved adequate funds from her teaching job to enroll in Oberlin Collegiate Institute in Ohio, one of the few colleges that accepted both men and women.

Oberlin may have accepted female students, but the administration was otherwise quite traditional. Although the women shared classes with the men, they were "excused" from participation in debates or rhetorical exhibitions and were prohibited from speaking publicly in coed groups. The education of women was geared toward moral and religious self-improvement in order to contribute to their God-given roles as wives and mothers.

Despite the clear regulations, Antoinette and her fellow female students constantly pushed the boundaries. They blatantly disregarded the rules by speaking in public; they reactivated a dormant ladies' association for the sole purpose of using the meetings to train themselves as public speakers; and they convinced their rhetoric professor to allow them to stage a debate in their coed class. By the time they graduated in 1847, Antoinette, her close friend Lucy Stone (who would later become Antoinette's sister-in-law and a vocal women's rights activist), and a handful of other women had acquired substantial public speaking experience.

Despite her enthusiasm, though, most of Antoinette's friends and family members were staunchly opposed to her pursuit of ordination. In fact, Lucy claimed in a blunt letter that Antoinette would "never be allowed to stand in a pulpit, nor to preach in a church, and certainly . . . never be ordained."[4] Though her feelings were bruised by her friend's lack of support, Antoinette was not swayed in her determination to study theology. While Lucy moved on to the women's rights public speaking circuit, Antoinette decided that she was not finished at Oberlin.

The Oberlin administration, however, refused Antoinette's admission into the graduate theology program. While the college allowed women a general education, it still had no intention of training women for professions other than teaching.

Finally, after much haggling, Antoinette and the administration settled on an uneasy compromise: she was welcome to sit in on theology classes, but she would not be supported in her ultimate goal of obtaining an advanced degree. Although Antoinette continued to appeal Oberlin's position during the three years she was enrolled in graduate school, she was not successful. When she completed her coursework in 1850, her name was not included in the official listing of the theology graduates. It would not be added until 1908.

Breaking Barriers

Although Antoinette spoke frequently in favor of both women's rights and the temperance movement, she considered herself first and foremost a Christian speaker, even at the risk of alienating her female companions. Lucy Stone and Elizabeth Cady Stanton eventually abandoned the church, concluding that religion was detrimental to the cause of women's rights. Even Lucretia Mott, a Quaker whose views aligned with Antoinette's, considered discussion of the Bible a waste of time. But for Antoinette, God and his Word were not simply a part of her public speaking platform; they were the whole focus. She viewed her faith as a fundamental part of her identity and a source of personal strength, which is why she did not abandon her goal of becoming an ordained minister in favor of becoming a women's rights activist. Antoinette did not aspire simply to be a public speaker; she yearned to speak specifically about God and his Word.

As a result of these convictions, Antoinette turned her attention elsewhere when she failed to convince Oberlin's administrators to ordain her. In 1853, after hearing her speak, a small Congregational church in South Butler, New York, invited Antoinette to become their pastor. On September 15, a huge crowd of friends and supporters gathered in the chapel to witness the historic occasion, the magnitude of which was not lost on Antoinette herself. "It seemed to me a very solemn thing when our three deacons and these clergymen all stood around me each placing a hand upon my head or shoulder and gravely admitting me into the ranks of ministry," she said.[5] For a salary of three hundred dollars a year, Antoinette was expected to preach two sermons every Sunday and minister to the sick and troubled members of the congregation.

News of the historic ordination spread like wildfire, and while some reactions were favorable, most were not. Few of Antoinette's female contemporaries, including Susan B. Anthony, considered her ministerial role beneficial in furthering the women's rights movement. They viewed her ambitions suspiciously, skeptical of her desire to expand women's opportunities in what they considered the anti-feminist hierarchy of the church. Other friends and family regarded her ministerial work as downright bizarre and wondered why she couldn't have chosen a more acceptable profession like teaching.

One by one, even the male church leaders who had initially supported Antoinette in her quest for ordination began to recant. Two years after her ordination, when Antoinette requested a certificate of authentication from Luther Lee, the minister who had preached the sermon at her ordination, he refused, backpedaling on his original support. "I do not see my way clear to give you such a paper as you ought to have as I did not ordain you," Lee told her. "All I did was to preach a sermon."[6] Until the late nineteenth century, some historians questioned whether Antoinette should actually be considered the first ordained female minister, although that distinction has come to be accepted by most history and religion scholars today.

"Was There Any God?"

Antoinette thrived during the early months of her ministerial work in South Butler, but the smooth sailing did not last long. Ostracized by most of her female and male peers, she struggled with feelings of abandonment and isolation. Worse, she also began to doubt both the orthodox Christian doctrine she was expected to preach and her personal faith. Early in her tenure at South Butler, Antoinette realized her liberal emphasis on divine mercy did not fit particularly well with the more traditional and conservative fire-and-brimstone style of preaching that was expected. At the same time, she began to question the authority of the Bible and her own understanding of God as love.

By the spring of her first year, Antoinette was frantic. "Suddenly I found that the whole groundwork of my faith had dropped away from me," she said. "I found myself absolutely believing in nothing. . . . Was there any God?"[7] Less than a year after she began her pastor duties, Antoinette left South Butler to return to her parents' house to rest. She never returned to ministry in an official capacity.

She did, however, return to public speaking. Although she was terrified that her exit from the church would be seen as evidence that her ordination had been a hoax, Antoinette no longer felt comfortable preaching in a church. Instead, she planned to rent a hall in New York City every Sunday, where she would preach the gospel to the masses. She also spent a significant amount of time visiting women in prisons, tenements, and asylums, then wrote about her experiences in a series of articles for the *New York Tribune*.

Despite her emphatic declaration that marriage would not interfere with her public speaking and writing, her marriage to Samuel Blackwell in 1856 and the subsequent birth of her five daughters (she also lost two children in infancy) did, in fact, dramatically impact her public speaking career. She wrote to Susan B. Anthony about the clothes she needed to sew for her daughters, her husband's garments that required mending, and her dirty house, in addition to "the whole winter store of coal and provisions to be taken in, a garden to be covered up from the frost, seeds to save, label and put up for spring, bulbs to store away, and shrubs to transplant. . . . This, Susan, is woman's sphere!"[8] Something had to give, and in the end it was Antoinette's public speaking aspirations. Her dream to preach the gospel in New York City was never fully realized.

From the confines of her own home, however, Antoinette discovered an occupation that better coincided with her family duties:

writing. Between 1869 and 1915, she wrote a number of theological, philosophical, and metaphysical articles and books. Her first project was a compilation of essays entitled *Studies in General Science*, in which she examined the dispute between the new science of Darwinism and traditional Christian doctrine. She also published several articles addressing the position of women in American society, particularly the issue of how women could balance intellectual work with household duties. She proposed a radical solution: that men and women share child-rearing and household responsibilities, and she admitted that she and her husband adhered to such an arrangement in their own household. "Mr. Blackwell, who was engaged in business and might have fewer hours to give to home occupations, declared himself more than willing to help me with home duties. This promise he generously more than redeemed for almost fifty years," Antoinette wrote after her husband's death.[9] In 1875 she published *The Sexes Throughout Nature*, arguably her most important book, in which she wrestled with the theory of evolution and gender differences.

An Untrodden Path

As her daughters matured and her parenting responsibilities eased, Antoinette reentered the public speaking circuit, lecturing on women's suffrage and advocating for equal pay for female factory workers. She also returned to organized religion after a more than twenty-five-year absence, and in 1878 she was recognized as a minister by the Committee on Fellowship of the American Unitarian Association. Although she preached regularly as an itinerant Unitarian minister, she never worked as a parish minister again.

Antoinette continued to write well into her later years and published her last book, *The Social Side of Mind and Action*, at age ninety, six years before her death in 1921. Her prolific writing served not only the public but also Antoinette herself, allowing her the space to wrestle with many of the spiritual questions that had erupted during her brief parish ministry and clarifying her thoughts on faith and theology.

Some might look at Antoinette Brown Blackwell's life and conclude that she failed to realize many of her dreams. After all, she served as a parish minister for less than twelve months, suffered through a significant faith crisis, and ultimately was not able to launch the speaking platform in New York City she had envisioned. Yet her life as a whole points to incredible perseverance and an unwavering dedication to her calling. In the face of daunting obstacles, Antoinette pressed on, determined.

Antoinette Brown Blackwell may not have perfected the balance of work and home, but she was among the first to venture successfully into uncharted territory. She navigated a male-dominated culture with endurance and grace, redefined the role of women in religion and ministry, and advocated for a woman's right for intellectual satisfaction, not at the expense of domestic responsibility, but in harmony with it.[10]

25

Josephine Butler

A Passionate Advocate for Prostitutes

(1828 – 1906)

S he stood at the bottom of the staircase and watched helplessly as her six-year-old daughter tumbled over the second-floor banister and hit the tile floor. The sight of the girl's limp and lifeless body, her blonde hair matted with blood and draped over her husband's arm, remained with Josephine Butler forever.

Her daughter's death left Josephine nearly paralyzed with grief. The home where the accident had occurred became a place of dread and horror, and shortly after their daughter's death, the Butler family moved from the small town of Cheltenham, England, to the larger, more industrial city of Liverpool. In an attempt to stave off her own pain, Josephine decided to dedicate her life to those who suffered even more than she did. "I became possessed with an irresistible desire to go forth, and find some pain keener than my own—to meet with people more unhappy than myself," she wrote. "I only knew that my heart ached night and day, and that the only solace would seem to be to find other hearts which ached night and day."[1] Josephine's search for pain led her to Liverpool's prostitutes.

A Passion for the Poor

As the daughter of a wealthy landowner, Josephine was accustomed to a comfortable, stimulating life as a child. Her father, John Grey, was the cousin of Earl Grey, the British prime minister who led the Whig administration between 1830 and 1834. John himself was a strong advocate of social reform and played a significant role in the campaign for the 1832 Reform Act and the repeal of the Corn Laws. John Grey was also an unusual Victorian father in that he encouraged the political and social education of his daughters. As a result, Josephine grew up to share her father's religious and moral principles and his strong dislike of inequality and injustice.

When she was seventeen years old, Josephine suffered through a "dark night of the soul," a period of several months in which she became obsessed with the question of why suffering existed. She spent hours alone in the pine forest near her home, wrestling with God and seeking an answer to her soul's conflict. Years later, when she looked back on this period, she concluded the struggle and despair had been sent by God himself, and she saw this period of darkness as essential in preparing her for her life's work.

In 1852 Josephine married George Butler, an academic and a clergyman. Though quite different in temperament—George was quiet and even-keeled, while Josephine was more dramatic and outspoken—the pair was well suited. They shared a common passion for the poor and both firmly believed that to be a follower of Christ required not only faith but action. George was also an advocate of an egalitarian marriage, and he was never anything but wholly supportive of his wife's work. "I am content to leave you to walk by yourself in the path you shall choose," George wrote to Josephine before they were married, "but I know that I do not leave you alone and unsupported for His arm will guide, strengthen and protect you."[2] As biographer

Joseph Williamson points out, this was not merely the passing zeal of a keen lover; it was a lasting promise that George kept for their entire marriage.

Josephine and George spent the first five years of their married life in Oxford, where George was a fellow at Exeter College. Oxford was a man's world—in fact, women were not allowed to dine in Christ Church until 1960—but that didn't dissuade Josephine from making her mark. She was the first woman to apply—and be accepted—for a library card at the Bodleian, the university library, and she breezed in and out of this male preserve with an armload of books on a regular basis. The Butlers also made a name for themselves when they allowed a "fallen woman"—the mistress of an Oxford professor—to live in their home after she was released from jail.

The Butler family spent eight years in Cheltenham, where George was vice principal of Cheltenham College. But after the untimely death of their daughter, Eva, in 1864, they couldn't bear to stay in the familiar surroundings any longer. When George was offered the position of principal at Liverpool College in 1866, they fled small-town life for the bustling urban seaport. Josephine was in search of human misery, and she didn't have to look far to find it in Liverpool.

Presumed Guilty

Liverpool was a huge seaport, with as many as ten thousand sailors in port at any given time. As Lisa Severine Nolland notes, "The combination of under-employed, unemployed and unemployable women with legions of sexually frustrated sailors with money in their pockets resulted in a thriving subculture of prostitution; indeed, the city was reputed as being 'the most immoral of all immoral places.'"[3]

The nature of the occupation makes it difficult to establish the exact number of prostitutes working in England during the Victorian period. Estimates range from 50,000 to 368,000. But one thing was clear to British authorities during the 1860s: the spread of venereal diseases, especially among the British Army and Royal Navy, was on the rise. In an effort to curb the spread of sexually transmitted diseases among the armed forces, Parliament passed the Contagious Diseases Act (CDA) in 1864, with amendments in 1866 and 1869. Not only did the acts allow the establishment of official brothels where prostitutes were under medical supervision, it also empowered police officers to arrest any woman suspected to be a prostitute and force her to submit to a medical examination. The CDA effectively abolished habeas corpus in Great Britain. A woman's guilt was presumed until she could prove herself innocent.

Josephine was quick to recognize the abuses that could, and did, result from the passage of the CDA. Innocent women and young girls were arrested on the whims of corrupt police officers or as the result of false information and were subjected to humiliating and painfully invasive medical procedures. Once branded as a prostitute, however innocent she was, a woman was doomed to a life of prostitution, as no other employment would be open to her. Women who refused to consent to the medical examination were imprisoned. Women found to be infected with venereal diseases were locked in a hospital for three months to be cured.

Incensed by what she considered a blatant violation of women's civil rights, Josephine knew immediately that leading the charge against the CDA was her God-given calling. At the same time, she feared what such leadership would require. "This is perhaps after all the very work, the very mission, I longed for years ago, and saw coming, afar off, like a bright star," she wrote in her journal in 1869. "But seen near as it approaches, it is so dreadful, so difficult, so disgusting, that I tremble to look at it."[4]

You can imagine her dread. Human sexuality and the details of venereal diseases aren't dinnertime topics, even today. And Josephine lived in Victorian England, a time when such subject matter would have been taboo. But unsavory conversations were the least of her worries. Both the British government and the medical professionals were interested only in slowing the spread of sexually transmitted diseases, regardless of whether their efforts deprived women of their civil liberty or whether their measures were successful. Josephine knew the entire male-dominated British government and the medical establishment would stand against her call for the repeal of the acts. In spite of all this, she stepped forward.

She Lived Love

Josephine accurately predicted her fate. When she spoke publicly against the CDAs, she was slandered and ridiculed, heckled and harassed. On more than one occasion she was pelted with dung and stones as she walked through the city streets. At a hotel where she was scheduled to speak, an angry mob broke through the windows and cornered her, threatening to set the building on fire if she went through with her speech. At another meeting in a hayloft on the outskirts of town, protesters sprinkled cayenne pepper over the floor in the hopes that the pungent spice would cause significant eye, nose, and throat irritation and render Josephine unable to speak. When that failed, they attempted to smoke Josephine and a group of women out of the building by igniting bundles of straw below them. She escaped by jumping through the trapdoor to the ground floor, then went ahead with the meeting at another hotel.

In her speeches Josephine emphasized the gender discrimination inherent in the CDAs. In the manifesto she wrote as head of the Ladies National Association for the Repeal of the Contagious Diseases Acts, she noted that it is "unjust to punish the sex who are the victims of vice, and leave unpunished the sex who are the main cause of the vice and its dreaded consequences."[5] She also warned that the acts set a dangerous precedent, implying that if a woman's rights could be violated, so could anyone's. "This legalization of vice, which is the endorsement of the 'necessity' of impurity for man and the institution of slavery of woman, is the most open denial which modern times have seen of the principle of the sacredness of the individual being," she declared.[6]

After thousands of miles traveled, thousands of petition signatures gathered, and hundreds of speeches given, Josephine and her repeal supporters finally declared victory. The Contagious Diseases Acts were repealed in 1886, seventeen years after Josephine launched her campaign. "Looking back over those years we can now see the wisdom of God in allowing us to wait so long for the victory," Josephine wrote in retrospect.[7] What started as a simple initiative for legislative repeal had grown into a movement with lasting impact, which, she later realized, had been God's intent all along.

Through it all, Josephine never lost faith in the belief that she was carrying out God's work. Asked to state her case before the twenty-five members of the Royal Commission, she spoke frankly and with conviction:

> Allow me to say . . . that all of us who are seeing the repeal of these Acts are wholly indifferent to the decision of this Commission. . . . We have the word of God in our hands, the Law of God in our consciences. . . . You may be sure that our action in this matter will continue to be exactly the same, even if the Commission pronounces the Acts to be highly moral. We shall never rest until this system is banished from our shores. I am able to speak with calm confidence, yet with humility, because I believe in the power of prayer. There are tens of thousands throughout this country, men and women who are daily praying to God that this legislation may be overthrown. The Acts are doomed for this country and for the colonies.[8]

Josephine Butler possessed a tremendous faith, a faith born out of tragedy and grief and fueled by her love for God and her desire to heal the brokenhearted. Like Jesus, she was particularly devoted to the outcasts, those shunned and disdained by the rest of society. And like Jesus, she was able to see past their degradation to love them as children of God, created in his image. "Love to the fallen, the outcasts, even the madly sinful," she once wrote. "Love to every human being however degraded who bears the impress of the Divine image."[9] Josephine Butler's philosophy of love and compassion wasn't empty rhetoric. She didn't merely preach love. She lived it.[10]

26

Catherine Booth

Mother of the Army

(1 8 2 9 – 1 8 9 0)

Distracted by the ruckus, she glanced up from her quiet game in the front yard to see a crowd of young boys taunting a drunken man as he was being forced down the street by a police officer. In a blink, she was at the man's side. Grabbing his hand, she walked with him the remainder of the way to the police station, her head held high against the jeers of the bystanders. She was only nine years old at the time, but Catherine Booth was already on a path to becoming a passionate advocate for the poor and oppressed.

Praying for Salvation

Catherine was a serious, reserved child. But her quiet nature didn't prohibit her from speaking out with uncharacteristic boldness when she felt called to do so. At the age of fourteen, for instance, Catherine became an impassioned spokesperson for the temperance move-ment. She read avidly on the subject, served as secretary of the junior branch of the local temperance society, and wrote prolifically for a variety of magazines. Promptly after dinner each evening she retired to her bedroom and wrote essays by candlelight, many of which were published anonymously in the leading magazines (for who would take the thoughts of a teenage girl seriously?).

When Catherine was sixteen she moved with her family to London, and it was around this time that she endured a crisis in her faith. Up to this point, Catherine had been a devout Christian. By the time she was twelve years old she had read the Bible aloud, cover to cover, eight times, and often she was unable to sleep until she had confessed her sins to God and felt forgiven and comforted by a sense of his love. But suddenly Catherine was inexplicably gripped by the fear that she had not received the Holy Spirit into her heart and was therefore not saved. "She felt that if the witness of the Holy Spirit to her own heart were not given, all her knowledge *about* God, *about* the practice of religion, would fail to satisfy," wrote her granddaughter and biographer, Catherine Bramwell-Booth. "She could not recall any particular place or moment when she had definitely stepped out on the promises of God and received the witness of the Holy Spirit to her salvation."[1]

Catherine obsessed over this fear for weeks until finally she awoke one morning to find that her deepest prayers had been answered. She slid her hymnal from beneath her pillow and, reading these lines, knew in her heart that she was saved: "My God, I am Thine, what a comfort divine, what a blessing to know that my Jesus is mine!" She later recollected, "The words came to my inmost soul with a force and illumination they had never before possessed. . . . I no longer hoped that I was saved; I was certain of it."[2]

Dearest Earthly Treasure

When Catherine was twenty-three she met her soul mate and hus-band, William Booth, by chance, on a carriage ride after he'd preached at her church. Because she was not feeling well, William had been asked to escort her home. As the carriage lurched over the unpaved road, the two acquaintances instantly and simultaneously realized that God intended their union. Later William wrote it was God himself "who in a most wonderful and providential manner has brought us together and then flashed into our hearts the sweet and heavenly feeling of a something more than earthly unison."[3]

The two wrote hundreds of letters to each other during their three-year engagement, frequently posting multiple letters in a single day. One written by Catherine stands out in particular, in which she argued for the biblically sanctioned authority allowing women to preach—an argument that would have great bearing on her future ministry and leadership in the Salvation Army.

"If God has given her the ability why should not woman persuade the vacillating, instruct and console the penitent, and pour out her soul in prayer for sinners?" Catherine wrote, to which her fiancé succinctly answered, "I would not stop a woman preaching on any account. I would not encourage one to begin. You should preach if you felt moved thereto; felt equal to the task. I would not stay you if I had the power to do so. Although I should not like it. I am for the world's salvation; I will quarrel with no means that promises help."[4] William clearly agreed with Catherine in theory, yet was not comfortable with the reality of a woman in the pulpit. Over time, though, his philosophy would change dramatically.

She Preaches

After William and Catherine were married in a quiet ceremony in 1855, the two began to travel together while William served as an evangelistic preacher. By 1858 Catherine had begun to teach Sunday school to children and women, although she was not confident of her abilities. Not long after, the mother of three young children (five more would follow) was stunned by a startling revelation as she walked to church one evening. Gazing through the dingy row-house windows, she glimpsed women sitting together at kitchen tables, gossiping and passing the time, and she felt called to bring them to God. "Would you not be doing God more service, and acting more like your Redeemer, by turning into some of these houses, speaking to these careless sinners, and inviting them to the service, than by going to enjoy it yourself?" she asked herself.[5]

Catherine stood still, looked up to heaven, and asked God to help her. And then she immediately approached a group of women sitting on a doorstep and invited them to church. Her courage fueled, Catherine knocked on the door of the next house and spoke about Jesus to the woman who answered. Thus began her twice-weekly evening visits to the slums to evangelize to the poor and destitute, a practice that would later be an important component of the Salvation Army's ministry.

Up to this point Catherine philosophically believed that women should be allowed to preach, but she was reluctant to pursue that calling herself. In fact, the very idea of standing before a crowd and preaching the Word of God filled her with anxiety, fear, and dread. That all changed on a stormy Sunday morning in 1860, as Catherine sat in the front pew with her four-year-old son, Bramwell, on her lap. As she listened to a visiting minister testify about obedience to God's will, she suddenly felt a voice urge her to do the same. At first Catherine resisted the voice, reminding herself that she was entirely unprepared. "You will look a fool and you have nothing to say," she heard another voice argue in her head. For Catherine, that "voice of the devil" was the deciding moment. "I have not yet been willing to be a fool for Christ. Now I will be one," she decided, rising and striding toward the pulpit where her husband stood.

Surprised to see his typically shy wife standing next to him before the congregation, William leaned toward her with concern. "What is the matter, my dear?" he whispered.

"I want to say a word," Catherine whispered back. William, shocked almost to silence, simply announced to the congregation, "My dear wife wishes to speak," before taking a seat in the pew.[6] Catherine went on to testify, confessing her sin of disobedience before the rapt congregation. By the time she was finished, several in the chapel were weeping audibly, and when William rose to his feet, he announced that his wife would preach again that evening.

Thus began nearly three decades of preaching and evangelizing for Catherine Booth. In fact, only a few weeks after this initial foray, Catherine stepped into William's place when he fell ill and covered his preaching duties for four months while he recuperated. With her traveling, preaching several nights each week, visiting "the men" (the alcoholics on the street), and caring for now four children—the eldest only four years old—Catherine's schedule was almost impossibly demanding. "It was not I that did this but the Holy Spirit," Catherine wrote later. "With four little children . . . it looked like an inopportune time, did it not, to begin to preach. . . . I never imagined the life of publicity and trial it would lead to. . . . All I did was to take the first step."[7]

It's interesting to note that later, when Catherine and William's eldest daughter, Kate, demonstrated a gift for preaching, Catherine initially objected. Perhaps she recalled her own rigorous regimen and the demands of balancing motherhood and domestic duties with a full-time preaching schedule. When she balked at the notion of Kate climbing to the pulpit, her son Bramwell suggested she bring her misgivings to God and talk with him honestly about her reluctance and fear. "In our conversation he fixed his eyes upon me and said, 'Mama dear, you will have to face this question alone with God, for God has as assuredly called Katie and inspired her for this work as ever He called you, and you must mind how you hold her back,'" Catherine reflected later.[8] Catherine, who never hesitated to talk directly and honestly with God, spoke to him that night behind the closed doors of her bedroom, and when she emerged, she gave Kate her blessing and promised God that she would never again stand in the way of his will for her children.

The Salvation Army Is Born

By 1870 the Salvation Army—known then as the Christian Mission—was well under way with William at the helm and Catherine as his trusted advisor. Discouraged by the church's refusal to support him as a full-time traveling evangelist, William broke from the Methodist Church in 1861 and with Catherine's blessing forged out on his own, despite the fact that it meant no steady income for his growing family.

The couple's vision of religion and evangelism departed dramatically from the norm. Instead of preaching in churches and meetinghouses, William spoke in tents, dance halls, taverns, and even graveyards and stables—anyplace that put him among the people who most needed salvation. "More than two-thirds of the working classes never cross the threshold of a church or chapel," he wrote. "It is evident that if they are to be reached, extraordinary means must be employed."[9]

The couple also strongly believed in the power of personal testimony and encouraged those already converted, from prostitutes to recovered alcoholics, to preach to the people directly. The Booths believed that God chose members of the uncultivated masses to be his messengers, his army of salvation. While William preached to the destitute and poor, Catherine concentrated on the wealthy, reaching congregations that could afford to give generously to support both their mission and the Booth family themselves.

By the end of 1878, the year the Christian Mission was officially renamed the Salvation Army, the organization employed 127 full-time ministers (more than one hundred of them recruited from the ranks of recent converts), and the total Sunday night congregation in churches and meetinghouses in London and beyond numbered more than 27,000. Modeled after the military, the Salvation Army had its own flag and hymns, and its ministers wore uniforms and were assigned ranks according to a hierarchy. William was known as the "General," while Catherine assumed the title "Mother of the Salvation Army." Several of their eight children followed in their parents' footsteps. Two of them, Bramwell and Evangeline, later became generals themselves.

Driven from the Familiar to the Unknown

Catherine suffered from serious illnesses almost her entire life. As a teenager she was bedridden by a severe curvature of the spine.

When she was an adult, exhaustion, depression, angina, and what's now thought to be Crohn's disease incapacitated her and, more than once, brought her to the brink of death. Her frail health, combined with an exhaustive preaching schedule, constant financial challenges, a relentless mission, and the unceasing job of raising eight children, made for an existence fraught with challenges and change. As her granddaughter Catherine Bramwell-Booth noted, "Catherine was continually driven by God out from the familiar to the unknown, and every new departure in her life demanded a new act of faith in God. To every fresh call and in the presence of every threatened loss or sorrow her response had to be 'I will trust and not be afraid.'"[10]

In dying, as in living, Catherine trusted and encouraged. In her last letter to her beloved Salvationists, she soothed them, always a mother, with these words: "The waters are rising, but so am I. I am not going under, but over. Don't be concerned about your dying; only go on living well, and the dying will be all right."[11]

Catherine Booth, Mother of the Salvation Army, died on October 4, 1890, in the arms of her beloved husband, surrounded by her children. Three days later more than fifty thousand people knelt by her coffin to pay their respects, bowing their heads beneath a sign that read, "Love one another and meet me in the morning," a quote from one of her messages. Many who attended the visitation and funeral were poor, their clothes shabby and unkempt, their faces ravaged and worn. Many had come to God through Catherine's preaching or her personal attention. Many were still alcoholics, prostitutes, and gamblers, just now taking their very first step toward God. These were Catherine's beloved people, her family. She would have been very much at home.[12]

27

Hannah Whitall Smith

God Is Enough

(1832 – 1911)

Slamming his hand down on the arm of the chair, her father made his declaration to the couple standing before him. "I will not have thee in my house any longer," he bellowed, his eyes meeting his daughter's. "Your ungodly doctrines are contaminating our family and have humiliated us amongst the Friends." Her brother stepped forward, insisting that Hannah leave their father's house and informing her that she was no longer welcome there or at her married sisters' homes. Hannah stumbled out the door toward the carriage, her husband's steadying grip on her arm. Branded a heretic and a disgrace and banned from her childhood home, she despaired of ever seeing her parents or her siblings again.

"Could Anything Be More Liberating Than That?"

Hannah Whitall strained against the Quaker sensibilities from the start. As a young girl, she resisted the demands of piety imposed by her elders, preferring instead to revel in the great outdoors. She struggled to reconcile the message she heard preached so often from the pulpit—a message of a dark world stained by sin—with her love of nature and the unbridled joy she experienced in the midst of God's creation. "How could such an angry, harsh God have created such a beautiful world?" she wondered.

Hannah continued to grapple with the nature of God long after her marriage to Robert Pearsall Smith in 1851 and the birth of her first two children, Nellie and Frank. During the afternoons while the babies napped, she often wrote in her journal, pouring her doubts and questions into its pages: "I [feel] myself cut off from God entirely. I [feel] like a sinking boat, tossed about by a mighty tempest on the godless deep of life, listening with anguished ears to the falling away of its ever breaking shore."[1] Not only did Hannah struggle to define God, she also began to doubt his very existence.

When five-year-old Nellie died of a bronchial infection three days before Christmas in 1857, grief rocked Hannah to her core. But surprisingly, her daughter's death proved to be a turning point in her faith. For the first time in two years, Hannah felt a sense of God's presence in the months following Nellie's death. "My precious child, my angel child, thou shalt indeed be, I trust, a link to draw me up to heaven," Hannah wrote in her journal just three days after her daughter's funeral.[2]

The following summer, determined to wrestle out her lingering questions, Hannah packed only one book when the family vacationed at the beach in Atlantic City: the Bible. Day after day, she sat in a lounge chair on the beach and immersed herself in Scripture while young Frank played in the waves. Finally, after weeks of searching for God's truth, she turned to chapter five in the book of Romans and read this: "While we were yet sinners, Christ died for us" (Rom. 5:8 KJV). Suddenly the image of the harsh and impenetrable God vanished, replaced by a God of infinite love and grace. "While I was yet a sinner, Christ died for me. Could anything be more liberating than that?" she wrote later in her journal, reveling in her new freedom in Christ.[3]

A Stumbling Block

Not long after her spiritual revelation, Hannah and Robert resigned their membership to the Society of Friends, and in 1859 Hannah was baptized by immersion at a Baptist church near her Philadelphia home. But while Hannah was at peace with her decision, her extended family—particularly her father, a devout Quaker—was appalled. They refused to accept her conversion and banned her, her husband, and their child from visiting. Devastated but undeterred, Hannah later wrote that although she was an outcast from her earthly father's house, she was comforted by the fact that she was not cast out by her heavenly Father. Ultimately, after several years had passed, her father softened and reconciled with Hannah and her husband.

During the 1860s Hannah's faith took another turn when she was introduced to the increasingly popular Methodist holiness movement. The Smith family had weathered several difficulties, including Robert's financial ruin and his subsequent breakdown, which resulted in a move from Philadelphia to a small town in New Jersey. Distanced from her church, Bible study, and friends, and exhausted from caring for her ill husband and her children (she now had five), Hannah struggled to find a spiritual home in New Jersey. When her dressmaker encouraged her to attend a Saturday evening holiness meeting with the local factory workers, Hannah, out of desperation, agreed. Initially she assumed the working-class people wouldn't have anything to offer her, but she was soon proved wrong. In those humble meetings and among those humble people, Hannah found the real Christianity for which she had always longed.

As she settled into her newfound religion, however, Hannah hit a roadblock. Followers of the holiness movement emphasized what was known as the "second blessing"—an experience that indicated the palpable presence of the Holy Spirit. Pray as she might for such an experience, Hannah was left without this conviction. She watched with a mix of joy and envy as her husband was transformed by the second blessing at a Methodist camp meeting during the summer of 1868. But although she felt on the verge of such a blessing, Hannah was never completely overcome with emotion, the clear sign that a baptism of the Holy Spirit had occurred. She often approached the altar with a handful of handkerchiefs, prepared for an onslaught of tears that never materialized. Why didn't she succumb to overwhelming emotion like so many others at the camp meetings? she wondered. She worried her lack of emotion made her less faithful and perhaps was an indication that she was not a believer at all.

Finally, after two years of relentless praying, Hannah concluded that the second blessing and its accompanying emotional response was simply the reaction of those with a more emotional disposition like her husband. To those with a rational, practical nature such as herself, spiritual truth was imparted as a growing conviction about the truth of the Gospels rather than a feeling. Hannah later explained this reasoning in her bestselling book *The Christian's Secret of a Happy Life*:

> I am convinced that throughout the Bible the expressions concerning the "heart" do not mean the emotions, that which we now understand the word "heart," but they mean the will, the personality of man, the man's own central self, and that the object of God's dealings with man is that this "I" may be yielded up to Him, and this central life abandoned to His entire control. It is not the feelings of the man God wants, but the man himself.[4]

The Woman Preacher: "A Traveling Barnum's Hippodrome"

Life grew increasingly difficult for the Pearsall Smiths during the 1870s. In August of 1872, their eighteen-year-old son Frank died of typhoid fever while the family was vacationing. That fall, Robert suffered a serious nervous breakdown, which led to the family's move to Clifton Springs, New York, where Robert was admitted to a sanatorium. While her husband recovered, Hannah wrote her first book, *The Record of a Happy Life*, about Frank's life, which was published and became a bestseller by 1874.

In 1873 Robert traveled to England per his doctor's orders. Hannah, pregnant at age forty-one with her seventh child, stayed behind and was surprised to hear that her husband, instead of resting in his time abroad, had embarked on a rigorous preaching schedule. Their baby, a girl, was delivered stillborn in August 1873. In the midst of her grief, Hannah threw herself into the public eye, not only writing but also speaking and preaching regularly in Philadelphia and Atlantic City.

When Robert, whose ministry in England had grown exponentially, urged Hannah to join him in Great Britain, she and the children set sail. By 1875 Robert was known internationally as a preacher in the holiness movement, and Hannah's reputation as a writer and speaker was growing as well. Still, she dreaded the hectic schedule. En route to England for the Brighton Conference in 1875, Hannah wrote to her sister, "I cannot tell thee how dreary the showlife I have to live this summer looks to me. . . . I feel just as if I were a sort of traveling Barnum's Hippodrome with a 'woman preacher' on show instead of a tight-rope dancer."[5]

However, Hannah didn't have the luxury or the time to bemoan her circumstances. With a deadline looming, she battled seasickness to write most of *The Christian's Secret of a Happy Life* aboard the steamer, a book she later admitted hadn't inspired her and was a burden to write. The book was published in 1875 and has since sold millions of copies. Hannah often pointed to the book's success as evidence that feelings and inspiration weren't as critical as faithfulness.

More than eight thousand people from all over the world attended the Brighton Conference that year. Hannah led two Bible study sessions each day, with between two and three thousand people attending each session, while Robert preached to thousands. A few weeks after the conference ended, however, scandal erupted when a British newspaper reported that Robert had engaged in inappropriate relations with a young female follower. The scandal destroyed Robert's reputation and career as a preacher. As a result, he experienced yet another nervous breakdown, becoming so weak and mentally fragile that Hannah could hardly rouse him from his bed in their hotel room to board the ship bound for America. By the time the couple returned to Philadelphia, disgraced and humiliated,

Robert's faith had virtually vanished, and Hannah was assuaged by doubt and depression.

God Is Enough

Although she was still speaking and leading Bible studies, Hannah felt like an imposter. She spent hours analyzing her own words in *The Christian's Secret of a Happy Life*, determined to find an answer to her most pressing question: why had God allowed this scandal to happen? For two years, between 1876 and 1878, her letters returned again and again to her questions and doubts. Still, she persevered in her faith and refused to give up on her God. While her husband abandoned Christianity in favor of Buddhism and continued to pursue adulterous relationships, Hannah surrounded herself with other Christians in an attempt to buoy her own faith. Slowly she grew more confident. "One thing I know, and that is that I am all the Lord's and that His will is infinitely and unspeakably sweet to me," she wrote to a friend in 1878. "And like a poor little child who has lost its way, I creep into the dear arms of my Father and just ask Him to carry me, since I cannot understand His directions. He doeth all things well and I can leave myself with Him."[6]

Hannah Whitall Smith went on to become a leader in the temperance and women's suffrage movements and an advocate for women in education. She also spoke and wrote about her faith and published several more books in her later years, including *Everyday Religion, or, The Commonsense Teaching of the Bible*; her spiritual autobiography *The Unselfishness of God and How I Discovered It*; and *God of All Comfort*.

Hannah Whitall Smith's critics have noted that the title of her most famous book, *The Christian's Secret to a Happy Life*, is ironic, given the difficulties she faced throughout her life. Why take advice from someone whose life was so fraught with disappointment? you might ask. How is Hannah Whitall Smith's life a model for happiness? She dealt with the deaths of her children; her husband's mental health issues, his multiple infidelities, and their increasing estrangement;

her daughter Mary's scandalous affair and subsequent divorce; her daughter Alys's depression and suicide attempt; and a prolonged custody battle for her two grandchildren. Yet in spite of these challenges, Hannah persevered in her faith, growing more confident in God's love as she aged.

The final words of her last book, published five years before her death, are a simple but powerful testament of her faith. "God is enough!" she wrote. "God is enough for time. God is enough for eternity. God is enough!"[7] It's true, Hannah Whitall Smith's understanding of happiness may not be typical, especially by modern standards. She understood that happiness was not created by success or fame, a perfect marriage, good health, or any of the parameters we often use to define it, but was in God alone.

28

Clara Swain

Healing Bodies, Ministering to Souls

(1834–1910)

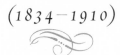

Clara Swain's arrival in India started off on the wrong foot. After traveling two months by ship over rough seas, she finally stepped ashore in Bombay to discover that the horses pulling her carriage refused to budge. In fact, one horse simply lay down in the middle of the dirt road. Clara wrapped her shawl around her shoulders and settled into a fitful sleep, surrounded by strangers and aware that the fires winking in the distance weren't for warmth or cheer, but to deter wild tigers from approaching the village.

When fresh horses were found several hours later, the group set off, traveling by carriage, rail, boat, and dooly over the Indian countryside and across the Ganges River, until they arrived three days later in Bareilly, the city in northern India where Clara would spend the next twenty-seven years of her life as a medical missionary.

Discovering Her Calling

Clara was born in Elmira, New York, in 1834, the youngest of John and Clarissa Swain's ten children. The family moved to Castile, New York, and when Clara was eight she officially joined the village Methodist church and declared herself a Christian.

Clara was a studious child. Not satiated by what she was offered in school, she often borrowed books from neighbors to read in her free time. She also discovered her gift of nursing at a young age when, as a teenager, she cared for a Presbyterian minister and his family as they suffered through the ravages of typhoid fever. After the minister and two of the children died, Clara stayed with the widow and her surviving children for many months as they recovered from their loss.

By 1859 Clara was teaching at a small school in Canandaigua, New York, but she chafed in the role. Though she taught for three years, she was frequently discouraged by the children's inattention and the mundane daily routine. In her heart, Clara knew her true calling. She yearned to be a doctor, and she waited patiently for an opportunity to present itself.

Opportunity knocked when Dr. Cordelia Greene invited Clara to train with her at the Castile Sanitarium. Three years later she was admitted to the Women's Medical College in Philadelphia, where she graduated in 1869. Clara A. Swain, MD, knew exactly how she wanted to put her degree to use. When the Women's Union Missionary Society of America invited her to serve as a medical missionary in India, Clara accepted. She departed from New York City on November 3, 1869, and arrived in Bareilly on January 20, 1870.

Physical and Spiritual Healing

Clara awoke on her first morning of duty, stepped outside her humble dwelling, and was greeted by a group of Indian women waiting for her, all in need of medical services. She treated fourteen patients that day, despite the fact that her trunk containing medicines and medical supplies had not yet arrived from America. Shortly after her arrival in Bareilly she also began to teach anatomy, physiology, and nursing classes to seventeen students—fourteen girls from a nearby orphanage and three married women. Many of her initial patients and students were already Christians. When one of the girls first saw the model of a skeleton hanging in the classroom, she said, "Oh, Miss Sahiba [the Indian word for *lady*, which is how Clara was addressed by her students and patients], how will this woman rise in the resurrection with her flesh in America and her bones in India?"[1]

By the end of her first year in India, Clara had treated more than 1,025 patients at the mission house and made an additional 250 home visits in the city and surrounding villages. Male doctors were not allowed to examine Indian women, and Clara was the only female doctor within hundreds of miles. She often combined Bible study with medical visits to village homes and would initiate conversations about Jesus and the Gospels with the native women. In 1875 she wrote in a letter,

> God has said that His Word shall not return unto Him void, so we may hope that the good seed of the Word which has been sown this morning may spring up and bring forth fruit in His good time. These people come to us with the utmost confidence believing that our medicines will cure their ailments whatever they may be or of how long standing, and while we endeavor to heal their bodies we are trying just as earnestly to minister to their souls.[2]

Later, after the hospital pharmacy had opened, she even included passages from Scripture on the back of the prescriptions so that every patient would "receive with her prescription a portion of the Word of Life."[3] Conversion was slow, but one by one, Clara began to see the results of her evangelizing. "How this pays for coming to India! It is better than the world or friends can give," she wrote to her sister after learning that a man, his wife, and her mother had declared their conversion to Christianity.[4]

A Gift from the King

Clara realized the need for a hospital almost immediately after her arrival in Bareilly. The mission house was not adequate for the number of patients she treated each day, and the home visits, all of which were made in the early mornings before the extreme heat of the day, were time consuming and exhausting. "If our work continues to increase we could care for many more if we had a suitable place for patients to remain with us, and it would save much of our time and strength," she wrote to her sister in 1870. "Hospitals, especially for women and children, are much needed in India, and if properly conducted might do much for their social and religious improvement as well as for the relief of their physical suffering."[5]

The problem was that the nawab of Rampore owned the property abutting the mission house. The nawab was a prince-like Muslim ruler of the region who not only resisted the introduction of Western medicine in India but swore he would never allow a Christian missionary in his city. Clara approached the nawab with great trepidation, requesting that he donate one acre of his estate for the construction of a hospital for women and children. Before the words were even out of the interpreter's mouth, the nawab interrupted him, granting not one but forty acres of his property, as well as a house, for the hospital. "We were unprepared for so generous a gift . . . and were not a little surprised at the Nawab's immediate and hearty reception of our request, and we accepted the gift with gratitude not to this prince alone, but to the King of the Universe, who, we believe, put it into his heart to give it to us," Clara later wrote.[6]

By 1874 construction of the Women's Hospital and Medical School, the first of its kind in all of Asia, was completed. It was laid out according to Indian custom, with separate apartments, each complete with its own kitchen, where patients could live with their family and cook their own meals. Caste laws prohibited the Indian women from eating the food prepared by Christians or members of other castes. Patients arrived with their extended family and several servants as well as animals and livestock in tow. It was not uncommon for a patient to stay in a hospital apartment with her husband and children; her own furniture arranged in the room; and the family's goats, horses, and oxen outside.

Explaining the Great Mystery

In 1885, after Clara was summoned to Ketri to care for the ailing wife of the raja (princely monarch), she accepted the offer to stay on as physician to the palace women. After wrestling with and praying about the decision for days, Clara felt God moving her to stay in Ketri, where, as the only Christian missionary within hundreds of miles, she saw great opportunity for her evangelical work. Not only did she offer medical services, but within weeks of settling at the palace she also asked the raja for permission to launch a school for girls. The raja accepted Clara's proposal and even offered each of her eighteen students a pound of wheat flour every morning, equal to what they would earn in a day's wages, to encourage their attendance. The raja also gave each of the young girls a new skirt and head covering so they could attend school in clean clothes, and he rewarded those with perfect attendance each week with an extra pound of flour on Saturday.

Clara and the raja's wife, the rani, grew close during the years Clara worked in the palace. Although the rani was Hindu, the two often read the Bible together, and Clara attempted to explain the concept of salvation through Christ to her. She admitted that she struggled in the process. "It is hard for earthly royalty to submit to the requirements of the King of kings," Clara wrote to her friend and former teacher, Dr. Greene. "They require submission from their own subjects but their religion teaches them that they may do what they please, their position in the world saves them."[7] She admitted that all she could do was pray that the Holy Spirit would become the rani's teacher and explain the great mystery that puzzled so many.

Clara also taught Bible study to the daughters of the raja and rani, although at one point, when the raja saw that one of his daughters was growing too knowledgeable in the Gospels, he forbade her to continue her studies. The rani interceded on her daughter's behalf, admitting to her husband that she too read the Bible and found it to be a good book and a comfort to her during times of trouble. "Let Bai read it, it will do her no harm," the rani implored her husband. The raja considered his wife's request for a few moments and then acquiesced on two conditions: that his daughter refrain from reading about killing cows and "too much about Jesus Christ."[8] A compromise was reached, and the rani and her daughters continued their study of Scripture.

Neither the rani nor her daughters converted from Hinduism to Christianity while Clara worked for them. Nevertheless, she remained hopeful that her teaching had not been in vain. Clara observed that the rani seemed to find in the New Testament what she had been in search of for years. Her immersion in the Bible made the raja anxious, but he did not attempt to halt the study. "He thought the Rani so grounded in the Hindu faith that the reading of the Bible would not move her," Clara wrote to her sister. "He does not understand the change in her mind which has already taken place."[9]

This Is My Country

Clara visited America twice to restore her deteriorating health, but she returned to India following each respite. While she admitted that she missed her family, she also couldn't ignore her life's calling. "I know you are disappointed that I decided to return to India," she wrote to loved ones in 1879, "but knowing so well the need of workers among the poor and destitute women of India I cannot but feel that my work is among them while I have strength to work anywhere, and I would much rather go back and die on the field than stay at home from a selfish motive."[10]

Today Clara Swain is honored with the distinction of being the first woman physician in India, as well as the first fully accredited female physician sent out by any missionary society into any part of the non-Christian world. Her impact on the people of India, particularly the women and children, was tremendous. Clara loved India and its people, and she considered India her true home. "This is my country, the land to which my Father has called me," she wrote.[11] It's clear that when God called Clara to offer her services to the Indian people, she didn't give them only her medical expertise. Clara Swain gave the people of India her whole heart.[12]

29

Amanda Berry Smith

Preaching in the Face of Racism

(1837–1915)

As an itinerant minister and evangelist in nineteenth-century America, Amanda Berry Smith had three notable strikes against her. She was a woman. She was uneducated. And she was black. None of these obstacles, however, prohibited Amanda from pursuing her God-given calling. She crossed gender, class, and racial barriers to live out her ministry, first in America and then overseas in England, India, and Africa.

Amanda Berry Smith was born a slave in Long Green, Maryland, the oldest of thirteen children, five of whom were born into slavery. Her parents, Samuel and Mariam Berry, lived on adjoining farms. Offered the opportunity by his mistress to "buy himself," Samuel labored at her dairy farm all day, then walked four miles to harvest in the neighboring fields until one or two o'clock in the morning, after which he walked the four miles home, slept for a couple of hours, and began his labors again the next morning. During what little spare time he could find, Samuel also made handcrafted brooms and husk mats to sell at the market. "He had an important and definite object before him and was willing to sacrifice sleep and rest in order to accomplish it," Amanda wrote in her 1893 autobiography. "It was not his own liberty alone, but the freedom of his wife and five children. For this he toiled day and night."[1] When Samuel had finally saved up enough, he purchased his own freedom and that of his wife and children.

The Great Mountain Becomes a Molehill

Amanda felt the first faint stirrings of belief as a thirteen-year-old, while attending worship services with her employer at a largely white Methodist church in Pennsylvania. But her yearning for God was quickly diminished by the racism she encountered there. Later, though she longed for deliverance, Amanda questioned the existence of God entirely. "How do you know there is a God?" she asked her deeply religious aunt as they stopped to gaze at a river during an afternoon walk. "My aunt turned and looked at me with a look that went through me like an arrow, then stamping her foot, she said: 'Don't you ever speak to me again . . .' And God broke the snare. I felt it. I felt deliverance from that hour."[2]

Throughout most of her life Amanda struggled as a black woman among white believers. Often she suppressed the urge to shout with joy in the midst of worship service, fearful that the white congregants would judge her. One Sunday morning, while listening to the white Methodist holiness leader John Inskip, Amanda clamped a hand over her mouth in an effort to hold still, the devil hissing in her ear, "Look, look at the white people, mind, they will put you out."[3] Later, though, as she left the church, a revelation prompted by Galatians 3:28, "Ye are all one in Christ Jesus" (KJV), temporarily quelled her fear:

> Somehow I always had a fear of white people—that is, I was not afraid of them in the sense of doing me harm, or anything of that kind—but a kind of fear because they were white, and were there, and I was

black and was here! But that morning on Green Street, as I stood on my feet trembling, I heard these words distinctly . . . the Holy Spirit had made it clear to me. And as I looked at white people that I had always seemed to be afraid of, now they looked so small. The great mountain had become a mole-hill. "Therefore, if the Son shall make you free, then you are free, indeed."[4]

Preaching in the Face of Racism

Amanda was preaching regularly by 1869, mainly at black churches throughout Brooklyn and Harlem, although occasionally at white churches, despite the fact that neither the Methodist Church nor the African Methodist Episcopal Church (AME) supported female preachers. Because she earned so little from preaching, she also worked as a washerwoman, taking in the washing and ironing from wealthier families and often working more than twenty hours at a stretch, simply to earn enough to pay the rent. Although she was married twice, her husbands provided little help. Her first husband, Calvin, whom she married at age seventeen, was killed in the Civil War. Her second, James, abandoned her and their young children. Several of Amanda's children died at a young age; only her daughter Mazie survived to adulthood.

Amanda prayed constantly while she labored over her endless domestic chores, grateful that the mundane work allowed her the opportunity to grow her relationship with God. "I found out that it was not necessary to be a nun or be isolated away off in some deep retirement to have communion with Jesus," she wrote. "Many times over my wash-tub and ironing table, and while making my bed and sweeping my house and washing my dishes I have had some of the richest blessings."[5]

In 1869, just as Amanda was comfortably settling into her ministry as a preacher in New York, she heard a call from God to "Go out," first to Salem, New Jersey, and later to the Methodist holiness camp meetings that were spreading up and down the East Coast under Inskip's leadership. Initially she resisted, stalling in Philadelphia for a week before finally heeding God's will and continuing on to Salem, where she remained for seven months.

Despite her earlier revelation outside the Green Street church doors, Amanda faced rampant racism at every turn, even as her ministry flourished. When she arrived at the Kennebunkport, Maine, camp meeting as a featured speaker in 1871, Amanda found herself the object of curiosity and disdain among the white crowds. There, Amanda wrote later in her autobiography, she learned the meaning of Hebrews 10:32–33 (NIV): "Remember those earlier days after you had received the light, when you endured in a great conflict full of suffering. Sometimes you were publicly exposed to insult and persecution; at other times you stood side by side with those who were so treated."

"There had been a great crowd all day, and everywhere I would go a crowd would follow me," Amanda wrote about her arrival at the camp meeting. "If I went into a tent they would surround it and stay till I came out, then they would follow me. Sometimes I would slip into a tent away from them. Then I would see them peep in, and if they saw me they would say, 'Oh! Here is the colored woman. Look!'"[6]

Later that evening, frustrated and humiliated after a day of public ridicule, Amanda walked into the woods to pray for relief. "I told the Lord how mean I felt because the people had looked at me. I prayed, 'Help me to throw off that mean feeling, and give me grace to be a gazing stock.'"[7] By the next morning, she was relieved of her anger and discomfort, "free as a bird" and liberated once again by God.

As church historian Chris Armstrong notes, Amanda Smith was a "barrier-crosser," overcoming multiple obstacles to forge new ground in American religious history. "Locked out of leadership within her own denomination, which wanted no part of having women serve as ordained ministers, frequently snubbed among both blacks and whites . . . Smith would become the only black *and* the only woman member (that is, leader) of the National Camp Meeting Association."[8]

Even in the midst of her increasing prominence and popularity as a speaker on the holiness camp meeting circuit, Amanda faced discrimination at every turn. In her autobiography, she recalled one incident in which a white woman boldly asked her if she thought all "colored people wanted to be white." Amanda replied, "No, we who are the royal black are very well satisfied with His gift to us in this substantial color."[9] She admitted, though, that the color of her skin was at times "very inconvenient," and she related an incident in which while traveling to California, she was forced to spend the entire night in a hotel lobby because her skin color did not allow her accommodations, dinner, or even a cup of tea. "I could pay the price—yes, that is all right," she wrote. "I know how to behave—yes, that is all right; I may have on my very best dress so that I look elegant—yes, that is all right; I am known as a Christian lady—yes, that is all right; I will occupy but one chair; I will touch no person's plate or fork—yes, that is all right; but you are black!"[10]

On another occasion, a white woman asked Amanda, "I know you cannot be white, but if you *could* be, would you not rather be white than black?" Again, Amanda answered succinctly, "I would rather be black and fully saved than to be white and not saved; I was bad enough, black as I am, and I would have been ten times worse if I had been white."[11]

On the other hand, Amanda had this to say to those who assumed she was always treated fairly and kindly: "If you want to know and understand what Amanda Smith has to contend with, just turn black and go about as I do, and you will come to a different conclusion. I think some people would understand the quintessence of sanctifying grace if they could be black for about twenty-four hours."[12]

While she often used humor to soften the sting of her commentary—she noted that it was a good thing God made her black because, given the option, she surely would have chosen pea-green, a color she was passionately fond of as a young girl—Amanda was very clear about the painful and destructive effects of racism. As Armstrong notes, Amanda's autobiography exemplifies her unique ministry, not only as a preacher from the pulpit and in print about the sanctified faith of the holiness movement, but also as a frank spokesperson about the realities of racism in postbellum America.

The Answer Is the Grace of God

Where, one might wonder, did Amanda Smith find the courage and strength to pursue her ministry in the face of such pervasive racism? How did she not succumb to bitterness and resentment in the midst of such daunting race, class, and gender discrimination? How did she persevere in a ministry that not only crisscrossed America but also led her to evangelize as the first black missionary in England, India, and Africa? The answer, Amanda would say, was the grace of God.

For her entire evangelistic career Amanda Smith preached that sanctification—the process of becoming holy through Christ—was the key to both personal salvation and earthly contentedness. It was her steadfast belief in sanctification that allowed Amanda not only to transcend anger and bitterness but also to work relentlessly for the greater good of all people, including her oppressors. "We need to be saved deep to make us thorough, all around, out and out," she wrote, "come up to the standard of Christians, and not bring the standard down to us."[13]

No matter the offenses and hardships she personally suffered, Amanda Smith would never stoop to sully Christ by lowering his standards. Her mission was to bring people, including her persecutors, up to Christ's standards. Her prayer for all people—"Lord, help the people to see"[14]—was simple, but it's a prayer just as relevant for us today.

30

Lottie Moon

The Unlikely Missionary

(1840–1912)

Charlotte "Lottie" Digges Moon died emaciated and penniless on Christmas Eve in 1912, aboard a ship en route from China to the United States. She had given herself physically, emotionally, and financially for nearly forty years as a Southern Baptist missionary in China. In the last months of her life, weighing only fifty pounds and desperately ill, she had literally starved herself, sacrificing her own rations in order to help feed the famine-ravaged Chinese people.

Lottie Moon died poor, but she left a rich legacy unmatched by any missionary who had gone before her. Little did she know that the fund she launched in 1888, today known as the Lottie Moon Christmas Offering for Foreign Missions, would grow to become the largest source of funding for the Southern Baptist Convention's overseas missions. In its first year the offering raised 3,315 dollars, enabling three female missionaries to work with Lottie in China.[1] In

213

2012 alone the offering raised more than 149 million dollars to support nearly 4,900 Southern Baptist missionaries around the globe.[2]

From Plantation Life to Mission Life

Lottie Moon was an unlikely candidate for missionary work. Born in 1840 into an affluent Baptist family, Lottie and her six siblings lived at Viewmont, a 1,500-acre slave-labor tobacco plantation in Virginia. Private tutors educated the children in the classics, French, and music, and all the Moon children received the best possible education and were encouraged to pursue whatever discipline inspired them. Lottie's sister Orianna was one of the first two Southern women ever to earn a medical degree. And Lottie herself went on to the Albermarle Female Institute in Charlottesville to become one of the first Southern women ever to receive a master's degree. By the time she completed her education, she was proficient in Latin, Greek, French, Italian, and Spanish and could read Hebrew fluently.

Despite her strict Baptist upbringing, Lottie wrestled with serious spiritual doubts. She was known as a skeptic at the institute, and her name was often included on the chapel prayer list. She frequently skipped Sunday morning service, and once, when an acquaintance asked why she wasn't in church, Lottie admitted that she'd chosen to read Shakespeare instead, which was "much better than a dry sermon." On another occasion, when a student asked her what the "D" in Lottie D. Moon stood for, she retorted, "It stands for 'Devil'— don't you think it suits me excellently?"[3]

Late one night, though, as Lottie struggled with insomnia, she made a decision that would change the course of her life: she decided to pray about her doubt. By morning, she had undergone a spiritual awakening. "She had always wielded an influence because of her intellectual power," said fellow student and lifelong friend Julia Toy. "Now her great talent was directed into another channel. She immediately took a stand as a Christian."[4]

With the Civil War finally over, their mother dead, and the family fortune obliterated, each of the Moon children was forced to fend for themselves. Lottie and a friend moved to Georgia, where they operated a school for girls. Yet despite the success of the school, Lottie felt restless and unfulfilled. Her sister Edmonia had recently been permitted to travel to China as a missionary with a married couple, and Lottie wondered if she as a single woman could carve out a path as a missionary as well, despite the strict constraints placed on women in public ministry. She found her answer in Scripture, concluding, "Our Lord does not call on women to preach, or to pray in public, but no less does He say to them than to men, 'Go, work in my vineyard.'"[5]

In October 1873, after twenty-five days at sea, Lottie stepped foot onto Shanghai soil and then traveled by mule to Tengchow, where she would live, with only two brief respites from missionary work, until her death in 1912.

Women's Work and Beyond

Lottie's assignment in China was "women's work"—namely, to teach young girls. While she accepted school teaching as a means toward ministry, teaching was not her primary objective. Personal and direct evangelism became her passion, and she began a slow but relentless campaign to allow female missionaries the freedom to evangelize.

Lottie often accompanied two seasoned missionary wives on "country visits" to the outlying villages. There she would share the gospel from morning until night from the back of a donkey, tucked into a cramped shack, or amid the dirt and dust of a front yard. She was frequently exposed to illness and disease and at the mercy of the relentless heat or cold. Despite her command of Chinese, as a foreigner she was always approached with suspicion and was often reviled as the "Devil Woman."[6] The Chinese peasants would stare at her, peeking around door frames and peering through windows as she sat outside on her bedroll and ate breakfast. "Have you ever felt the torture of human eyes bearing upon you, scanning every feature, every look, every gesture?" she wrote to H. A. Tupper, corresponding secretary of the Foreign Mission Board. "I feel it keenly."[7]

215

Regardless of the fact that she was scrutinized as a foreigner and an outcast, Lottie persevered, tirelessly introducing the Chinese peasants to the message of Christ. "As I wander from village to village," she said, "I feel it is no idle fancy that the Master walks beside me, and I hear His voice saying gently, 'I am with you always, even unto the end.'"[8]

Lottie dreamed of establishing a chain of mission stations in the interior of China, and since she was virtually working alone by this point, it was up to her to bring that dream to fruition. She settled on Pingtu, a city one hundred miles inland from her base in Tengchow. She was the first Southern Baptist woman to open a new mission outpost, and she was the only foreigner living in Pingtu; renting a four-room, dirt-floor house for twenty-four dollars a year; and living as the Chinese did. No one she knew spoke English.

She often sat on a stone or a pile of straw on the threshing floor and chatted with the women as they came to prepare their grains. "We must go out and live among them, manifesting the spirit of our Lord," she wrote in a letter to Tupper. "We need to make friends before we can hope to make converts."[9] For seven years Pingtu was Lottie's primary operating base, although she maintained her home in Tengchow and occasionally retreated there for a much-needed respite.

Beginnings: The Lottie Moon Christmas Offering

During her time in Pingtu, Lottie penned the letter that would mark the beginning of the annual Christmas offering. Lottie's famous letter, which was printed in *The Foreign Mission Journal*, pointedly held up the Methodist women's fund-raising methods as an example. "They give freely and cheerfully. Now the painful question arises, 'What is the matter, that we Baptists give so little? Whose is the fault?' Is it a fact that our women are lacking in the enthusiasm, the organizing power, and the executive ability that so conspicuously distinguishes our Methodist sisters?"[10] Lottie urged the Southern Baptist women to follow the lead of the Methodists and dedicate the week prior to Christmas as a time for prayer and missions support.

Ongoing Hardship

During her many decades in China, Lottie weathered war, famine, and revolution, including the First Sino-Japanese War, the Boxer Rebellion (which forced her to flee for a time to Japan), and the Chinese Nationalist uprising. The Boxer Rebellion escalated in 1900, resulting in the deaths of thousands of Chinese Christians and foreign missionaries. Warned against visiting Pingtu, which was suffering through violent attacks, Lottie traveled there in a sedan chair, disguised in a Chinese man's robe, her hair slicked back beneath the red-buttoned cap that designated the officials. In Pingtu she visited thirteen imprisoned Baptists, but other than giving spiritual encouragement, she was unable to help them. Her own life at risk, she was forced to escape to Tengchow.

"I fear you work yourself too hard," wrote R. J. Willingham, who replaced Tupper at the Foreign Mission Board.[11] Yet in response to Lottie's continuous appeals for help, Willingham could do nothing; the funds were simply not available.

Later, when Lottie was finally able to take a leave in the United States for a much-needed reprieve (she took only two furloughs from missionary work during her entire forty years overseas), her family tried to convince her to retire. "Oh, don't say that you don't want me to return," Lottie pleaded. "Nothing could make me stay. China is my joy and my delight. It is my home now."[12]

In 1904, at age sixty-three, she sailed in an economy cabin from San Francisco back to Tengchow, where she was content to don Chinese robes and sixty-seven-cent, cardboard-soled fabric shoes and resume work once again. "I constantly thank God that He has given me work that I love so much," she wrote to Willingham.[13] Ultimately, though, Lottie's greatest joy—her work—would lead to her death.

In 1909 Lottie received stunning news—her beloved sister Edmonia had committed suicide. Lottie confided in no one, keeping the news to herself and soldiering on despite her intense grief. She threw herself into her work with renewed determination and passion, most likely in an effort to fill the huge void left by her sister. By

1912 Lottie was the only missionary working in Tengchow—most of her colleagues had been claimed by death or ill health; a few of the younger missionaries were serving in distant villages and other regions. No one was around to notice that Lottie had worked herself to the point of physical and emotional collapse. Obsessed with the concern that Chinese children were dying of starvation during the famine, Lottie sacrificed her own food for the women and children in her village. When a missionary medical doctor was finally brought in to treat her, she weighed only fifty pounds and was diagnosed with self-starvation and severe depression. Her only hope for survival, the mission doctor reported, was to return to America.

In her cabin with a nurse by her side, she whispered the words of the song "Jesus Loves Me" as the ship slowly made its way toward America. But Lottie didn't make it back to her home soil. While docked in Kobe, Japan, on Christmas Eve, 1912, Lottie opened her eyes for the last time, smiled, and raised her fists together in the Chinese greeting as her spirit rose up to meet God. The last entry in her account book, in her own script, showed that she had given her last dollar to the Famine Relief Fund.

Lottie Moon left a tremendous legacy. The Christmas Offering for Missions named in her honor has raised more than three billion dollars since its inception in 1888. But beyond that, she continues to serve as an inspiration and a role model for modern-day Christians who aspire to live out God's Word. She compels us with this question, one she asked more than a century ago but is still relevant today: "Are there not some, yea many, who find it in their hearts to say, 'Here am I; send me?'"[14] Lottie Moon heard the call and answered yes.

31

Fanny Crosby

My Story, My Song

(1840–1915)

Huddled in her bunk, heading homeward up the Hudson River from New York City, five-year-old Fanny Crosby was soothed by the sound of the water lapping against the hull. Earlier in the day she and her mother had received a dire report from the eye specialist: there was no hope for recovery. Fanny would remain blind for the rest of her life. Yet she did not despair. As she lay in ever-present darkness, the sound of the water slapping rhythmically against the wood, the waves seemed to call out encouragement to her. "I never lost faith in the great Father above," she wrote. "I know that the river waves were His, and that I had heard His voice."[1]

Most people don't consider their suffering a gift from God, but Fanny Crosby was an exception. In fact, she repeatedly acknowledged that her blindness was a blessing: "I verily believe it was His intention that I should live my days in physical darkness, so as to be better prepared to sing His praises and incite others to do so."[2]

And sing his praises she did. Fanny Crosby wrote more than nine thousand hymns over the course of her ninety-four years, including some, such as "Blessed Assurance" and "Safe in the Arms of Jesus," that are regularly sung in worship services today. She wrote so many hymns that she was forced to use nearly two hundred pseudonyms over the span of her career, for fear that the hymnals would be filled with virtually her name only from front to back.

She also penned more than one thousand poems; published two bestselling autobiographies; worked tirelessly for New York City missions in Hell's Kitchen, the Bowery, and the Tenderloin; and traveled nationally as a public speaker. It's clear that Fanny Crosby never let blindness—or any other obstacles, for that matter—stand in the way of fulfilling God's vision for her life.

"Contented I Will Be"

Frances Jane "Fanny" Crosby was born in 1820 in the village of Brewster, fifty miles north of New York City. When she was six weeks old, she developed inflammation in both eyes, which led to blindness. Her mother, Mercy, and her maternal grandmother raised her. Her father, John Crosby, died before her first birthday.

Determination was a hallmark of Fanny's personality, even when she was a young child. At age eight, she wrote her first poem:

> Oh, what a happy child I am,
> Although I cannot see!
> I am resolved that in this world
> Contented I will be.
> How many blessings I enjoy
> That other people don't!
> So weep or sigh because I'm blind,
> I cannot, nor I won't!

By age ten Fanny could recite from memory the Pentateuch and the four Gospels, and she desperately hungered for education. She

I'm writing to write guest posts or do Q&A interviews that you can post on your blog on release day or in the days following. Please email me at **michellederusha1@gmail.com** if you are interested in that.

- Spread the word on your favorite social media channels: Facebook, Twitter, Google+, Pinterest—tag with #50Women.

- Pin images of the 50 Women cover to your relevant boards on Pinterest.

- Pin 50 Women "pinables" to Pinterest and share them on Facebook or as a Twitter pic. Find a selection of images on http://michellederusha.com/50Women—tag with #50Women.

- Share your favorite quotes from 50 Women on Facebook and Twitter. Tag with #50Women.

- Ask your local library and/or church library to order a copy of the book.

- Ask your local independent bookstore to carry 50 Women.

- Purchase copies to give as gifts—Christmas is around the corner!

And most importantly, help generate excitement by word of mouth. Tell your BFF about the book, your mom, your manicurist, everyone!

Friends, I pray that you see yourself and God's infinite grace and love in the stories of these 50 women. Thank you for journeying with me.

Love,

Michelle

Harriet Tubman

Corrie ten Boom

Dear Friends,

Thank you so much for your participation in this launch team. I am so excited about the opportunity to introduce you to these 50 amazing women! I know some of the women in this book will be familiar to you, but I am hoping and praying that you are inspired and encouraged by many others in the book as well. Every time I finished writing a chapter, I told my husband, "This woman was definitely my favorite!" I have a feeling you're going to feel the same way about each of these sisters in faith.

I learned from my last book release that the launch team is about far more than promotion. The encouragement, community, and friendship we found in that group was such a gift, and I feel confident the same will happen with this group too. So thank you for being a part of it—I'm excited to see how we will grow in our faith together.

50 Women Every Christian Should Know: Learning from Heroines of the Faith releases **September 16, 2014.** I've created a list of ideas you might consider to help spread the word, especially on **September 16 and in the days following.** These suggestions are all optional— we'll do what we can, knowing God's got this book in his hands.

These suggestions are listed in order of importance, so if you choose one or two, please start at the top:

- *Write a review of the book and post it on Amazon (and Barnes & Noble, Christian-Book.com, and Goodreads). It doesn't need to be long or fancy—a few lines is plenty. You can copy and paste the same review to every website.*

- *Post a review of 50 Women on your blog on release day, September 16, or in the days following.*

Lottie Moon

Katharina Luther

prayed each night for God to give her light, referring not to a cure for her blindness but to her quest for knowledge. "I had long been contented to bear the burden of blindness: but my education—my education—how was I to get it? I felt like I was in danger of growing more and more ignorant every day."[3] Not long after, Fanny's prayers were answered when she was accepted by the New York Institution for the Blind, where she remained for twenty-three years: twelve as a student and eleven as a teacher of grammar, rhetoric, and history. There she met her husband, fellow student, teacher, and organist Alexander van Alstyne, whom she married in 1858 and who wrote the music to many of her hymns.

The school fueled Fanny's determination and acknowledged what she'd always suspected: with God's help, she could overcome any obstacle. "Whatever we determined to do, if within the average power of man or woman, we could, with God's help, do—the same as if we had the blessings of sight: and at it we went with a will."[4]

Old-Fashioned Hymn Composing

From the time she was a young girl, Fanny was moved by the music she heard every Sunday in church. "With the ultra-acute hearing which generally accompanies blindness, I could distinguish every word of the hymns . . . and they were in many cases a refreshment to my young soul. Even in childhood, I began to wonder who made those hymns; and if I could ever make one that people would sing."[5] She published her first hymn, "An Evening Hymn," in 1843, and shortly after that she set a lofty goal for herself. She aimed to bring one million people to Christ through her hymns, and throughout her life she kept a careful account of those reportedly saved by her lyrics.

Fanny described her writing process as old-fashioned, acknowledging that she began each hymn-composing session with prayer, asking God to provide her with inspiration. She advised aspiring hymn writers not to force the process: "True hymns may be said, in one sense, to make themselves; although they must be given to human instruments through which to work."[6]

She often received her lyrics in a flash, which she attributed to divine inspiration. Such was the case with the creation of one of her most famous hymns, "Safe in the Arms of Jesus." On April 30, 1868, the musician Howard Doane knocked on Fanny's Manhattan apartment door. "I have exactly forty minutes before I must meet a train for Cincinnati," he said. "I have a tune for you. See if it says anything to you."

After Doane hummed the melody, Fanny immediately clapped her hands and exclaimed, "Why, that says, 'Safe in the arms of Jesus!'" She dashed into her bedroom, kneeled on the floor, and asked God to provide her with the words quickly. Within thirty minutes, she'd composed the poem in her mind and dictated it to Doane, who made it to the station in time to catch his train.[7]

Many years later, in her autobiography *Fanny Crosby's Story of Ninety-Four Years*, she revealed her life's greatest loss: the death of her infant, Frances. Some biographers suggest that "Safe in the Arms of Jesus" was inspired by her daughter's death, although Fanny never acknowledged that in her own writing, nor did she ever talk about her daughter. Regardless, the hymn offered comfort and hope to hundreds of grieving mothers. Reverend John Hall of New York City's Fifth Avenue Presbyterian Church once told Fanny that her hymn had given more "peace and satisfaction to mothers who have lost their children than any other hymn I have ever known."[8]

Fanny never learned to write properly, so she composed a hymn entirely in her head and then would "let it lie in the writing-desk of [her] mind" until she was ready to prune and shape it into its final form. She was passionate about what she feared would become "the lost art of recollection" and often urged friends and fans to practice memory exercises. "The books of the mind are just as real and tangible as those of the desk and the library shelves—if we only will use them enough to keep their binding flexible, and their pages free from dust."[9] Finally, she would wait until her husband or a friend was available to transcribe the hymn for her as she recited it, and then the hymn would be set to music by one of the composers with whom she regularly worked. Fanny typically earned one to two dollars per song, with the rights of the song retained by the composer or publisher.

Rescue Mission Work

Despite her prolific hymn writing, Fanny most desired to be known as a mission worker, especially in the later years of her life. In 1880, at the age of sixty, she made a commitment to God to serve the poor. Later, in an interview that was published in the March 24, 1908, issue of the *New Haven Register*, Fanny stated her chief occupation not as hymnist but as mission worker.[10] For the last several decades of her life, she lived separately from her husband in some of the poorest neighborhoods in Manhattan so that she could be closer to those she served. "From the time I received my first check for my poems, I made up my mind to open my hand wide to those who needed assistance," she wrote in her *Story of Ninety-Four Years*. "During these ninety years I have never served for mere pay."[11]

Fanny lived by her word. Not only did she financially support more than a half dozen city missions, she also volunteered almost daily at a number of them and spoke publicly as a passionate advocate for the poor at YMCAs, churches, and prisons. When she died, a provision in her will provided the funds to launch the Fanny Crosby Memorial Home for the Aged in Bridgeport, Connecticut, which operated for more than seventy years before the property was donated to the Bridgeport Rescue Mission.

She was also creatively inspired by her mission work, and many of her hymns were written as a direct response to the people who knew her as "Aunt Fanny" at the inner-city missions. One of her most famous, "Rescue the Perishing," was written after a speech she gave to blue-collar workers in Cincinnati and later became, as her composer Ira Sankey called it, "a battle-cry for the great army of Christian workers throughout the world."[12]

Nothing pleased her more than hearing that one of her hymns was a catalyst for a person's conversion to faith. "God has given me a wonderful work to do, a work that has brought me untold blessing and great joy," she wrote. "When word is brought to me, as it is from time to time, of some wandering soul being brought back home through one of my hymns, my heart thrills with joy, and I give thanks to God for giving me a share in the glorious work of saving human souls."[13]

Daily Rejoicing

It's easy for us to conclude that Fanny Crosby was a phenomenally hopeful, optimistic, and faithful person, and much of her own writing supports that claim. However, a closer look at her autobiographies hints that she was not immune to periods of discouragement. It was during these times especially that she looked to God for hope and sustenance. She was as pragmatic about her faith as she was about both her blindness and her gift for poetry and song, and it's clear that she accepted every facet of her life as a gift from God: "For me, life has been short of many things that some people would probably rather die than be without. That is their misfortune—not mine. It is not the things I've missed, or never had, which make me sorrowful. It is the things I have had in full measure in which I rejoice daily."[14]

So many of Fanny Crosby's hymns capture her deep faith and love for God, but the refrain of one of her most famous and familiar hymns, "Blessed Assurance," may express it best in a few simple words:

> This is my story, this is my song,
> praising my Savior all the day long.

Fanny Crosby was blessedly assured of Jesus' love throughout all of her ninety-four years. That unwavering faith is the essence of her story . . . and her songs.[15]

32

Pandita Ramabai

A Stream of Living Water

(1858 – 1922)

Weak, emaciated, and literally starving to death, the five members of the Ramabai family were faced with a dire decision: retreat into the nearby forest to die, or disgrace themselves by begging for food. They chose death.

As famine raged across India, Anant Shastri Dongre and his wife, Laxmibai, had donated the family's entire savings to the Hindu gods in the hope that they would be relieved of their suffering. At last the day came when they had spent every cent and eaten the last of their rice. The family stayed eleven days and nights in the forest, where they subsisted on water, leaves, and a handful of dates. Both Anant and Laxmibai succumbed to starvation, along with their eldest daughter.

For more than three years after the deaths of their parents and sister, Pandita Ramabai and her brother wandered more than four thousand miles on foot. The siblings survived by eating wild berries and the occasional handful of grain soaked in salted water. They walked barefoot and slept under bridges. Once, in an attempt to find refuge from the cold, they dug two grave-like pits in a riverbank and buried themselves in sand, leaving only their heads exposed. They visited sacred places and temples; bathed in sacred rivers; fasted and performed penance; and worshiped gods, trees, animals, and Brahmans. "We had fulfilled all the conditions laid down in the sacred books, and kept all the rules as far as our knowledge went, but the gods were not pleased with us, and did not appear to us," Pandita wrote.[1] Finally, their faith extinguished, they settled in Calcutta.

Unanswered Prayers

Born in her father's ashram, a religious community four thousand feet above sea level on the forested slopes of the Western Ghats, Pandita Ramabai was raised in an atypical Hindu household. Her father was a renowned Brahman scholar, orthodox in all his beliefs and practices but one: Anant believed that women should be educated in Sanskrit and have access to the Hindu holy texts. He taught Pandita's mother, who then educated her own children, including her two daughters. Anant's ideas about the education of women were nothing short of radical for the time.

Pandita, her parents, and her siblings traveled the countryside as pilgrims, reading the *Puranas* (the Hindu religious texts) in public. By the time she was twenty, Pandita had memorized eighteen thousand verses of the *Bhagavata Purana*. These readings served two purposes: they absolved the reader and listeners of sin, and they provided the reader with an honest living. People who gathered to listen to the *Puranas* were obligated to present gifts to the reader, including food, flowers, sweets, money, and clothing.

The system worked well for many years, until Pandita's elderly father became too feeble to withstand the constant travel. Because the family members had, as Pandita described, "grown up in perfect ignorance of anything outside the sacred literature of the Hindus,"[2] they were unfit for work and unable to earn a living. Their high caste prohibited them from doing menial labor or begging. "In short, we had no common sense," said Pandita, "and foolishly spent all the money we had in hand in giving alms to Brahmans to please the gods, who, we thought, would . . . make us rich and happy. . . . But nothing came of this futile effort to please the gods—the stone images remained as hard as ever, and never answered our prayers."[3] Their savings spent or donated, Pandita's family succumbed to the famine that swept through India between 1874 and 1876.

Converted and Baptized but Still Wandering

Pandita experienced her first taste of Christianity in Calcutta, where she finally settled after three years of wandering the Indian countryside. While curious and puzzled—she later wrote that when the Christians knelt to pray with their eyes closed, she assumed they were paying homage to the chairs they knelt in front of—she was not impressed. Pandita received her first copy of the Bible from these curious Christians, but she found the stories and language inaccessible and considered it a waste of time.

While in Calcutta, Pandita also delved more deeply into the sacred Hindu texts and was shocked to discover how women were viewed:

> Women of high- and low-caste, as a class were bad, very bad, worse than demons, unholy as untruth. . . . The only hope of their getting this much-desired liberation from Karma . . . was the worship of their husbands. The husband is said to be the woman's god; there is no other god for her. This god may be the worst sinner and a great criminal; still HE IS HER GOD, and she must worship him. She can have no hope of getting admission into Svarga, the abode of the gods, without his pleasure, and if she pleases him in all things, she will have the privilege of going to Svarga as his slave, to serve him.[4]

This did not sit well with Pandita. In fact, she lost all faith and hope in Hinduism as a result of her studies. "My eyes were being gradually opened," she wrote. "I was waking up to my own hopeless condition as a woman, and it was becoming clearer and clearer to me that I had no place anywhere as far as religious consolation was concerned. . . . I wanted something more . . . but I did not know what it was that I wanted."[5] Disenchanted with her culture and religion, Pandita made a bold move that shocked her peers: she married a Bengali lawyer, a man far below her Brahman caste.

Despite her husband's reservations, Pandita turned toward Christianity. By chance she discovered and read a Bengali translation of the Gospel of Luke, and not long after she met a Baptist missionary who explained the book of Genesis to her, a story that was unlike anything she'd ever read before. The story struck her as true, though she admitted she couldn't give any reasonable explanation for believing it.

After her husband died less than two years into their marriage, Pandita defied societal expectations by traveling with her young daughter to England. Widows in nineteenth-century India were considered social pariahs with virtually no rights and no status. Not only was a widow not allowed to marry again, but she was seen as the cause of her husband's death and thus was viewed with fear and animosity. Forced to shave her head, the widow was allowed to eat only one meal per day and typically served as a household slave.

Pandita, on the other hand, refused to accept this lot. Ignoring expectations that she would retreat into her role as a widow, Pandita set her sights on a career in medicine and traveled to England to study there. While she stayed with a group of nuns, Pandita experienced a change of heart that refocused her energy from medicine to mission work. At the convent, for the first time in her life, she met women who were rehabilitated at a rescue home and who had subsequently rededicated their lives to the service of others. "I had never heard or seen anything of this kind done for this class of women by the Hindus in my own country," she wrote. "Here I came to know that something should be done to reclaim the so-called fallen women, and that Christians . . . were kind to these unfortunate women, degraded in the eyes of society."[6]

After reading the fourth chapter of the Gospel of John, Pandita acknowledged that Christ was indeed the Savior he claimed to be and that "no one else but He could transform and uplift the down-trodden womanhood of India and of every land."[7] A few months after her arrival in England, Pandita and her daughter were baptized into the Church of England.

Despite her conversion and baptism, though, Pandita struggled in her newfound faith. At times she still felt empty and unfulfilled, striving toward something in her faith but unsure of exactly what. She found the myriad Christian denominations, which she called "a Babel of religions," confusing and even unnecessary, noting that such a proliferation of sects led to arguments and indicated a lack of unity. She also disagreed with much of the church doctrine. Pandita finally concluded that although she believed in Christ, "I shall not bind myself to believe in and accept everything that is taught by the church; before I accept it I must be convinced that it is according to Christ's teaching."[8]

"But a Drop in the Ocean"

After a visit to the United States in 1883, Pandita returned to Bombay and opened the Sharada Sadan (House of Learning), a residential school that trained girls and young women as teachers and nurses. She felt particularly called to help child widows. Given in marriage by their parents to a high-caste man at four or five years old, the girls were typically servants in their husband's household until they were old enough to fulfill the traditional role of a wife. If, however, they became widowed, they were cast out of society and often turned to prostitution as the only means of survival.

Initially, Pandita did not directly instruct the students in religion, although she did read the Bible to them and pray with them every day. However, following a spiritual epiphany in 1891, she changed her approach to Christian education and evangelism. Eight years after her baptism in England, Pandita realized that although she had found Christian religion, she had not found Christ. As a result, she ceased reading books about the Bible and began to study the Bible itself, meditating on the messages God gave her. "There were so many things I did not understand intellectually," she wrote. "One thing I knew by this time, that I needed Christ, and not merely His religion."[9] As a result of this epiphany, Mukti Sadan, which opened to provide shelter, sustenance, and education during the famine of the late 1890s, offered secular and Christian education and trained the girls to lead useful Christian lives.

Pandita was the first to admit that as a Brahman, a member of the high caste, she was a stranger to the conditions and needs of the so-called fallen women of India. Yet ever since she had witnessed the dramatic transformation of the fallen women in England, she felt compelled to help these same women in India, many who were "married to the gods" and employed by the priests as prostitutes in the Hindu temples.

In 1899 Pandita opened Kripa Sadan, the Home of Mercy. By 1900, in the midst of the famine, the home housed more than 350 girls and women, and altogether, Sharada Sadan, Mukti Sadan, and Kripa Sadan provided food, shelter, and education to more than one thousand girls and women. Still, the needs were overwhelming. As Pandita wrote in 1900,

> My heart is burdened with the thought that there are more than 145 million women in this country who need to have the light of the knowledge of God's love given to them. All the work being done . . . in this vast country is but a drop in the ocean. It will be a very small help to add our particle to that drop. But every particle added will increase the drop, so it will be multiplied and permeate the ocean until it becomes a stream of the living water that flows from under the throne of God, to give life and joy to this nation.[10]

In 1889 Pandita stood before two thousand delegates of the National Social Congress in Bombay. As she prepared to speak about two resolutions for gender reform, she waited at the podium for the crowd to quiet. "It is not strange, my countrymen, that my voice is small," she began when she had the audience's full attention, "for you have never given a woman the chance to make her voice strong!"[11] Pandita Ramabai may have viewed her work as merely a drop in a vast ocean, but in giving voice to the voiceless, in speaking for the oppressed, she walked in the footsteps of Jesus.

33

Amy Carmichael

The Winning of Souls

(1867–1951)

"Go ye." She heard the words audibly, as clearly as a human voice. And then again, "Go ye," the command crashing through her subconscious like a lightning strike. It was, without question, the voice of God, calling Amy Wilson Carmichael to pursue mission work. And so, one year later, on March 3, 1893, Amy Carmichael leaned against the deck rail of the *Valetta* as it slowly steamed away from the shores of Tilbury, England. Her friends and family sang hymns to her from the wharf as the Japan-bound ship faded into the horizon. Little did she know at the time that she would spend the remainder of her eighty-three years as a missionary overseas.

No More Fit for a Missionary Than a Puppy

Even at a young age, service was an integral part of Amy's life. After her father died when she was seventeen, Amy, the oldest of seven children, helped her mother raise her siblings in their tiny village of Millisle, Ireland. She also dedicated herself to various good works, first launching a Bible study in Belfast with a small group of mill girls called the "shawlies" (named for the shawls they wore as head coverings because they were too poor to buy proper hats), and later beginning a similar ministry with factory workers in Manchester, England.

It was during her time in England that Amy met Keswick Convention co-founder and Quaker Robert Wilson, whom she affectionately called the D.O.M. ("Dear Old Man"). Wilson, whose name Amy adopted as part of her own before she left for her first missionary trip to Japan, filled the role of both spiritual advisor and father figure for Amy.

Amy was chosen as the Keswick Convention's first missionary. Fifty years later she would declare that she was "no more fit to be a Keswick missionary than a Skye terrier puppy,"[1] yet Amy never let her inexperience deter her from what she considered her God-given calling. Initially she served in Japan for fifteen months and then for a very brief period in Ceylon (now Sri Lanka), but it wasn't until she applied to and was accepted by the Church of England Zenana Missionary Society that she found what was to become her lifelong mission. She sailed for India in 1895. Once Amy set foot on Indian soil, she never returned home.

"The Winning of Souls"

Amy was challenged and sometimes even frustrated by missionary work in India. Not only did she find the native language, Tamil, daunting, she was also exasperated by what she called the nominal Christianity that had resulted from the great conversion sweep of the early nineteenth century. Furthermore, she discovered that the Indian caste system was virtually impenetrable. Those in the lower castes "lived in a sort of twilight, far from the true Gospel light,"[2] while the elite upper castes—the Brahmans, the Vellalas, and the trade guilds—barred from their homes anyone they considered unclean, including foreigners and especially missionaries. Despite the formidable obstacles, Amy was relentless, traveling to and camping in villages, reading the Gospels aloud, praying with women, and endeavoring to convert Indians to Christianity one soul at a time.

She poured every ounce of her personal energy and faith into her calling, and nothing irritated Amy more than lackadaisical missionary work. "O to be delivered from half-hearted missionaries! Don't come if you mean to turn aside for anything. . . . Don't come if you haven't made up your mind to live for one thing—the winning of souls," she wrote to one young woman.[3] On the other hand, she also made it clear that even the most dedicated missionaries were not above the rest of the human race in nobility or purity: "Don't imagine that by crossing the sea and landing on a foreign shore and learning a foreign lingo you 'burst the bonds of outer sin and hatch yourself a cherubim.'"[4] Amy knew that missionary or not, she was as flawed as any other human being.

She was also disdainful of any attempt to entice potential converts to Christianity with anything but pure Scripture. On one occasion, for instance, her Indian assistant Saral suggested they teach women to knit with a bit of pink wool while talking about Jesus and the Gospels at the same time. Amy refused; the pure Gospel was more than enough and certainly didn't need to be prettied up or made more tantalizing than it already was. As her biographer Elisabeth Elliot wrote, "To try to help God with pink fancywork was, she felt, plain unbelief."[5]

A Crack Opens Right at Her Feet

In early March 1901, Amy experienced a life-altering event that rooted her to India for life.

A Christian woman by the name of Servant of Jesus came upon a seven-year-old girl named Preena who stood alone outside a church in the village of Pannaivilai, not far from a Hindu temple where her mother had abandoned her as a devotion to the gods. The next morning, Servant of Jesus delivered Preena, who had run away from

234

the temple, to Amy. From this child, Amy learned about the lives of these temple girls and women, known as devadasis—details that turned her life upside down. After hearing firsthand about the prostitution these girls endured, often at a shockingly young age, Amy knew instantly that her life had taken a dramatic turn: "Sometimes the broad smooth levels of life are crossed by a black-edged jagged crack, rent, as it seems, by an outburst of the fiery force below," she wrote later. "We find ourselves suddenly close upon it; it opens right at our feet."[6]

Three months after Preena's arrival, Amy had already become known as Amma (from the Tamil word *ammal*, meaning "mother") to four more orphans. By 1916 the single, dilapidated bungalow that had housed a handful of orphans, many of them temple children, had grown into the Dohnavur Fellowship, with twelve nurseries and dozens of infants, toddlers, and young children. In 1918 the Fellowship rescued its first young boy, and by 1926 between seventy and eighty boys had also been adopted by what Amy came to call the Family.

A Different Drummer

Amy intended that life at her mission would be different. As Elisabeth Elliot noted, "Amy Carmichael was marching to a different drummer. . . . She had a vision of holy living. She would not deviate from that no matter how well-established, rational, and practical the ways of older missions seemed to be."[7] Amy's vision for life at the mission was based entirely on two principles: love, which she called the Gold Cord, and prayer.

In her early days at Dohnavur, Amy was a thorn in the side of other missionaries and Indian Christians, who considered her practices too radical. She didn't accept nominal Christianity; she insisted on blending in with the Indians by wearing saris and doing work that many considered beneath her; and she refused to ask outright for funds that were desperately needed, relying instead on prayer and God's will. "We do not tell when we are in need unless definitely asked, and even then not always," Amy wrote. "We rely upon the verses which assure us that our Father knows our needs, and we take it that with such a Father, to know is to supply."[8] Time and time again, Dohnavur was provided with exactly the resources needed at exactly the right time, from the funds necessary to expand the compound in the early years to the resources to construct the hospital that continues to serve thousands of Christians, Muslims, and Hindus living in the countryside surrounding Dohnavur today.

Amy's nontraditional missionary style extended to worship as well. Although she was officially a member of the Church of England Zenana Missionary Society, she didn't exactly adhere to Anglican doctrine. When a Dohnavur boy was once asked if he was Church of England, Wesleyan, or Baptist, he simply answered, "I am Christian." Amy practiced and taught her children to practice nondenominational Christianity, which she interpreted as the literal New Testament. In 1925 the Dohnavur group severed all ties in an amicable split with the Church of England Zenana Missionary Society and other England-based missionaries. It was simply best for each to go its separate way.

Knowing that life in Dohnavur was intense and difficult, Amy prayed relentlessly that God himself would send missionaries to join her, and she encouraged young missionaries to pray long and hard about the decision. She wrote detailed letters to those considering mission work at Dohnavur, urging them to spend as much time reading Scripture as possible to prepare themselves for the battlefield that lay ahead. "We follow a stripped and crucified Savior," she said to a group of newcomers. "Those words go very deep. They touch everything—motives, purposes, decisions, everything. Let them be with you as you prepare your spirit for the new life."[9]

Amy never shied from telling the straight truth about missionary life, no matter how harsh. When she wrote matter-of-factly in *Things as They Are* about the atrocities perpetrated against temple children, her publisher returned the manuscript, citing it as too negative and discouraging. When asked to edit the material to make it more palatable, she refused, and even when the book was finally published several years later in 1903, the public was disappointed.

They yearned for success stories of hope and redemption, not the hard, unsweetened truth as Amy presented it.

"Do Anything, Lord"

On the morning of October 24, 1931, Amy prayed a very specific prayer: "Do anything, Lord, that will fit me to serve Thee and to help my beloveds."[10] Later that same afternoon, on a trip to inspect property that had been offered to the Dohnavur Fellowship to rent, she stumbled into a shallow hole, breaking her leg, dislocating her ankle, and twisting her spine. She never anticipated that the "anything" she had prayed for earlier that morning would manifest itself in the life of an invalid for her remaining twenty years. The woman who had spent sixty-three years in a blur of ceaseless activity for the benefit of others was now confined to bed, immobile, in constant pain, and almost entirely reliant upon the help of others.

God, however, was not done with Amy yet. As it turned out, she could accomplish a great deal even from bed. And what he desired most of all was for her to tell her story.

Initially she resisted. Amy was not interested in telling her personal story. She had always avoided the limelight, even going so far as to prohibit anyone from ever taking photographs of her (only a handful of images of Amy exist today), so she was certainly reluctant to bare her soul on paper for the public to read. But God's will prevailed. Amy completed *Gold Cord*, an account of the establishment of the Dohnavur Fellowship, and went on to write thirteen more books during her confinement, for a total of thirty-five books over her lifetime. She also wrote hundreds of songs and poems and thousands of letters, both to prospective missionaries and to her "beloveds," the Dohnavur children. Before she died in 1951, Amy wrote a letter to each member of the Family, in which she conveyed encouragement, hope, thanksgiving to God, and, above all, love.

Five simple questions guided Amy's writing: Is it true? Is it helpful? Is it kind? Is it necessary? Does it have the "seed of Eternity" in it? For Amy, it was imperative that she tell the truth, no matter how difficult or harsh. "There is a false suavity about most that is written from this land now," she wrote. "We are so afraid to offend, so afraid of stark truth, that we write delicately, not honestly." Delicacy, Amy felt, was dangerous. "Our smoothness glides over souls," she said. "It does not spur them to action."[11] And for Amy—even a bedridden, immobile Amy—action was everything.

The Face of Jesus

When biographer Elisabeth Elliot interviewed members of the Family after Amy's death, she found most of them would not acknowledge any flaws in their leader. "She was perfect," said one. "She must have been a sinner—the Bible says we all are—but I never saw it," said another.[12] Amy, of course, would have been appalled by this. She knew she was far from perfect—her flaws ranged from stubbornness, occasional self-righteousness, and a controlling nature to the tendency to complain about her ill health. Yet these flaws were generously overshadowed by her enormous gifts: loyalty, humility, courage, faith, obedience, trust, and a tremendous zeal for serving others.

The Dohnavur Fellowship thrives today and has ministered to thousands of needy children—a living testament to Amy Carmichael's unwavering commitment to God and his people. As one young missionary stated after she was taken to meet the elderly Amy for the first time, "I have seen the Lord Jesus."[13] The same could be said about Amy. It's clear from her life and legacy that Amy Carmichael saw Jesus when she looked into the face of each and every person she encountered during her eighty-three years on earth.[14]

34

Ida Scudder

God Knocked and She Answered

$(1870-1960)$

Ida Scudder had no intention of becoming a missionary, despite the fact that foreign missionary work ran deep in her family's blood. Since the time her grandparents had dedicated their lives to missionary work in Ceylon five decades before Ida was born, the Scudder family had been known for their Christian work overseas. But Ida was determined not to follow suit. She had other plans for herself, plans that included marriage, a family, and a comfortable life in America—plans that changed on a single night, when three knocks at the door dramatically altered the course of her life forever.

The Unlikely Missionary

Ida Scudder was born in India in 1870 to missionary parents. Her father, John Scudder, was a third-generation medical missionary, and more than forty members of her family had dedicated their lives to missionary work as well. Ida came to America as a young girl when her parents were granted a furlough. Her father returned to India alone, and two years later her mother joined him, leaving Ida with relatives in Chicago. She was fourteen years old; nearly ten years would pass before she would see her parents again.

After she graduated from high school, Ida attended a women's seminary founded by evangelist Dwight Moody in Northfield, Massachusetts. She was decidedly against joining the family tradition and instead focused primarily on finding herself a husband. As biographer Dan Graves notes, "If asked to define the good life, [Ida] would have replied 'America and marriage to a millionaire.'"[1] Having spent several years in India as a child, Ida knew exactly what a life in that country entailed. She had witnessed famine with her own eyes, helped her parents feed starving children, and glimpsed corpses stacked on the dusty streets. In her mind, India was a horrible place—dirty, hot, noisy, and smelly, filled with the sick and the dying, the destitute and the hopeless. India was a place Ida would never set foot in again if she could help it.

As it turned out, Ida was called back to India for a reason even she couldn't ignore. When her father cabled to inform her that her mother was gravely ill, Ida departed for India almost immediately and, a few weeks later, arrived in the south India village of Tindivanam. After her mother recovered, Ida was pressured by her family to join their missionary efforts. She found herself directing a school for young girls, yet she still clamored to return to the United States and fully intended to do so as soon as she could free herself from her parents' grip.

One evening, as Ida sat reading, three knocks on her door derailed those plans. When she opened the door at the first knock, a high-caste Brahman stepped out of the shadows on the veranda and pleaded with her to assist his child-wife, who was in labor and dangerously near death. The Indian midwives had done all they could to no avail, the man explained—would she help? Ida was at a loss. While her father, John Scudder, was a skilled doctor, she had no medical skills whatsoever. But when she promised to send her father to the man's home as soon as he was available, the Brahman refused. He would not allow his wife to be attended by a male doctor.

Not long after the man left, Ida heard a second knock, but when she stepped onto the veranda, expecting to see the Brahman man again, she was greeted by a Muslim man instead. His wife was also dying in labor, but when Ida's father offered to assist, the man refused. No man outside his family had ever glimpsed his wife's face, and he could not allow a foreign male to touch her. Neither Ida nor John could convince the man to change his mind.

Later that evening, Ida again heard footsteps on the veranda, and to her horror, a high-caste Hindu approached her, pleading for her to help his laboring wife. He too refused John Scudder's assistance. In all three cases, Ida was not able to do anything to help.

She lay awake the entire night in anguish and prayer, begging God to make his will clear. Ida desperately wanted to return to America, to a life of comfort and ease. But she couldn't dismiss the thought of the three women who were left with no one to help them, simply because their culture prohibited contact with men.

Early the following morning, as she tossed and turned in dawn's gray light, she heard a somber beat thrumming through the village—a death toll. Her servant reported the news she had dreaded: all three women had died in labor during the night. That same day, Ida made her decision: she requested permission from her mother and father to return to American to enroll in medical school. Later Ida wrote that during that long night, she had met God face-to-face for the very first time in her life.

Female Doctor, Fund-Raiser Extraordinaire

Ida's ambition to attend medical school was not implausible, even for a woman in the late nineteenth century. Elizabeth Blackwell had already paved the way when she became the first American woman to earn a medical degree in 1849. And Methodist missionary Clara Swain had been serving as a doctor in India since 1869, a full fifteen years before Ida enrolled in the Women's Medical College in Phila-delphia. That said, female missionaries, particularly medical mis-sionaries, were still few and far between in the early 1900s. In fact, as the only female medical missionary within hundreds of miles, Ida treated more than five thousand patients in the first two years of her medical practice in India.

Although she initially enrolled in the college in Philadelphia, when Cornell Medical College in New York City opened its doors to women, Ida transferred there to take advantage of the school's stellar reputation. She received her medical degree from Cornell in 1899 and immediately began to make plans to return to India. Determined to open a hospital for women in India, Ida focused on fund-raising in America, and she managed to raise more than ten thousand dollars in a single week, thanks in part to a generous con-tribution from the president of a Manhattan bank, who had heard about Ida's ambitions.

Ida intended to open the medical practice with her father, but only months after she returned to India, John Scudder died from cancer. To add to her difficulties, the Indian people were initially suspi-cious of a female doctor, and Ida had few patients during her early months of practice. But after she successfully treated a high-caste Hindu woman's eye infection, word spread, and soon Ida's waiting room—the veranda of her house—was full. It wasn't long before Ida was treating more than one hundred patients a day, with the number continuing to grow. At one point she saw nearly five hun-dred women in a single day, and she often took her medical practice on the road to villages, operating on the roadside and traveling by oxcart. The need was tremendous. In a country in which there was one doctor for every ten thousand people, Ida's services were but a drop in the ocean.

Ida opened the Mary Taber Schell Hospital for women in 1902, but it was soon readily apparent that she would need to open a medical college to train nurses as well. Male critics were skeptical that she would enroll more than a handful of women, but 151 applicants applied for admission in 1918, the school's first year.

As Ida's work grew, larger and larger sums were required to defray expenses and update equipment, the lion's share of which was raised by women's groups from four different denominations. In the early 1920s, when Ida heard that her medical school would be eligible for a one-million-dollar Rockefeller grant *if* two million dollars could be raised privately, she returned to America to focus on fund-raising. She successfully raised the required funds, which were used to build the Vellore Medical Complex. Now known as the Christian Medical College and Hospital in Vellore, it's one of India's largest and most prominent medical facilities.

Back in the 1940s, however, Ida faced her most difficult challenge to date. As her medical school and hospital began to flounder under heavy financial burdens, Ida could think of only one viable solution that would save the school. She proposed to make it coeducational, a suggestion that infuriated many of her donors. Thousands of supporters, primarily women, had raised millions to support medical missions for women in India, and they were not interested in seeing that mission "diluted" by the inclusion of men. As Hilda Olson, a governing board member of the Vellore Medical Complex, stated, "Vellore is as you say, God's work, but I would like to add God's work *for women*."[2] She suggested that every dollar that had been raised in support of the medical school for women over the past few years should be returned to the donors if the school went coed.

The debate simmered for years, with the governing board bitterly divided over the issue, each side refusing to concede. Some of Ida's staunchest supporters became her most vocal critics during this time, accusing her of disloyalty and selling out on the mission's vision.

Finally, in 1947, the board agreed to admit men to the college. Although the battle left her depressed and anxious, Ida had remained focused during the entire process on what she believed was God's will. "First ponder, then dare," she advised. "Know your facts. Count the cost." But, she cautioned, remember that in the end, money is not the most important object. "What you are building is not a medical school. It is the kingdom of God," she reminded the board. "Don't err on the side of being too small. If this is the will of God that we should keep the college open, it has to be done."[3]

A Lesson in Obedience

Ida became widely recognized for her achievements during her own lifetime. She was so esteemed in India, people who met her would often kneel or bow down before her in homage. Many Indians worshiped her as the incarnation of a god, and many clamored to touch her, believing they would be healed by her mere presence.

When she retired in 1946 at the age of seventy-five, Ida continued to serve as an advisor at the hospital for another decade. She also taught a weekly Bible study class to both women and men, frequently entertained friends and dignitaries at her home, and played a vigorous game of tennis. Although she wasn't as spry as she was at sixty-five, when she handily beat a teenager who had complained about playing a "granny" in the tournament, at eighty-three she still boasted a mean serve.

Ida Scudder's legacy is an obvious one. Today the forty-bed hospital she founded in 1902 has grown into a 2,600-bed teaching hospital that treats 1.9 million outpatients and 120,000 inpatients annually, performs more than 3,500 surgeries each month, and delivers more than 15,000 babies every year.[4] Perhaps less measurable but no less important is the lesson Ida teaches all of us about obedience. Many of us can surely relate to the strong-willed self-assurance Ida demonstrated as a young girl—she had envisioned a clear plan for herself, a plan that did not include India. However, when God turned that plan on its head, Ida reacted not with her usual defiance and stubbornness but in obedience. As a young girl, Ida had claimed she would never return to India. Instead, she served there more than sixty years until the day she died. When God knocked, Ida Scudder answered with a willing heart.

35

Thérèse of Lisieux

The Little Way

$(1873-1897)$

She waited, shifting from one foot to the other and wringing her hands as the long line inched forward. No one spoke. The shuffling of feet and the clinking of rosary beads were the only sounds heard in the grand room as the pilgrims filed toward the seated figure. Craning to catch a glimpse of the distinguished face and robed form of Pope Leo XIII, Thérèse watched from her place in line as each pilgrim kneeled silently in front him, bending low to kiss first the foot and then the hand of the pontiff before receiving his benediction.

Thérèse was on a mission. She had resolved to break the reverent silence during her brief audience with the pope, to ask him to bless her entry into the Carmel cloister at the age of fifteen, a full six years ahead of the typical entry age. But as one pilgrim and then another took their turn with Pope Leo, Thérèse began to lose her nerve, especially when a papal guard reminded the visitors that conversation with the Holy Father was strictly forbidden. Panicked, she whirled around to face her sister, Céline, who stood in line behind her. "Speak!" Céline urged.

Suddenly it was Thérèse's turn. Her eyes on the ground, she kneeled before Pope Leo, lowering her head to kiss his slipper. Then, as the pope presented his hand to her, Thérèse raised her tear-streaked face, looked the pope in the eye, and whispered her question with conviction. "Most Holy Father, I have a great favour to ask of you. Most Holy Father, in honour of your Jubilee, allow me to enter Carmel at fifteen!"[1]

Pope Leo, Thérèse wrote later, gave her his full attention, bending down so that his head nearly touched hers, "as though his black and profound eyes wanted to penetrate me into the recesses of my soul."[2] But before he could answer, the vicar-general of Bayeux interrupted. Standing to the right of the pope and familiar with Thérèse's unrelenting zeal to gain admission to the Carmelite monastery at Lisieux, he stated curtly that local church authorities were already investigating Thérèse's request.

"Well, then, my child," Pope Leo said gently, "do whatever the authorities decide." Undeterred, Thérèse clasped her hands together and pressed them onto the pope's knees. "O! Most Holy Father," she implored, "if only you would say yes, everyone would be willing!" Before the papal guards forcibly removed Thérèse from the room, she heard Pope Leo's response: "He looked at me very fixedly and pronounced these words, weighting each syllable in a penetrating tone, 'Come now . . . come now . . . you will enter if God wills it.'"[3]

Five months later, Thérèse was accepted into the convent at Lisieux as a Carmelite postulant.

Saved from Grief

Marie-Francoise-Thérèse Martin was born weak and ill with a failure to thrive. At two days old, she was whisked by her despairing mother to the countryside, where a peasant woman with a houseful of her own children nursed and cared for her. Rose raised Thérèse in her humble cottage, pushing her through the fields in a wheelbarrow full of hay and wrapping her in her apron as she went about her work, until, at fifteen months old, Thérèse was finally strong enough to return home to her parents and sisters in Alencon.

Thérèse's pleasant childhood didn't last long. When she was four years old, her mother succumbed to breast cancer at the age of forty-six. As the youngest children, Thérèse and her sister Céline were shielded from their mother's suffering, but they were both summoned to her bedside to witness the sacrament of last rites during her final hours. It was a pivotal moment in Thérèse's life and faith. She remembered kneeling in the corner of the bedroom as the priest administered the sacrament to the still, gray form in the bed. Later, she recalled kissing her mother's cold forehead. On her way out of the bedroom, she glimpsed a coffin towering upright in the hallway outside the door.

Later Thérèse admitted to her sister that her mother's death changed her, and that it was only God who saved her from her grief: "If God had not lavished His beneficent rays on His little flower, she would never have been able to acclimatise herself on this Earth."[4] Previously an exuberant and even mischievous child, Thérèse was now serious and sensitive, prone to tears and bouts of melancholy and hysteria.

She was also increasingly drawn to God and the religious life. The first word Thérèse learned to read was *heaven*, and it's said that at a young age she informed her father that her name was written in heaven. She told him that she had glimpsed the letter *T* in the constellation of Orion on a bright winter night and considered it a sign. At age nine, she approached the mother prioress of the Carmel convent to seek entrance as a postulant and was undeterred when she was informed she must wait until she was at least sixteen. Later the mother prioress amended the age to twenty-one, further delaying Thérèse's entrance.

A Sudden Maturation

In addition to her mother's death, Thérèse cited one other event that profoundly impacted her spiritual life. On Christmas Eve 1886, when Thérèse was thirteen years old, she experienced what she called her "complete conversion," a moment in which she matured from a child to an adult in a single instant.

It was just after one in the morning, and Thérèse, her sisters, and their father had returned home from midnight Mass at the cathedral in Lisieux. Thérèse was eager to discover what treats Father Christmas had left in her empty shoes, which had been arranged, as was the Christmas Eve custom, on the hearth. But as she climbed the stairs, she overheard her father mutter to her older sister that Thérèse was too old for such nonsense, and he hoped this year would be the last of the silly tradition. Thérèse was crushed by her father's callous words, but instead of dissolving into tears as she typically would have, she steeled herself, entered the living room, and delighted over her gifts as if she hadn't overheard a word. Later, she said that Christmas Eve was the moment she crossed from childhood to adulthood. "Thérèse instantly understood what had happened to her when she won this banal little victory over her sensitivity, which she had borne for so long," observes Ida Gorres in her biography *The Hidden Face*. "She had been vouchsafed a freedom which all her efforts had been unable to win."[5]

Following this revelation and "complete conversion," Thérèse pursued her goal of entering the convent at Lisieux with renewed determination. First she approached the bishop of Bayeux for his permission and then later Pope Leo XIII himself while she was on a pilgrimage to Rome with her father and sister. Finally, on April 9, 1888, Thérèse, wearing white velvet trimmed in swans' down, a bouquet of white lilies in her hand, was led by her father down the center aisle of the chapel to be received as a postulant. Kneeling before the priest, she renounced all earthly pleasures and then was led into the convent, where her shoulder-length hair was shorn to her scalp and she exchanged her luxurious clothing for the brown tunic, white cloak, scapular, and sandals of the Carmelite novice.

The Little Way

Confined within the convent's walls, Thérèse felt her ambition to serve her God intensify with each passing day. Simply being a nun, she felt, was not enough. "To be Thy spouse, O my Jesus, to be a daughter of Carmel and by my union with Thee to be the mother of souls, should not all this content me?" Thérèse pondered. Yet she was not content. She yearned for more, to be a "priest, an apostle, a martyr, a doctor of the church. . . . Martyrdom was the dream of my youth and the dream has only grown more vivid in Carmel's narrow cell."[6]

Finally, after much contemplation, Thérèse understood a way in which she could fulfill her desire to serve the Lord. Her service would not, as she had once imagined, be realized through dramatic acts as a martyr or even through ecstatic visions, as was the case for Teresa of Ávila and other mystics. Instead, Thérèse vowed to serve God through the smallest, seemingly most insignificant acts of love. While reading Paul's first letter to the Corinthians, Thérèse found her answer in what she called the *petite voie*, or the "little way."

"I realized that love includes every vocation, that love is all things. . . . Beside myself with joy, I cried out: O Jesus, my Love, my vocation is found at last—my vocation is love!"[7] Thérèse later wrote to her sister Céline that she aimed to strip herself of self, to descend lower toward humility, rather than aspire to greater and greater heights. Thérèse's little way was a means to live out her devotion and service to God in the people and circumstances of everyday life. "In my Little Way," she said, "there is nothing but very ordinary things; little souls must be able to do everything that I do."[8] As biographer Vita Sackville-West noted, Thérèse aimed "not to do extraordinary things, but to do ordinary things extraordinarily well."[9]

Thérèse approached her daily tasks at the convent as a tangible way to illustrate her love for God and others. Even the smallest duty, from maintaining the altar as a sacristan to serving in the laundry room, became an opportunity for Thérèse to demonstrate her devotion to God.

She also aspired to love her fellow nuns as deeply and purely as she could—even those with the most difficult personalities. In fact, Thérèse often requested to minister particularly to the most grouchy and quarrelsome nuns at Lisieux. She noted that one of her most taxing trials during her time at the convent was presented in the form of a fidgety nun, who continuously clanked her rosary beads during contemplative prayer, distracting Thérèse so that she literally sweated in annoyance and frustration beneath her habit. Over time and with conscientious discipline, Thérèse trained herself to listen attentively to the irritating noise, transforming the cacophony into a concert of prayer for Jesus.

Thérèse's little way sounds ordinary and routine, but every step of it was steeped in love. Ironically, her little way was simple and direct, but it required the utmost fortitude and commitment day in and day out.

Fulfilling the Vocation of Love

When Thérèse succumbed to tuberculosis in September of 1897, she died in obscurity, known by few beyond the walls of the convent. She would have remained that way, undoubtedly forgotten among the many thousands of nuns who had gone before and come after her, had her prioress not released Thérèse's autobiographical manuscript just days after her death. The book was first read in convents, but it spread across the countryside, and soon the Carmelite convent at Lisieux was inundated with book orders from around France and beyond. Stories of miraculous cures of those in possession of Thérèse's *The Story of a Soul* began to surface, until finally her fame rose to the attention of Rome itself.

Thérèse was canonized on May 17, 1925, by Pope Pius XI, only twenty-eight years after her death. Just three years later, a young Albanian nun named Agnes Gonxha Bojaxhiu would take the name Teresa in honor of Thérèse of Lisieux. Today we know that nun as Mother Teresa.

The whole of Mother Teresa's life and labor bore witness to the value of small acts done faithfully and with love, just as her predecessor and role model had done before her. Likewise, we too can look to Thérèse of Lisieux as a guide on our own faith journeys. Her simple, direct way of seeking and serving God is not complicated or unique.

It's not limited to a chosen few. It doesn't require a particular set of skills or a certain education. Rather, Thérèse's little way of serving God in our ordinary, everyday lives is a practice open to each one of us. We simply need to take the first step toward fulfilling this vocation of love.[10]

36

Mary McLeod Bethune

Enter to Learn, Depart to Serve

$(1875-1955)$

T he girls huddled together in the darkness, peering over the
windowsills of Faith Hall. They watched, barely able to breathe,
as more than one hundred men on horseback and on foot, all of them
with white sacks cinched over their heads, paraded behind a burning
cross down Second Avenue toward the campus gates. Entering the
school grounds, the Klansmen encircled the building, the trample
of horse hooves and human feet thundering into the silent night. A
single shrill scream pierced the stillness, followed by another and
another as the girls broke into panic, crouched inside the dark hall.

Suddenly, cutting through the hysteria, a voice rose calm and
steady, singing the lyrics of a comforting hymn. One by one the
terrified girls joined in, singing, "Be not dismayed whate'er betide,
God will take care of you," as the hooded men marched out the
campus gates.[1] Later that night, the last of her students comforted

and tucked into bed, Mary McLeod Bethune continued to repeat the hymn to herself as she lay awake. She thanked God again and again for protecting her students and her school.

An Education and a Mission

Legend has it that Mary McLeod was born with her eyes wide open. "She'll see things before they happen," the midwife said as she handed the infant to her mother. Mary was the fifteenth of seventeen children born to former slaves Samuel and Patsy McLeod. Most of her siblings had been born into slavery, but by the time Mary came into the world, her parents were free. Her mother worked as a cook for her former master, and her father farmed cotton. They lived in a tiny log cabin near Mayesville, South Carolina.

Although she was born into freedom, Mary saw plenty of evil with her own young eyes. On a birthday trip to town one year she witnessed an angry crowd of white men lynch an innocent black man. She also suspected her father was routinely cheated when his cotton was ginned, baled, and weighed, but since she couldn't read the numbers on the scales, she couldn't prove it.

That all changed the year Mayesville's Presbyterian Trinity Church opened a school for black children and Mary was allowed to attend. The next time she accompanied her father to the cotton gin, she was able to read, write, and calculate well enough to observe that the scales registered something different than the white man claimed. When she quietly corrected the overseer, noting that the scales read 480 pounds, rather than 280 pounds, he paused for a moment, looked Mary straight in the eye, and then agreed that he had made "a mistake." It was a small victory but an important one to young Mary.

Nearly the whole town turned out to the Mayesville depot to see Mary off in 1887 when she departed for Scotia Seminary in North Carolina. She stayed at Scotia on full scholarship for five years and from there went directly to Chicago, where she was admitted to the Mission Training School at the renowned Moody Bible Institute. Of the approximately one thousand students at Moody, Mary was the only African American.

During her two years at Moody, Mary stayed focused on her goal: to serve as a missionary in Africa. But when the time came for her to apply to the mission board of the Presbyterian Church, she was bitterly disappointed with their answer: there were no openings for "Negro missionaries" in Africa.

Missionary to America

Mary wasn't one to wallow in disappointment for long. Realizing that foreign missions work was out of the question, she refocused her attention on a new mission: the education of American black children. "Africans in America needed Christ and school just as much as Negroes in Africa. . . . My life work lay not in Africa, but in my own country," she later acknowledged.[2]

Newly married, with an infant son of her own (her husband eventually abandoned the family and returned to South Carolina in 1907), Mary relocated her family to Florida, first to Palatka, where she ran a small school, and then to Daytona. With $1.50 as a down payment on a two-story rental building, Mary opened the Daytona Literary and Industrial School for Training Negro Girls in 1904. She had six female students, plus her own young son. Discarded boxes and packing crates from the nearby businesses were used as desks and chairs. Mary's own seat at the head of the classroom was a barrel turned upside down.

At the end of a long day of teaching, Mary baked sweet potato pies to sell early the next morning on the construction lines in order to supplement the funds needed for the school. She also wrote leaflets that described the school's mission to distribute on street corners in the business district, and she often went door-to-door in the evenings, fund-raising nickel by nickel and dollar by dollar.

Mary's school for girls grew quickly. In just over two years, more than one hundred girls were enrolled, many of them boarders. She also taught adults in the evenings and held a Bible study on the weekends. When it was time to scout out a new, larger property to accommodate her growing student enrollment, Mary found the perfect spot: a lot adjacent to the town dump, on the fringe of the black neighborhood. Known by the locals as Hell's Hole, the price for the lot was two hundred fifty dollars, far more than the five dollars Mary had in savings. Still, by then Mary had acquired a reputation for honesty and hard work, and the landlord took her at her word when she assured him she would raise the rest.

In addition to relentless fund-raising, Mary also established a board of trustees comprised of some of the area's most upstanding white male citizens. She set her sights on James Gamble, co-founder of Procter and Gamble, who wintered one town over from Daytona. Upon meeting her in person, Gamble admitted that when Mary had written him, he assumed she was a white woman. But when he visited her classroom a few days later, he and four other guests were so impressed by what she had accomplished with so little that all five men agreed to serve on her board.

In October 1907 the Daytona Literary and Industrial School for Training Girls officially opened its brand-new building on the grounds of the former Hell's Hole. Although Faith Hall was largely unfurnished and partially unfinished, with a dirt floor, unplastered walls, and no indoor plumbing, the school was up and running. Its motto was inscribed in two parts in the main hall: "Enter to learn" over the front door, and "Depart to serve" over the back door.

On Sundays, Mary hosted community meetings that were initially associated with the temperance movement and attended by blacks only. But as Mary's popularity and fame grew, the audience was soon comprised of a mix of both blacks and whites. Conversation often centered on race relations, and guests were encouraged to sit wherever they wanted, a practice that was decidedly radical for the time. Mary never submitted to Florida's rigid segregation laws; she simply invited all visitors, black or white, to sit wherever they pleased.

The Daytona girls' school continued to grow, and by 1911 some of its first enrollees were doing high school work. When she suggested to the board that the school aim for secondary accreditation, Mary was met with strong opposition. The board believed eight grades were adequate for the education of black children. Mary, appalled that the board still did not understand her philosophy—that what was good for one was good for all—threatened to close the school and start anew elsewhere. Later that night, Mr. Gamble knocked on her door and insisted that as chairman of the board, he would support her no matter what.

In 1923 the girls' school merged with the Cookman Institute for Men to become the coeducational Bethune-Cookman College. The college, which was one of the few places where African American students could pursue a college degree, is still in existence today, enrolling more than 3,500 students on an eighty-acre campus in Daytona Beach. Mary served as president of the college until she retired in 1942.

Milestones

You might assume the school provided more than enough work for Mary, but her influence was not limited to Florida. In fact, today she is best known for her work on the national level with the National Council of Negro Women, an organization Mary founded in 1935 to represent a number of groups working on critical issues for African American women. She also served as a special advisor on minority affairs to President Franklin D. Roosevelt and as director of the Division of Negro Affairs of the National Youth Administration (NYA).

When Aubrey Williams, director of the NYA, first approached Mary to inform her that President Roosevelt had created a special position for her as administrator of the Division of Negro Affairs, Mary balked. Feeling overwhelmed and underqualified for a job of such magnitude, she refused to accept the offer until Williams insisted she was the only woman President Roosevelt wanted for the position. "Do you realize that this is the first time in the history of America that an administrative government office has been created for one of the Negro race?" he asked.[3] Such a grand statement surely unnerved Mary further, but she accepted the challenge.

In 1936, as part of her effort to focus attention on racial inequality, she organized the Federal Council on Negro Affairs, which became known as the Black Cabinet. Comprised of African Americans who had been appointed to various government agencies, the group first met in August 1936 at Mary's Washington, DC, apartment. They focused on how African Americans could be better represented in the administration and how they could best benefit from New Deal programs. "The responsibility rests on us," Mary told the group. "We can get better results by thinking together and planning together. . . . Let us band together and work together as one big brotherhood and give momentum to the great ball that is starting to roll for Negroes."[4]

It's easy to look at Mary's myriad accomplishments and forget the immense burden she shouldered as an African American woman who broke innumerable barriers. At times, Mary's work at the national level was lonely and discouraging. At one point, after she overheard a disparaging comment from a white woman in attendance at one of the First Lady's afternoon teas, Mary wrote in a journal, "I looked about me longingly for other dark faces. In all that great group I felt a sense of being quite alone." A few sentences later, though, she acknowledged the importance of her role:

> Then I thought how vitally important it was that I be here, to help these others get used to seeing us in high places. And so, while I sip tea in the brilliance of the White House, my heart reaches out to the delta land and the bottom land. I know so well why I must be here, must go to tea at the White house. To remind them always that we belong here, we are part of this America.[5]

Despite facing constant humiliation, Mary did not succumb to bitterness or hatred. "Love, not hate, has been the foundation of my fullness," she wrote in her spiritual autobiography. "When hate has been projected toward me, I have known that the persons who extended it lacked spiritual understanding. . . . Faith and love have been the most glorious and victorious defense in this 'warfare' of life, and it has been my privilege to use them."[6]

Two years before her death, Mary sat at her desk in her Florida home and penned her last will and testament. As she noted, her worldly possessions were few, but the principles she had derived from her life's work were, in her words, the legacy she passed on to her people:

> I leave you love.
> I leave you hope.
> I leave you the challenge of developing confidence in one another.
> I leave you a thirst for education.
> I leave you a respect for the uses of power.
> I leave you faith.
> I leave you racial dignity.
> I leave you a desire to live harmoniously with your fellow men.
> I leave you finally a responsibility to our young people.[7]

"If I have a legacy to leave my people," she stated in her last will and testament, "it is my philosophy of living and serving."[8] Mary McLeod Bethune lived that philosophy each day of her eighty years, and she left each one of us her legacy of living and serving to follow as well.

37

Faye Edgerton

Good News for the Navajo

(1889-1968)

On a stifling August day in 1956, a middle-aged woman opened her mailbox and pulled out a package airmailed from New York City. Braced against the brisk Oklahoma wind, she stood at the end of the dusty driveway and tore open the wrapping to reveal a hardcover volume, its pages edged in red, the title, *Diyin God Bizaad: Aha'deet'a Aniidii*, in gold script. It was the Navajo New Testament, the first-ever translation of the New Testament into the language of the Navajo Indians. The book was the culmination of Faye Edgerton's lifework.

Too Frivolous for a Missionary

When a friend learned of Faye Edgerton's decision to serve as a Christian worker in Korea, she exclaimed, "Faye is the last person I thought would be a missionary—she's so frivolous!"[1] As a teenager growing up in Hastings, Nebraska, Faye was much more concerned with dances, parties, and boys than much anything else. While she did well in school and regularly attended the Presbyterian church where her father was an elder, Faye admitted that she was generally a willful and self-centered child. "I lived a truly worldly life all through my girlhood," she said. "None of our crowd had any strong convictions about anything. We just wanted to have a good time."[2]

All that changed two years after her high school graduation, when she became gravely ill with scarlet fever. The illness caused complete, but thankfully temporary, hearing loss, and the weeks of silence during her convalescence gave Faye ample opportunity to reconsider her priorities. When she recovered, Faye entered the Moody Bible Institute in Chicago, determined to dedicate her life to Christ as a foreign missionary. After graduation she spent four years teaching the Bible to recently converted Christian women in Korea. When Faye returned home to Hastings, the Presbyterian missionary board assigned her to work on a Navajo reservation in Arizona, a decision that opened the door to her life's work.

Good News for The People

The education of Navajo children in 1924 was based on the philosophy of assimilation. Suppression of the Navajo language was standard practice in government and mission schools. Children were encouraged to speak English only; the use of Navajo was considered backward and inhibitive to real progress. Faye communicated to The People, as the Navajos referred to themselves, with the help of an interpreter, but she longed to talk with them in their own language. Little by little, as her busy schedule on the reservation permitted, she began to teach herself Navajo. Recalling how beneficial it was for the Koreans to read the Bible in their own language, she dreamed of an accurate Navajo translation of the Bible. She was also increasingly frustrated by extemporaneous translations that puzzled or misled Navajo Christians. "I remember one fine man who was interpreting a message on the prodigal son," she wrote. "When the missionary told of the father's word, 'Bring hither the fatted calf and kill it; let us eat and be merry,' the interpreter said, 'Let us eat and be *married*'!"[3]

In 1944 Faye finally took a major step toward fulfilling her dream as a Navajo translator when she joined Wycliffe Bible Translators. "Our God is a God of wonders," Faye wrote home in October 1944. "He has led me on and given me the opportunity to do the thing that I feel He has been calling me to do for some time."[4] But before Faye could begin work on translating the Scriptures to Navajo, she had to master the language. She settled into a house trailer in a grove of piñon trees on the Navajo reservation land called Yellow-at-the-Edge-of-the-Woods. There in New Mexico, among The People, she immersed herself in their language. "God has answered the prayer of many years in allowing me to live thus where no English is spoken," Faye wrote to her family. "I am depending on Him and your prayers for me, that I may master this language, conceded to be one of the most difficult in the world."[5] Often she sat on a sheepskin rug on the dirt floor of a hogan (the traditional home of the Navajo), a stack of 3x5 cards beside her, listening to conversations and jotting down tidbits of the language at a time. Later she spent hours analyzing the note cards and memorizing what she had written.

Threatened by an unusually severe winter in her trailer high up on the Continental Divide, Faye later moved to Farmington, New Mexico, to live on the grounds of the Navajo Methodist Mission School. There she taught Navajo reading in exchange for room and board. Dr. Eugene Nida, Faye's mentor at Wycliffe, suggested she give Scripture translation a try by revising the Gospel of Mark, which had been published in Navajo several years before. She was assisted by Geronimo Martin, a blind Navajo. "His keen mind was only made keener and his spiritual life deepened by his affliction," said Faye of Geronimo. "He was a strict teacher of his language. As I read back a translation he would detect even the faintest error in pronunciation—which reflected an error in spelling."[6]

Faye split her time between translation and teaching. A new alphabet was now being used by the specialists working at the Bureau of Indian Affairs, and Faye helped to create some of the materials used in the bilingual schools. She was often torn between her two tasks—translation for the Navajos and literacy of the Navajos, knowing that a translated Bible would be useless for The People if they could not read it.

One Who Draws Fish Up out of Water

By 1946 Faye had completed the revision of Mark and moved on to Paul's letters. The translation work was arduous, requiring hours of grueling, detailed research. Not only did Faye need to ensure the Navajo grammar was correct, but she also regularly consulted Greek lexicons, teasing out the origins of phrases, words, and expressions in order to most accurately convert them to the language of The People. "In the process of transforming thoughts into another verbal mold, Faye was the bridge between two worlds, a link between two languages," writes Ethel Emily Wallis in her biography, *God Speaks Navajo*. "The onus of explaining what the original text meant rested upon her. And often the manner of expressing the thought of a biblical concept in the Indian tongue was worlds away from either Greek or English!"[7]

For example, the concept of fishing was an especially difficult one to convey in Navajo, which has no word for *fishing*. Not only were there few bodies of water on the reservation, in the Navajo culture it was taboo to eat fish. As a result, the entire concept of fishing, including how to describe the activity and the purpose of it, was foreign to the Navajo. As Wallis observes, in the Navajo language the verbal expression of an action includes an element of the word specifying the shape of the object used in a given action. Not only was there no general word for *fishing* in Navajo, but the two different acts of fishing with a line versus fishing with a net had to be distinguished. Therefore, a man fishing with a line was described as "one who draws fish up out of (water) by means of a ropelike object," while a man fishing with a net was translated as "one who draws fish up out of (water) by means of a flat, flexible object."[8]

Other occupations were much easier to convey. Sheepherding, for example, is a common occupation among Navajos, and Faye and Geronimo were delighted to find that the many references to and parables about sheep were among the easiest to translate. Likewise, silversmithing is one of the main industries of the tribe, resulting in a relatively simple translation of the account of the silversmiths' riot in Acts. The word "silver" was described as "metal which is white," while a silversmith was translated as "one who pounds metal which is white"—a seemingly awkward phrase in English, but the most compact and accurate Navajo equivalent.

When Faye and her team reached the book of Revelation, they were ecstatic to be nearing the end of the project, only to discover that the variety of musical instruments mentioned in Revelation are not part of Navajo culture, which only includes the drum and a type of flute called the *dilni*. As a result, in the holy concert in Revelation 18, *pipers* was translated as "those who whistled through dilni," trumpeters "played the brass dilni," and harpists "played the wood that sings."[9]

When conveying the concept of anxiety, Faye used a word that in Navajo means "that which prickles or irritates, like a pin sticking into the flesh." For example, in 1 Peter 5:7, which in English translations urges the reader to cast their worries onto Jesus, the Navajo verse is translated as, "The things that are constantly sticking into you, turn them over to me, for I am interested in you and caring about you."[10]

Each time the translators completed a book, Faye read it aloud to a team of Navajos to test for errors. Missionaries across the denominational spectrum were also consulted. Finally, after more than ten years of painstaking labor, Faye, Geronimo, and another Navajo translator, Roger Deal, finished the Navajo New Testament and sent the final manuscript off to the New York City publisher. Still, the question remained: would the New Testament actually be read and used by The People? Would the Navajos pay seventy-five cents for it? Although it was a low price made possible by a subsidy through the American Bible Society, it was still more than many Navajo families could afford.

Faye and her team didn't have to wait long for their answers. The first edition of 2,500 volumes sold out in five months; two subsequent printings sold out just as quickly. By the end of 1967, the book had been reprinted seven times, with 14,500 copies in hogans, missions, and schools across the reservation. The People had spoken their approval.

Up Next: Apache, Inupiat, and Hopi

Now that her life's mission was accomplished, one would think Faye would have rested on her laurels, but that wasn't the case. Soon after the Navajo New Testament was published, The People began to clamor for the entire Bible to be translated into their own language. Faye oversaw the revision of Genesis and Exodus, which had been translated by early missionaries, as well as the translation of the Psalms. Together these three books, along with translations of Joshua, Ruth, and Jonah, were published by the American Bible Society in 1966. Then Faye turned her attention to the Apaches.

The fact that she didn't know the language didn't stop Faye; she and her friend and colleague Faith Hill simply moved into a house trailer on the border of the San Carlos Apache Reservation in Arizona and made friends with the people. Ten years later, the Apache New Testament was published by the American Bible Society. A year later, at the age of seventy-seven, Faye flew to Fairbanks, Alaska, where she spent the summer working with fellow translators on the Inupiat New Testament. A year before her death she worked as a consultant on the Hopi New Testament, and just one month before she died Faye was still working on a new revision of the Navajo New Testament. She never stopped translating God's Word for The People—a people who had, over a lifetime, become her people too.

Most of us who speak English as our first language probably don't give much consideration to the Bibles that sit on our nightstands and on the bookshelves in our homes. We have dozens of English translations from which to choose, and many of us own more than one version. The Navajo, on the other hand, had no such choice.

They stumbled through God's Word in a language that wasn't their own, a language that didn't always make sense and wasn't always clear—that is, until Faye Edgerton found her mission. As fellow translator Roger Deal said, "This is not just a missionary talking to us in another language—this is God's word in Navajo. It is just like God talking!"[11] Faye Edgerton wasn't just any voice for The People. She was the voice of God speaking in Navajo.

38

Edith Stein

A Sacrifice for Her People

(1891–1942)

When the grim-faced nun stood at the doorway of her cell and informed her that two SS officers had summoned her to the gate, Edith knew exactly what awaited her. She lay her pen down next to her manuscript and followed the sister down the dark hallway to the front entrance of the convent. The officers on the other side of the iron bars stated that Edith had five minutes to gather her belongings. A few minutes later when she reached the convent gate, her sister Rosa was already there. Edith took her sister's hand and led her to the car. "Come, Rosa," she encouraged. "We're going for our people."[1]

Pope John Paul II beatified Edith Stein as a martyr in Cologne in 1987. "We bow down before the testimony of the life and death of Edith Stein, an outstanding daughter of Israel and at the same time a daughter of the Carmelite Order, Sister Teresa Benedicta of the Cross, a personality who united within her rich life a dramatic synthesis of our century," the pope said. "It was the synthesis of a history full of deep wounds that are still hurting . . . and also the synthesis of the full truth about man. All this came together in a single heart that remained restless and unfulfilled until it finally found rest in God."[2]

Edith was canonized as a Roman Catholic saint by him eleven years later, more than fifty-five years after she was killed by the Nazis at Auschwitz.

A Quest for Truth

Edith Stein was born on Yom Kippur, the Jewish Day of Atonement, in Breslau, Germany, the youngest of eleven children in a devout Jewish family. From the time her father died when Edith was just two years old, her mother, Auguste Stein, always considered Edith her husband's last testament. Although Edith accompanied her mother to the synagogue and participated in the fasts and other rituals of Judaism, she abandoned her faith by the time she completed secondary school. "I consciously decided, of my own volition, to give up praying," she said.[3] Instead, she enrolled in the University of Breslau to study philosophy, to "search for the ultimate grounds for being, the quest for truth taking the place of childhood faith."[4]

After Edith graduated with honors, she enrolled in the Gottingen School to pursue graduate work under her mentor, Edmund Husserl, who pioneered the revolutionary method of phenomenological research. Phenomenology, the study of the development of human consciousness and self-awareness, greatly appealed to Edith in her search for truth. Ironically, it was one of the influences that led her back to faith. "With good reason we were repeatedly enjoined to observe all things without prejudice, to discard all possible 'blinders,'" she wrote in her autobiography, *Life in a Jewish Family*. "The barriers of rationalistic prejudices with which I had unwittingly grown up fell, and the world of faith unfolded before me."[5]

As World War I descended, Edith continued to both move toward faith and struggle against it. At one point she visited Frankfurt

Cathedral, where she witnessed a woman enter the sanctuary with a shopping basket on her arm and kneel in a pew for a brief prayer. Edith, who up to this point had experienced religious people praying only during an actual church service, was intrigued by the fact that this woman prayed in the midst of her everyday life, as if she were engaging in an intimate conversation with God. Later Edith wrote that she never forgot that scene.

Around the same time, her good friend and fellow phenomenologist Adolf Reinach, who had converted to Protestantism with his wife a few years prior, was killed on the battlefields of Flanders. Edith dreaded visiting Adolf's widow, but when she did, she was amazed by Frau Reinach's hope and her ability to console her husband's mourners. Shortly before her death, Edith recalled the experience to her friend, Jesuit priest Father Hirschmann: "It was my first encounter with the Cross and the divine power it bestows on those who carry it. . . . That was the moment my unbelief collapsed and Christ shone forth—in the mystery of the Cross."[6]

Still, torn between her strong foundation in science and philosophy and the unfamiliar but powerful pull of Christ, Edith resisted faith. As she wrote later, an atheist can learn of the existence of God through personal experience yet still resist him, refusing to respond by holding God at arm's length. She knew an intellectual willingness to believe was not enough. God required a full and complete surrender to achieve complete transformation, but Edith was simply too afraid to acquiesce.

All that changed with a book Edith picked off a friend's shelf. The book was Teresa of Ávila's autobiography, and once Edith turned the first page, she couldn't stop until she had read it cover to cover in a single night. She found in Teresa's autobiography confirmation of what she had suspected for a while: that God is not a God of knowledge but a God of love. According to Teresa, our inner resistance is healed and transformed via interior prayer, and so, at Teresa's prompt, Edith embarked on a journey of quiet, meditative prayer. "The Spanish mystic told [Edith] to let the intellect rest in prayer, to let God come to her in solitude and silence, without the props of earthly consolations," biographer Waltraud Herbstrith explains.[7] Edith relinquished her dependence on a rationalist worldview and surrendered herself entirely to God in prayer.

She embraced her new quest with gusto, purchasing a catechism and daily missal and attending her first Mass. Immediately after that Mass, she approached the priest and asked him to baptize her. Surprised, the priest informed Edith that an extended period of study typically preceded baptism in the Catholic Church, but undeterred, Edith suggested that the priest test her knowledge. She passed the test with ease and was baptized into the Roman Catholic Church shortly after, on New Year's Day 1922. She took Teresa for her baptismal name. Edith Stein had finally found the truth she had pursued so relentlessly for thirty years.

Atonement

After her conversion Edith abandoned her dream of a professorship and accepted a job teaching German at St. Magdalena's, a school run by Dominican nuns. She refused a salary beyond what was necessary for clothing, room, and board, and she dedicated herself entirely to her students and to serving the inner-city poor. She also persisted in her practice of contemplative prayer, and when she spoke to both religious women and laywomen alike, she suggested they do the same. Every woman, she urged, should try to find "breathing spaces" in her day, moments in which she can center herself and rest in God. "God is there [in these moments] and can give us in a single instant exactly what we need," she explained. "Then the rest of the day can take its course, under the same effort and strain, perhaps, but in peace."[8]

Edith also worked as a translator, first translating the letters and diaries of Cardinal Newman from his pre-Catholic period, then Thomas Aquinas's *Quaestiones Disputatae de Veritate*. Her spiritual mentor encouraged her to write her own philosophical works as well. Little by little, Edith began to return to academic work as she realized it was possible to pursue scholarship as a service to God. As a result of this revelation, in 1932 she accepted a lectureship position for the Roman Catholic division of the German Institute for Educational Studies at the University of Münster, where she successfully combined scholarship and faith in her work and her teaching. She sought to be a tool of the Lord, endeavoring to bring anyone she connected with to Christ.

The year 1933 was a dramatic turning point for Edith. With the Nazi takeover and the large-scale offensive against the Jews, her life's purpose and calling began to crystallize. She realized Jesus' cross was being laid on the Jewish people—her people—and herself. As "one of the few who understood this [and] had the responsibility of carrying it in the name of all,"[9] she was willing to accept this burden and prayed to God to show her how. She was convinced that her calling included admission into the Carmelite convent in Cologne, and she was accepted into the convent in October of 1933. Her mother was devastated by Edith's decision, and their parting was excruciating—a step, Edith admitted later, "that had to be taken in the absolute darkness of faith."[10] Although Edith wrote to her mother faithfully from the convent, she never received a reply.

The situation in Germany worsened dramatically with the SS attack on November 8, 1938. Enclosed behind the convent walls, Edith was safe as Jews were driven from their homes during the night, their businesses confiscated or destroyed, and their synagogues burned. But her prioress knew Edith would not remain protected for long. She arranged to have Edith driven across the border to Holland under cover of darkness on New Year's Eve. A year later, her sister Rosa, who had also joined the Carmelites, narrowly escaped arrest as she fled from Belgium to Holland and was reunited with Edith in Echt.

As biographer Waltraud Herbstrith notes, Edith's escape to Holland should not be misconstrued as a flight from reality but rather her "entrance into the redeeming action of Christ."[11] She clearly stated her intentions in a letter written to her prioress just before the start of the war:

> Dear Reverend Mother: please permit me to offer myself to the Heart of Jesus as a sacrifice of atonement for true peace, that if possible the

reign of Antichrist might be broken without another world war and a new social order might be established. I would like to do it today, if I could, since it is already the final hour. I know I myself am nothing, but Jesus desires it, and I am sure he is asking it of many others in these days.[12]

Edith felt a sense of peace even as the Nazis invaded Holland in 1940. Although she applied for a Swiss visa and was accepted by Carmel of Le Paquier, a convent in Switzerland, when she realized Rosa would not be allowed to accompany her, she chose to remain in Echt.

On August 2, 1942, the moment she had anticipated arrived: all Jewish Catholics were ordered under arrest, including members of the Catholic religious orders. Edith and her sister Rosa were brought to a temporary camp in Amersfoort and then herded with 1,200 other Jewish women onto a train and brought to Westerbork, the central detention camp in north Holland. Edith occupied her time in the camp by caring for the abandoned children, washing their clothes, cleaning the living quarters, and comforting them. In the middle of the night on August 7, 987 Jews were awakened and loaded onto yet another train. The train stopped at Breslau, Edith and Rosa's hometown, on its way to Auschwitz. No one from the transport survived. Edith Stein, her sister Rosa, and more than one thousand others were killed in the gas chambers of Auschwitz on December 9, 1942.

It's natural for us to feel intimidated by Edith Stein, a woman who humbly and bravely offered her very life for God and considered her sacrifice an atonement for the horrors inflicted upon her people. How can we compare ourselves to a woman who made the ultimate sacrifice? we reason. Yet the prescient words she penned in 1930 are just as applicable to those of us who face far less dire circumstances: "Every time I feel my powerlessness and inability to influence people directly, I become more keenly aware of the necessity of my own holocaust."[13] Although she literally sacrificed herself for her love of Christ, Edith argued that each of us must die to ourselves in order to live as humbly, obediently, and lovingly as

271

Jesus Christ desires. If you've lived as "a person more or less contented with himself, the time for that is over," she challenged.[14] It's not about us, she reminds us matter-of-factly. We do not have the power to influence and impact others on our own. We, like Edith Stein, are simply his instruments.

39

Corrie ten Boom

Under His Wings You Shall Trust

$(1892-1983)$

Corrie and Betsie ten Boom. Being transported to Ravensbrück concentration camp.[1]

These eleven words, scrawled on a scrap of paper and squeezed through a slit in the boxcar and into a stranger's hands, were Corrie and Betsie ten Boom's only hope of getting a message to their family. The day before, more than seven hundred male prisoners had been executed at the work camp outside of Vught in occupied Holland, where the sisters had been imprisoned for the last few months. Now Corrie, Betsie, and hundreds of other women were herded into freight cars, where they would spend three days crushed by stench, filth, and the bodies of their fellow prisoners as they traveled deep into Germany toward one of the most notoriously brutal death camps in existence.

The Hiding Place

Only months earlier, Corrie and her older sister Betsie were living comfortably with their father, Casper, a watchmaker, in a cozy home above their watch repair shop in Haarlem, Holland (their mother had died several years earlier). From the outside, the ten Boom home, which they called the Beje, looked perfectly ordinary. But behind the brick walls and the tiny storefront, circumstances were anything but.

As the Second World War raged, the ten Boom home had become a refuge, part of the underground resistance movement for hiding and protecting Jews from the Nazis. The ten Booms hid as many as seven Jews and members of the Resistance in their "hiding place," a secret room behind a hidden wall in Corrie's third-floor bedroom. Some stayed for long periods, others for only a day or two before being transferred to another safe house. Corrie recalled hearing dire warnings from her father's friends, who were worried that he would surely face imprisonment if he persisted in hiding Jews. She also remembered his determined reply: "I am too old for prison life, but if that should happen, then it would be, for me, an honor to give my life for God's ancient people, the Jews."[2]

The Raid

On the morning of February 28, 1944, Corrie, sick in bed with influenza, vaguely registered the sound of a buzzer ringing. Dulled by fever and a fierce headache, she struggled to make sense of the incessant noise. Suddenly she bolted upright in bed. The buzzing alarm wasn't a drill. It was a raid.

Six refugees—four Jews and two members of the Resistance—dashed past her bed in a panicked frenzy and scrambled into the hiding place. Seconds after Corrie lowered the secret panel and leapt under the blankets again, a member of the Gestapo loomed at the foot of her bed. He demanded she dress and follow him downstairs, where she, her father, her two sisters, and other family members who'd gathered at the house that morning for a prayer meeting were beaten and interrogated while the officers searched for the hidden Jews. The Gestapo waited, seizing anyone who came to the shop under the auspices of watch repair. At the end of the day, thirty-five captives were hauled to prison. Although they ransacked the house, the Gestapo didn't find what they sought most. The Jews were never discovered, and forty-seven hours later, they were freed from the cramped space behind Corrie's bedroom wall and taken to new safe houses. Four of the six survived the war.

While being interrogated by the Gestapo, Corrie's father was offered the opportunity for freedom. "I'd like to send you home, old fellow," the chief officer said. "I'll take your word that you won't cause any trouble." Corrie heard her father's solemn answer: "If I go home today, tomorrow I will open my door again to any man in need who knocks."[3]

In her preface to *Prison Letters*, Corrie wrote that as they huddled on the floor of the police station that night, "God used Father to prepare each of us in a special way for the unknown times that lay ahead. Father asked my brother Willem to read Psalm 91 and then Father prayed. 'He that dwelleth in the secret place of the most High shall abide under the shadow of the Almighty. I will say of the Lord, He is my refuge and my fortress: my God; in him will I trust.'"[4]

A few hours later, outside the gates of Scheveningen federal penitentiary, Corrie exchanged her last words with her father: "Father!" she called as she and Betsie were led to their cells, "God be with you!" Before the metal door slammed shut, she caught his reply: "And with you, my daughters."[5]

Casper ten Boom died a prisoner ten days later.

Companionship and Grief

Corrie and Betsie spent four months at Scheveningen—Corrie in solitary confinement, Betsie in a cell with several other inmates. It was there they each learned by letter from their sister Nollie, who had been released, that their father had died in prison. "During my months of solitary confinement I often felt lonely and afraid," Corrie wrote in the introduction to *Prison Letters*. "In such moments I recalled that last night with my father, sharing Psalm 91 and praying. I could remember some of those verses, especially that, 'He shall cover thee with his feathers, and under his wings shalt thou trust . . .' I would close my eyes and visualize that kind of protection . . . and with that thought in mind, I would fall asleep."[6]

Four months after they arrived at Scheveningen, Corrie and Betsie were transferred to Vught, a German concentration camp for political prisoners in the southern part of Holland. Although living circumstances were more challenging at Vught, the sisters were overjoyed to be reunited. Corrie described her time at Vught as "a baffling mixture of good and bad."[7] On one hand, she was grateful for the clandestine prayer meetings she and Betsie held around their bunk at night, as well as for the companionship of other people after months in solitary confinement. But, she wrote, "What I had not realized in solitary confinement was that to have companions meant to have their griefs as well."[8]

It wasn't long before Corrie would endure a personal grief of her own. The relative ease of life at Vught came to an abrupt halt when the ten Boom sisters were loaded into the boxcar that transported them and eighty other prisoners—filthy, reeking from sitting in their own waste, and nearly perished from thirst—to Ravensbrück concentration camp, deep in the heart of Germany.

A Lamp unto Her Feet

"'Ravensbrück!' Like a whispered curse, the word passed back through the lines," Corrie later wrote. "This was the notorious women's extermination camp whose name we had heard even in Haarlem. That squat concrete building, that smoke disappearing in the bright sunlight—no! I would not look at it. As Betsie and I stumbled down the hill, I felt the Bible bumping between my shoulder blades. God's good news. Was it to this world He had spoken it?"[9]

Corrie had carried her Bible with her all these months, stealthily hidden in a pouch that she suspended down her back beneath her threadbare dress. At Ravensbrück, she and Betsie clung to God's Word as a lifeline. The reason they were there, engulfed by such seemingly pointless suffering, was clear to both the sisters: "From morning until lights-out, whenever we were not in ranks for roll call, our Bible was the center of an ever-widening circle of help and hope."[10]

The suffering was relentless: brutal physical labor; little to no food; crowded, putrid sleeping platforms, with the women stretched feet-to-face without even adequate space to turn over or sit up. Each week they were paraded naked before leering guards for the "medical inspection." But despite the ceaseless punishment and humiliation, God's Word kept the sisters and dozens of other women steady. Corrie described the nights spent huddled under one weak lightbulb, the Bible open on her lap, as a preview of heaven. Women of all faiths and nationalities gathered around as Scripture verses were passed up and down the aisles in French, Polish, Russian, Czech, and back into Dutch.

When Corrie's faith faltered, as it did more than once during her time at Ravensbrück, her sister steadfastly shone God's light. "Betsie, how can we live in such a place!" Corrie wailed when she first glimpsed Barracks 28, where 1,400 women shared a flea-infested space designed to hold four hundred, with nine to a platform bed intended for four. When her sister answered, "Show us. Show us how," Corrie realized Betsie was praying. "More and more the distinction between prayer and the rest of life seemed to be vanishing for Betsie."[11] Corrie observed her sister's unfailing faith and found hope.

He Is Deeper Still

As the frigid December wind howled through the barren concentration camp, Betsie grew weaker and weaker, finally unable to stand on her own for the 4:30 a.m. roll call. It was then she began to speak about her plans for the future. First she talked excitedly about a home in Holland, where ex–war prisoners would recuperate amid peace and quiet. Later she spoke of refurbishing a German concentration camp where "the people warped by this philosophy of hate" would be rehabilitated and learn to love. And finally, the day before she died, Betsie pulled her sister down close to where she lay on the floor of the ramshackle hospital ward and whispered her last vision into Corrie's ear: "We must tell them that there is no pit so deep that He is not deeper still. They will listen to us, Corrie, because we have been here."[12]

The next morning, Corrie gazed through the filthy hospital window as the nurses lifted her sister's emaciated body in a sheet and laid it on the floor next to the other corpses. Three days later, Corrie was called to the camp's headquarters, where she was handed a certificate. She held it in her hand, reading the single word again and again, unable to process its meaning: *"Entlassen."*

Released.

From Visions to Reality

Corrie later discovered that her release had been an accident, or, as she considered it, a miracle. In 1959, fourteen years after she was freed, Corrie visited Ravensbrück, where she learned that a clerk had mistakenly recorded her prisoner number on a list of those to be released instead of where it was intended: the execution list. One week after she gained her freedom, every woman Corrie's age and older was executed at Ravensbrück.

In the months and years following her return to Haarlem, Corrie ten Boom concentrated on fulfilling her sister's dying visions. With the help of a generous patron, she established a rehabilitation home in Holland for war victims and, later, a second rehabilitation facility for Germans at a former concentration camp in Darmstadt. Finally, at age fifty-three, Corrie launched a worldwide ministry that took her to sixty countries over thirty-three years to share her and Betsie's story and to convey an unwavering message of hope in Jesus. Later, she funneled the proceeds from her books—*A Prisoner and Yet, The Hiding Place, Tramp for the Lord, In My Father's House,* and *Prison Letters*—into her ministry. She died at her home, which she'd named

Shalom House, in Los Angeles, California, on April 15, 1983—her ninety-first birthday.

Corrie ten Boom, her father Casper, her sister Betsie, and her entire extended family suffered unimaginable horrors for their convictions. Some of us may wonder if we would have made the same choices in such dire circumstances. Thankfully, most of us cannot even guess at an answer. What we can be sure of, though, is that the ten Boom family trusted entirely in God and his Word. Even when their faith faltered, even when darkness threatened to prevail, the Word of God cast a light of hope. Corrie and her sister Betsie lived deep in the pit and suffered more than most of us can possibly fathom. Only Corrie survived, but she lived to proclaim what her sister knew: that his love is indeed deeper still.[13]

40

Dorothy Sayers

A Reluctant Prophet

(1893–1957)

The *Daily Telegraph* called it a "triumphant mixture of religious feeling, scholarship and plain humanity."[1] The writing was deemed exquisite and spiritually gripping by laypeople and clergy alike, including an Anglican priest, who urged his parishioners to buy tickets to see *The Zeal of Thy House* and to approach it as a religious experience in and of itself. For many Christian writers, this kind of praise would not have been out of the ordinary. But Dorothy Sayers was not your typical Christian writer. In fact, she didn't consider herself a Christian writer at all but a mystery writer, an author of detective novels first and foremost. Dorothy wrote popular books about murder, suspense, and intrigue, which she considered her "proper job," insisting that her foray into theology later in her life was purely accidental. She was, as her biographer and friend Barbara Reynolds called her, a reluctant prophet, albeit an influential one.

On a Whim

Educated at home by her academic father (who was headmaster and chaplain of the Choir School at Christ Church College, Oxford, and later the rector at a small country church), her spirited mother, and a number of governesses, Dorothy spent much of her youth isolated from her peers, amusing herself by reading, writing poetry, and inventing imaginative stories. When she was fifteen, she left the tiny village of Bluntisham-cum-Earith to attend boarding school in Salisbury, where the students and teachers viewed her as odd, awkward, and standoffish. She was relieved to graduate in 1912, scholarship in hand, to attend what she called "the holy city"—Oxford University.

Dorothy majored in modern languages, and although she passed her final examinations with honors in 1915, because Oxford didn't acknowledge female graduates, she did not officially receive her degree until 1920. In the meantime she went to work, first for a small publishing firm in London and later at an advertising agency, where she wrote snappy copy for Guinness beer and Coleman's mustard. To fill the time while in between jobs, Dorothy conceived the character of amateur sleuth Lord Peter Wimsey and wrote *Whose Body?*, the first of more than a dozen novels and short stories still widely read today.

Guilt and Grief

While Dorothy's professional life was stable and productive, her personal life erupted into chaos in 1923. Heartbroken after the demise of a serious relationship with writer John Cournos, she found herself pregnant by a casual boyfriend who had no inclination to marry her or parent the child. Two days before her due date, finally realizing she couldn't change the man's mind, she checked into a private maternity home in Southbourne, a seaside resort town far from Oxford and her parents' town, where she secretly delivered a baby boy.

Two days before, Dorothy had written to her cousin Ivy, begging for her help with what she described as a "friend's" infant. Ivy agreed to care for the child. A few weeks later when Dorothy knocked on Ivy's door, baby John Anthony in her arms, she confessed she was his mother, insisting that her cousin keep her secret. Ivy honored her promise. Dorothy's parents died never knowing their daughter had borne them a grandson.

Always a pragmatist with an uncanny ability to compartmentalize her emotions, Dorothy quickly resumed business as usual. A few weeks after the birth she returned to work at the ad agency, telling colleagues only that she'd been ill. She kept up pretenses at the office and with her friends and family because she felt she had no other choice, but deep inside she suffered not only from terrible guilt and shame but also from grief over the loss of the child. Later, in the early years of her marriage to Oswald Atherton Fleming (who was known as Mac), she hoped her husband would eventually adopt John Anthony, but that plan never materialized.

Some of her biographers suggest that Dorothy did not truly want a child in her life. While Cournos's refusal to have children was cited as one of the reasons for their breakup, Dorothy also admitted to friends that she didn't much care for children. Her attitude toward John Anthony was businesslike at best. She was involved in his life from a distance—she wrote him letters, sent Ivy money for his care, and visited from time to time—but she also understood that the child could, and should, have only one proper mother. She was known as his "aunt," and it wasn't until many years later, when John Anthony applied for a passport and saw Dorothy's name listed as his biological mother, that he realized her true relationship to him.

Dorothy the Diva

As her popular detective series began to produce a reliable income and a steady stream of royalty checks, Dorothy was finally able to risk venturing outside her standard genre. When Canterbury

Cathedral approached her to write a religious play for a festival in 1937, she snapped up the opportunity. The response to *The Zeal of Thy House* was tremendous. Audiences from the public to the clergy to the media were enchanted, and she was soon asked to write a series of religious plays to be broadcast on the BBC Radio's children's hour.

Dorothy may have compartmentalized her emotions when it came to her personal life, but she didn't suppress her opinions when it came to her job. She was notoriously difficult to work with—stubborn, impatient, inflexible, and at times downright self-righteous. When the producer's assistant questioned whether the play's language was over the heads of the young audience, Dorothy fired back a scathing response. "I knew how *you* would react to those passages," she fumed. "It is my business to know. But it is also my business to know how my *real* audience will react, and yours to trust me to know it."[2] Dorothy deemed the assistant an unliterary critic, threatened the producer, and eventually tore up the original contract. As a result, a new contract was written, she was assigned the producer she'd originally wanted to work with, and the play was broadcast as part of BBC Radio's regular programming rather than the children's hour. In short, Dorothy got exactly what she'd wanted all along.

No "Bible Talk"

Dorothy's religious writing appealed to audiences in part because her contemporary language was so accessible. She also was not afraid to push boundaries and challenge the norm. As biographer James Brabazon notes, "Dorothy's particular blend of scholarship, imagination, vigour and homely realism was a revelation to radio listeners. Here was the sacred story springing to life in a way they had never heard it before."[3] Some, though, objected to her modern, colloquial style—like the *Daily Mail*, which ran the accusatory headline, "BBC 'Life of Christ play' in US Slang," and the Protestant Truth Society, which petitioned the prime minister to have Dorothy's plays banned.

But Dorothy stood by her convictions. "Nobody, not even Jesus, must be allowed to 'talk Bible,'" she wrote to her BBC producer. It must "appear as real as possible, and above all . . . Jesus should be presented as a human being and not like a sort of symbolic figure doing nothing but preach in elegant periods . . . even at the risk of a little loss of formal dignity."[4]

Dorothy approached her translation of Dante's *Divine Comedy*, which she considered her best work, the same way: as a dramatist. She was surprised to find Dante funny, lively, and even bawdy at times, and she aimed to convey these often-overlooked characteristics in her translation in order to distinguish it from the many translations of *The Divine Comedy* already available on the market. "I think the trouble with [other translations] is that they have far, far too much reverence for their author," she wrote. "They are afraid to be funny, afraid to be undignified; they insist on being noble, but they end up being prim. But prim is the one thing Dante never is."[5] At the time of her death thirteen years later, Dorothy had completed *Inferno* and *Purgatorio* and had begun *Paradiso*, which was finished by her friend (and later biographer) Barbara Reynolds.

Saved by a God-Given Intellect

In spite of her success as a Christian writer, Dorothy was never entirely comfortable in her role as an author-evangelist, even after her most famous religious plays, *The Mind of the Maker* and *The Man Born to Be King*, were broadcast on BBC Radio. She preferred to create art for its own sake, trusting that the moral would emerge, rather than create what she called propaganda art forms. "I do not know that I am much good at speaking about religious life, being a great deal stronger on doctrine than on practice," she once quipped to a church audience.[6] She also wrote, "I've got labeled as a writer of Christian Apologetics, but God knows it is the last thing I ever wished to be."[7] Dorothy didn't even like to talk about religion with her peers. Once, after a meeting with both clerics and laity at the

BBC, she griped in a letter to a colleague, "It sent me out in a mood for a stiff gin-and-tonic and the robust company of my heathen friends."[8]

A deep spiritual struggle lay at the heart of Dorothy's discomfort with religious writing. When her friend, the scientist and theologian John Wren-Lewis, accused Dorothy of staying within the safe confines of church dogma rather than sharing her personal spiritual views, she responded with candid humility, offering a rare glimpse of her inner spiritual state. "I am quite without the thing known as 'inner light' or 'spiritual experience.' . . . Neither God, nor (for that matter) angel, devil, ghost or anything else speaks to me out of the depth of my psyche. . . . I am quite incapable of 'religious emotion.'"[9]

While Dorothy undoubtedly struggled with this lack of an emotional connection to God, she was neither apologetic nor regretful. Rather, she embraced her pragmatic approach to faith. "Since I cannot come through God through my intuition, or through my emotions, or through my 'inner light' . . . there is only the intellect left," she wrote to Wren-Lewis. "Where the intellect is dominant it becomes the channel of all the other feelings. The 'passionate intellect' is *really* passionate. It is the only point at which ecstasy can enter. I do not know whether we can be saved by the intellect, but I do know that I can be saved by nothing else."[10]

Dorothy was difficult and, at times, a diva. But she was also a survivor—fiercely independent, brilliant, and bold. One can't help but respect and even admire her spunk, sass, and wit, and in many ways, her brash irreverence and frank demeanor contribute much to her appeal. She spoke her mind, argued passionately for what she believed, and wasn't afraid to risk being disliked in order to stand behind her convictions.

We, of course, are the beneficiaries of Dorothy's sharp intellect, which fueled her imagination and allowed her to create not only an entertaining detective in the enduring character of Peter Wimsey but an approachable, "human" Jesus and a host of accessible biblical stories as well. She also left us a unique and lasting legacy in the example of her honest, pragmatic approach to faith. Rather than grieve her lack of emotional connection to God, she celebrated the fact that God had gifted her with a unique avenue to pursue a relationship with him via her inquisitive, analytical mind. In doing so, Dorothy Sayers offers hope and comfort to those who come to God not through intuition or emotion but through the kind of passionate intellect that was her hallmark.[11]

41

Dorothy Day

Love Your Neighbor

$(1897-1980)$

When Dorothy Day knelt at the Shrine of the Immaculate
Conception and prayed that God would use her talents to
help the poor, she had no idea that a nomadic socialist would provide
the answer to her prayers. The next day, just back from reporting on
the hunger march in Washington, DC, Dorothy answered a knock
on her New York City apartment door. A stranger, the French immi-
grant and street soapbox philosopher Peter Maurin, stepped across
the threshold and began speaking at once, almost as though "he
were taking up a conversation where it had been left off," Dorothy
recalled later.[1] Distracted by her daughter, who was ill with the mea-
sles, Dorothy only half listened to Maurin's rambling speech, but she
did glean four of his points loud and clear. Maurin wanted to found
a radical, religious newspaper. He wanted to launch what he called
"houses of hospitality" to care for the poor and the unemployed. He

wanted to organize agrarian-based communities to shift America's focus away from industrialization.

And he wanted Dorothy to lead all three initiatives.

Receiving "a Call, a Vocation, a Direction"

Dorothy was born into a family of journalists. Her father, John Day, reported on the racetracks and wrote a racing column for the *New York Morning Telegraph*. All but one of the five Day children grew up to become journalists. The family moved frequently during Dorothy's early years, from Brooklyn to Oakland and finally to Chicago, after the 1906 San Francisco earthquake burned the newspaper that employed John Day to the ground. In Chicago they lived in a tenement over a tavern until her father found work again.

The Days were not religious—John was a self-proclaimed atheist, although he always carried a pocket Bible with him. As a result, Dorothy was not introduced to organized religion until the pastor of the neighborhood Episcopal church convinced John and his wife, Grace, to allow their children to attend services on Sunday mornings. Almost immediately Dorothy fell in love with the language of the Psalms, and the hymns filled her heart with a joy she had never before experienced.

Dorothy's political tendencies took root during her last year of high school. Her brother Donald worked for a socialist newspaper, and Dorothy pored over each issue, engrossed in the work of the American labor movement. She was also mesmerized by Upton Sinclair's description of Chicago's stockyards and slaughterhouses in his novel *The Jungle*. Dorothy often walked her infant brother in his carriage along the grim West Side of Chicago, where she was surprised to find beauty in the midst of poverty: "The odor of geranium leaves, tomato plants, marigolds; the smell of lumber, of tar, of roasting coffee; the smell of good bread and rolls and coffee cake coming from the small German bakeries. Here was enough beauty to satisfy me." Walking these streets as a young girl, she knew that "from then on my life was to be linked to theirs, their interests were to be mine: I had received a call, a vocation, a direction to my life."[2]

A Return to Religion

Dorothy fought her religious inclinations for a long time. During her two years at the University of Illinois and, following that, her employment as a reporter at the New York socialist daily *The Call* and the antiwar magazine *The Masses*, she was surrounded by people who disdained organized religion and considered themselves atheists. Yet at the same time, Dorothy couldn't bring herself to abandon God altogether. Bit by bit, she found herself drawn to the practice of worship, prayer, and Scripture reading. She told herself she read the Bible for its literary value, but when she roomed with three young Catholic women in Chicago, she also began to attend Mass with them on Sundays and on holy days.

In 1927, when her daughter Tamar was born, Dorothy's longtime partner Forster Batterham, an anarchist and an atheist, objected to her desire to have the infant baptized in the Catholic Church. Dorothy held her ground: "I did not want my child to flounder as I had often floundered. I wanted to believe, and I wanted my child to believe, and if belonging to a Church would give her so inestimable a grace as faith in God, and the companionable love of the Saints, then the thing to do was to have her baptized a Catholic."[3] Five months later Dorothy returned to the same church for her own baptism, an act that marked the end of her relationship with Forster.

Despite her decision, Dorothy was wracked with guilt. The day after her baptism, as she kneeled during Mass, she felt like a hypocrite and a betrayer of the oppressed and the poor. "Here I was, going over to the opposition, because the Church was lined up with property, with the wealthy, with capitalism, with all the forces of reaction." How could she balance such seeming disparity between the church itself and her personal drive for social justice? "How I longed to make a synthesis reconciling body and soul, this world and the next."[4]

The answer to her questions came five years later, when a knock on the door revealed Peter Maurin on her doorstep. She wrote,

> I felt keenly that God was more on the side of the hungry, the ragged, the unemployed, than on the side of the comfortable churchgoers

who gave so little heed to the misery of the needy and the groaning of the poor. I had prayed that some way would open up for me to do something, to line myself up on their side, to work for them, so that I would no longer feel that I had been false to them in embracing my new-found faith. The appearance of Peter Maurin, I felt with deep conviction, was the result of my prayers.[5]

Radical Religion, Radical Hospitality

On May 1, 1933, part one of Maurin's four-point plan came to fruition when 2,500 copies of the first issue of *The Catholic Worker* were printed and distributed for a penny a copy to the radicals and workers who crowded New York City's Union Square to celebrate May Day. Dorothy had taken Maurin's idea of launching a newspaper seriously. She produced the paper on a typewriter at the kitchen table in her Brooklyn apartment, scraping together fifty-seven dollars for printing by delaying payment on her utility bills.

By December, one hundred thousand copies of the paper were printed each month, and readers rallied behind *The Catholic Worker*'s unique voice and content, a melding of the radical and the religious. Soon immigrants, the unemployed, and the homeless appeared at Dorothy's apartment, interested in helping with the paper. Stanley Vishnewski, a seventeen-year-old Lithuanian boy, ran errands and sold papers on street corners. When a shabby, unemployed man nicknamed Big Dan knocked on Dorothy's door after walking the streets looking for work all day in the rain, he asked to soak his blistered feet in hot water, stayed for the night, and never left. Big Dan, with his booming voice and personable nature, sold more papers on the streets than anyone. Every person "employed" by the paper was a volunteer, working for nothing more than soup and bread.

When the paper's editorial offices expanded into the former barbershop below Dorothy's apartment, the staff began to serve lunch and offer accommodations to anyone who needed them. When *The Catholic Worker* moved into a larger building on Mott Street in 1936, which became its home for the next fourteen years, it officially became more than a newspaper. The second part of Maurin's vision blossomed during the Depression, when hundreds of men formed breadlines outside the building every morning. Dorothy described the men as "grey . . . the color of lifeless trees and bushes and winter soil, who had in them as yet none of the green of hope, the rising sap of faith."[6]

By the end of 1936 there were thirty-three Catholic Worker houses across the country. Dorothy was often criticized for helping those who came to the Catholic Worker for aid. She was accused of ignoring the "deserving poor" in favor of drunks and the lazy freeloaders. Readers often asked her how long the people were allowed to stay at the Catholic Worker. "We let them stay forever," she replied. "They live with us, they die with us, and we give them a Christian burial. We pray for them after they are dead. Once they are taken in, they become members of the family. Or rather they always were members of the family. They are our brothers and sisters in Christ."[7]

Striving for a New Social Order

Not all of the Catholic Worker's initiatives were successful. While Maurin insisted that the organization needed to move toward supporting an agrarian-based society, the farming communes they founded on Staten Island and in Easton, Pennsylvania, were eventually abandoned due to strife between those who lived there.

The newspaper struggled as well during the Spanish Civil War of 1936. Dorothy, an ardent pacifist, refused to take sides in the war, despite the fact that the Catholic Church supported Francisco Franco, the fascist dictator of Spain. As a result, the paper lost two-thirds of its readers. Later, following America's entry into World War II after the attack on Pearl Harbor, Dorothy announced that the paper would maintain its pacifist stand. "We will print the words of Christ who is with us always," Dorothy wrote. "Our manifesto is the Sermon on the Mount."[8] Not all members of the Catholic Worker communities agreed. Fifteen houses of hospitality closed in the months following America's entry into the war.

Likewise, during the Vietnam War, many young members in Catholic Worker communities were imprisoned for refusing to co-operate with conscription, while others did alternative service. Nearly everyone in the Catholic Worker communities took part in protests. Many went to prison for acts of civil disobedience, including Dorothy, who was arrested several times during her lifetime.

One of Dorothy's last arrests was in 1973, when she was jailed in California for picketing at several vineyards in support of local grape pickers. She was frequently criticized by contributors to the newspaper, who wanted to ensure that their gifts would be used to feed the hungry rather than to publish what they considered pro-paganda. "Bread lines are not enough, hospices are not enough," she responded. "I know we will always have men on the road. But we need communities of work, land for the landless, true farming communes, cooperatives and credit unions. . . . The heart hungers for the new social order wherein justice dwelleth."[9] For Dorothy, the Catholic Worker movement could never simply be about hospitality; it needed to be a movement of deep social change.

"Don't Call Me a Saint"

Dorothy's life was not squeaky-clean. She had an abortion when she was in her twenties. Shortly after, she married another man on the rebound, a union that lasted slightly over a year, and then lived with Forster for four years in a common-law marriage. Some have argued that she was a Communist as well, although that claim has been largely refuted. Despite her flaws, since her death in 1980 many within the Roman Catholic Church have insisted that Dorothy Day should be canonized as a saint.

Dorothy would have been the last person to accept the title of saint, or any title at all, for that matter. Throughout her life she de-fied labels and refused to be defined in a certain way or boxed into a particular category. "Don't call me a saint," she once quipped. "I don't want to be dismissed so easily."[10] For Dorothy, sainthood didn't require an elaborate canonization process; it was much simpler—and much more difficult—than that. "To put love into action, we must do all for the love of God," she wrote in her journal. "It is out of our common lives, filled with ordinary actions, that we are supposed to increase in love, to become saints."[11]

She took Jesus' instructions to "love your neighbor as yourself" (Luke 10:27) to heart. She loved her neighbors day in and day out through the most ordinary of actions. Her neighbors ate what she ate. They sat at the same table. They slept where she slept, in beds and on couches down the hall. They used her bathroom and brushed their teeth at her sink. Their children played with her daughter. For Dorothy Day, there were no boundaries and no limitations on the definition of neighbor. Her neighbor was everyone, because in her eyes, every person was a brother or a sister in Christ.[12]

42

Gladys Aylward

The Small Woman Who Did God's Great Work

(1902–1970)

She held her breath and prayed silently as she sat in the straight-back chair, her hands folded in her lap. The stern director of the China Inland Mission shuffled through a stack of papers on the desk, sighing and shaking his head as he reviewed the results of her examinations. When he finally spoke, the young woman leaned forward to hear him, praying fervently for a positive answer. She was gravely disappointed. The director reported that her grades were subpar. Worse yet, he felt her advanced age, twenty-six, would prevent her from adequately learning the Chinese language. In light of these two setbacks, the director informed the young woman that it was pointless for her to continue to prepare for foreign missionary work. Gladys Aylward's dream of serving in China was crushed.

From Parlor Maid to Preacher

Gladys Aylward was born in London to working-class parents. As the daughter of a mailman and the oldest of three siblings, she didn't have the luxury or the means to dedicate years to her education. Instead, by the age of fourteen she was already working long hours as a parlor maid and a housekeeper. When she could snatch a few minutes between chores, she would slip into her employer's personal library and page through one of his many books about China, a country whose people and culture fascinated her.

Though raised in the Anglican Church, Gladys was not particularly religious. At a revival with a friend when she was eighteen, however, she was convicted by the preacher's message, which emphasized the importance of giving one's life over to God. The message struck a chord in Gladys's heart and awakened a desire to serve in the missionary field. Given her fascination, China seemed like a natural fit—until, that is, her grades and her age deemed her unfit for the China Inland Mission program.

Despite the setback, Gladys was undeterred. During her downtime, she sharpened her preaching skills, evangelizing from a soapbox in Hyde Park to an audience of jaded London commuters. Little by little, a penny at a time, Gladys saved enough money to purchase the cheapest ticket to China—via the Trans-Siberian Railroad. She argued with the travel agent, who insisted the route was impossible, given the war raging between Russia and China. "We do not like to deliver our customers dead," the agent informed her.[1] Gladys ignored him.

After two years of hard labor and penny-pinching, Gladys kissed her parents and her sister good-bye and departed from Liverpool Street Station, bound for China. She had ninepence in coins, two one-pound travelers' checks, her Bible, a fountain pen, and her tickets and passport tucked into her corset. She carried a suitcase in each hand, a kettle and a saucepan tied to the handles with twine.

No Time for Crying

The travel agent had been right: the journey by rail, ship, and even at one point on foot, from London, across Siberia and Manchuria, and finally into China, was arduous. Gladys slept several nights on frigid train platforms across Siberia, grateful for the one blanket she had packed. After many weeks of grueling travel, Gladys arrived in the mountain village of Yangcheng in northern China. As she entered the tiny village, a group of children screamed and jeered, running from her in terror. Two Chinese women picked up dried clumps of mud and flung them at her. "It happens every time I go out," seventy-four-year-old missionary Jeannie Lawson informed the bewildered Gladys, greeting her at the doorstep of her home. "They hate us here. They call us *lao-yang-kwei*, foreign devils. It's something you'll have to get used to."[2]

Gladys also had to get used to the executions that regularly occurred in the market square. Not long after she arrived, she witnessed a man beheaded with a single blow from a curved sword blade while a crowd of onlookers cheered. As the head rolled across the stones, Gladys burst into tears. Later, Jeannie explained matter-of-factly that Gladys hadn't come to China to cry over every horrible sight she witnessed, or even to change China's laws. "We'll try to change these things through the love and wisdom of Jesus Christ, by making them understand truth and justice," she said, "but we won't do it by running home blubbering our eyes out."[3]

Knowing Yangcheng was an overnight stop for mule caravans and travelers passing through on the trading route, Jeannie and Gladys decided to open an inn. They called it the Inn of Eight Happinesses, and they advertised flea-free sleeping quarters, good food, and entertaining stories. The Chinese loved stories, Jeannie reasoned, so once the women had the travelers in the door, they would share the gospel stories with them and hope that the travelers would then carry the message to other parts of China.

The only problem, of course, was that the muleteers avoided the Inn of Eight Happinesses, preferring to sleep on the street rather than cross the threshold of the fearful "foreign devils." When shouting her sales pitch from the doorway of the inn failed to entice the travelers, Gladys took action, grabbing the reins of the lead mule and leading it toward the courtyard so the muleteers didn't have any choice but to follow.

Eventually the business flourished, and Gladys continued to run the inn on her own after Jeannie died. She also took on myriad additional responsibilities. As a government-appointed foot binding inspector, Gladys traveled from village to village, not only inspecting young women's feet and notifying the rural residents that the ancient custom of foot binding must cease, but also spreading the gospel wherever she went.

As time passed, both Gladys's command of the language and her reputation improved. At one point, summoned to the scene of a prison riot, the panicked prison director pleaded for her to help. "If you preach the truth—if your God protects you from harm—then you can stop this riot," he reasoned as they stood outside the gate. Gladys was terrified, but she knew she couldn't refuse the challenge. "Fail now, and you are finished in Yangcheng," she thought. "Abandon your faith now, and you abandon it forever!"[4] Miraculously, the rioting convicts listened to her, and Gladys's intervention eventually resulted in reforms at the prison. From that day on, Gladys was known as Ai-weh-deh, "the Virtuous One."

Breaking the Law for the Lord

Along with wayfaring travelers, Gladys began to take orphaned and neglected children into the inn as well. When she was reprimanded for challenging a government official about the lack of child-protection laws, she responded with a declaration of her own: "I have to inform you . . . that I did not come to China only to observe your laws. I came for the love of Jesus Christ, and I shall act upon the principles of His teaching, no matter what you say."[5] Just minutes after that pronouncement, Gladys stopped on the street and bought an orphan for ninepence, the money she had in her pocket. The girl, who was six or seven years old at the time and came to be known as Ninepence, lived with Gladys until she was married. By 1938, one hundred orphaned children lived at the inn.

When the Japanese began to bomb the mountain villages in 1937, Gladys identified herself with the Chinese people so intimately that she refused to leave even as artillery shells began to fall. "Do not wish me out of this or in any way seek to get me out, for I will not be got out while this trial is on," she wrote in a letter to her mother. "These are my people; God has given them to me; and I will live or die with them for Him and His glory."[6] Because she knew the mountainous terrain well from her travels, she worked as a spy for the Chinese soldiers, scouting behind enemy lines and reporting back to the Chinese nationalist officers. Though she considered herself Chinese by adoption and she deeply loved her people, she knew the information she passed on to the nationalist officers resulted in the loss of Japanese lives, a fact that kept her awake long into each night.

For a long time Gladys was able to blend in with the other Chinese refugees and thus continue her intelligence work undetected. Eventually, however, the Japanese learned about her espionage efforts. One day Gladys was shocked to read a leaflet tacked to the city gate announcing a one-hundred-dollar reward for "The Small Woman, known as Ai-weh-deh."

Early the next morning the Japanese fired at her as she dashed through the back gate of the walled city. Bullets ricocheted off the rocks around her, and as one grazed her back, she tore off her coat, balled it into a bundle, and dropped it behind her as a decoy. Bullets tore her discarded coat to shreds as Gladys wormed her way through the weeds on her belly and tumbled into the shallow moat. Pulling herself out of the water on the other side, she buried herself in the stalks of a dense wheat field, where she hid from the Japanese soldiers until darkness fell. After daylight faded she began the trek through the mountains toward Yangcheng. Two days later she reached the Inn of Eight Happinesses, where she gathered all one hundred orphans and prepared to flee to the safety of Sian, more than one hundred miles away.

Occasionally the group of refugees was offered shelter in a barn, but often they spent the nights in caves or in the open, huddled on the ground in the frigid mountain air. There was little to eat or drink—a handful of millet and a cup of water at most, and Gladys often gave her small portion to a hungry child. Gladys and the older children carried the young ones for miles at a time, encouraging them with hymns, prayer, and entertaining stories. Occasionally the slopes were so steep the group formed a human chain, passing the younger children from hand to hand down the mountainside. Twenty-seven days after they had set out with little but the clothes on their backs, Gladys and her orphans arrived at the refugee center. Every child had survived. Gladys, however, was near death, suffering from severe malnutrition, typhus, pneumonia, and exhaustion.

God's Second Choice

Although the doctors doubted she would survive, Gladys eventually recovered from her illness. It didn't take her long to resume her ministry of sharing the gospel in the villages and prisons in and around Sian. When the Communist government forced her to leave China in 1948, she returned to Britain, and when she sought reentry into China ten years later, the Communist government denied her. Instead, she settled in Taiwan, where she founded the Gladys Aylward Orphanage. She worked as a missionary in Taiwan until her death in 1970.

Gladys earned a fair degree of fame among Westerners when the movie *The Inn of the Sixth Happiness*, based on the biography *The Small Woman* and featuring Ingrid Bergman in the lead role, was released in 1957. Gladys was appalled by the movie, which took generous liberties with the details of her life, including embellishing her relationship with the Chinese colonel Linnan, whom she met during the war. Although she loved Linnan and even considered marrying him at one point, she never so much as kissed him and was horrified by the film's love scenes, which she felt sullied her reputation.

Hollywood portrayals aside, Gladys Aylward should be recognized for her contributions to Christian history and esteemed as an example of perseverance in the face of daunting odds. Refusing to be defined a failure and determined to overcome her educational shortcomings, she circumvented the traditional missionary route and took matters into her own hands, traveling alone into the unknown in order to heed what she knew was God's calling for her life.

"I wasn't God's first choice for what I've done for China," she once said to a friend. "There was somebody else. I don't know who it was—God's first choice. It must have been a man—a wonderful man, a well-educated man. I don't know what happened. Perhaps he died. Perhaps he wasn't willing. And God looked down and saw Gladys Aylward."[7] God didn't see a "small woman" in Gladys Aylward. He saw Ai-weh-deh, the Virtuous One—a woman who would do great things in his name.[8]

43

Simone Weil

The Uncompromising Christian

$(1909-1934)$

Turning her face to avoid the scorching blast, she slid the tray of huge copper bobbins into the inferno. A few minutes later, lifting the lid of the furnace with a large hook, she pulled the red-hot bobbins from the flames and then repeated the process again, over and over, stopping only for one fifteen-minute lunch break. For more than eight hours every day, she bent over the furnace, her pay dependent on the number of pieces finished. "Upon taking up your post at the machine you must kill your soul . . . kill your thoughts, feelings, everything," she wrote in her journal about her work on the factory assembly line. "You must suppress, purge yourself of all of your irritation, sadness, or disgust; they would lessen the pace. You must even abolish joy."[1] The most puzzling aspect of this scenario was that the factory worker who penned these words was an affluent, highly educated professor of philosophy. Simone Weil was not forced by poverty to toil on the assembly line; she deliberately chose to be there.

301

A Rare Strength of Mind

Born in Paris in 1909 to wealthy Jewish parents, Simone Weil was an intelligent child. By the time she was five years old, she was routinely reading the daily newspaper aloud to her family. She mastered Greek and several other modern languages in her early teens and would often speak in rhymed couplets or ancient Greek with her older brother, Andre, who was a brilliant mathematician. Because their mother deemed few educators skilled enough to teach her children, both Simone and Andre attended more than a half dozen schools and were instructed by several private tutors during their elementary and secondary school years.

From a very young age Simone also exhibited a heart for the world's poor and suffering. When she was six, she gave up sugar in an act of solidarity with the soldiers fighting in World War I, and she later befriended and mailed care packages to a French soldier on the front lines. When she was ten, while on vacation with her family, Simone gathered the chambermaids, porters, and desk clerks at the hotel and urged them to form a trade union. A few months after the end of World War I, her parents discovered her marching alongside workers in a union demonstration, singing "The Internationale" and chanting for better wages and hours.

At age sixteen Simone enrolled in the prestigious Lycée Henri IV, where she studied French, English, history, and philosophy. She was strongly influenced by her philosophy instructor, Émile Chartier, better known as Alain, who encouraged her writing and invited her to submit essays to the journal he published. Under his tutelage, Simone adopted Alain's central beliefs in intellectual responsibility, social justice, and, most important, the spiritual potential in manual labor. Upon graduation, Alain noted that his star student was "an excellent pupil" with a "rare strength of mind." He predicted Simone would "succeed brilliantly if she does not embark on obscure paths," and that she would attract much attention along the way.[2]

Attract attention she did indeed. Around the time she entered the lycée, Simone adopted an unusual fashion style that she adhered to for the rest of her life. With an unruly mop of black hair; huge tortoiseshell glasses that dwarfed her delicate features; and clothing resembling that of a destitute monk, with a dark cape, an ankle-length skirt, and boyish, flat-heeled shoes, Simone stood out as unusual and a bit bizarre. For her, style was a political expression. "It would be better if everyone dressed the same way and for the same amount of money," she told a teenaged friend. "That way . . . nobody would see our differences."[3] Adding to the effect was the fact that Simone was frightfully thin, due to her practice of severely limiting portions or abstaining from food altogether to make a political statement. Some scholars claim that she suffered from anorexia, and hospital records indicated that severe malnourishment was a contributing factor to her premature death from heart failure at the age of thirty-four.

"More Beautiful Than the Bourgeois"

Simone also took Alain's philosophy of manual labor to heart. While enrolled at the Sorbonne, she spent her summer vacations not lounging on the beach with her family but digging potatoes for ten hours a day at a Normandy farm and fishing off the coast with a four-man crew. She believed in a proto-Marxist view of work, concluding that manual labor was the truest road to self-knowledge and truth.

One day, sitting next to a friend on the subway, Simone pointed to a man wearing factory overalls, noting, "You see, it's not just in a spirit of justice that I love them. I love them naturally, because I find them more beautiful than the bourgeois." When another friend pointed out that she was the daughter of wealthy parents, Simone answered, "That's my misfortune, I wish my parents had been poor."[4]

Yet for Simone, work wasn't simply a philosophy. She believed in its value and lived it. By the time she had accepted a job teaching philosophy in the French lycée system, she was known as the Red Virgin and had aligned herself with the working class. She regularly wrote for several left-wing publications, organized and participated in worker strikes, campaigned for better working conditions, and

taught night classes to miners, in addition to her daily teaching responsibilities at the lycée.

Finally, in 1934, Simone made a dramatic move when she decided
to take an unpaid sabbatical from the lycée system to work in a factory. She moved out of her parents' spacious apartment and rented
a tiny maid's room, vowing to live exclusively on what she earned on
the grueling assembly line. As was often the case with Simone, she
took her pledge to the extreme. When she visited her mother and
father for Sunday supper, she left what she estimated to be the cost
for her meal on their dining room table. The gesture irritated her
parents, who, though they supported her, could never quite understand or accept their daughter's radical choices.

Taken Possession

Although her parents were Alsatian Jews who had moved to Paris
after Germany's annexation of Alsace-Lorraine, they were also self-
proclaimed atheists. As a result, Simone was raised in a nonreligious
household. Simone later claimed her year in the French factories as
one of the most pivotal in her life, not only because of the political
lessons she drew from her months on the assembly line, but also
because of the impact of the experience on her spiritual life. It
was during this time that the first subtle references to her personal
spiritual transformation began to emerge in her writing. She wrote
that during those months in the factory, she felt that she had "no
right to anything, that every moment of suffering and humiliation
must be received as grace."[5] Later, she described the experience to
her spiritual mentor, the Dominican priest Father Joseph-Marie
Perrin, this way: "Until then . . . I knew quite well that there was a
great deal of affliction in the world, I was obsessed with the idea,
but I had not had prolonged and firsthand experience of it. As I
worked in the factory . . . the affliction of others entered into my
flesh and my soul."[6]

Shortly after her year of factory work, Simone experienced her first
real moment of conversion. While vacationing with her parents in

Portugal, she watched a candlelight religious procession in the town square of the small fishing village. As she listened to the fishermen and their wives sing "ancient hymns of heart-rending sadness," she was suddenly gripped by the conviction that "Christianity is preeminently the religion of slaves, that slaves cannot help belonging to it, and I among others."[7] Unsure of what to do with this epiphany, she kept the knowledge to herself.

Two years later, in 1937, Simone experienced a second conversion moment while visiting the Chapel of Santa Maria degli Angeli in Assisi, where Saint Francis used to pray. Years later, she described the experience to Father Perrin, noting, "something stronger than I was compelled me for the first time in my life to go down on my knees."[8] Again, though, at the time it happened she largely kept quiet about the experience, unwilling to admit to others, and perhaps to herself, that she was moving toward a commitment to Christianity.

Finally, a year later, while meditating on a poem by the sixteenth-century poet George Herbert, she was struck once and for all by the magnitude of Christ's love. As she repeated the memorized stanzas to herself, Simone reported later, "Christ himself came down and took possession of me."[9] While she would never completely abandon her political and philosophical writing, this was the moment that prompted Simone to turn her full attention to theology.

Heretic or Theologian?

Simone later acknowledged that she believed she had been a Christian from the start. "I always adopted the Christian attitude as the only possible one," she wrote in her posthumously published collection of essays, *Waiting for God*. "I might say that I was born, I grew up and I always remained within the Christian inspiration. . . . From my earliest childhood I always had also the Christian idea of love for one's neighbor, to which I gave the name of justice."[10] While she may have "adopted a Christian attitude" and "remained within the Christian inspiration," Simone was not technically a Christian, at least by the church's definition, because she refused to be baptized

305

and resisted much of the Roman Catholic Church's doctrine. As biographer Stephen Plant observes, "Weil's understanding of God and what it means to live within the 'Christian inspiration' diverged greatly from what was acceptable to a priest like Perrin."[11]

In addition to refusing baptism, Simone also expressed little concern for salvation. At one point she even declared, "The Cross alone suffices. If the Gospel totally omitted any reference to Christ's resurrection, faith would be far easier for me."[12] Biographer Francine Du Plessix Gray wryly notes that perhaps the concept of the resurrection was too joyful for Simone, who led the life of an ascetic and avoided pleasure at all costs. In addition, Simone could not accept the church's history of excommunicating those whose theology did not align perfectly with its doctrine. "I love God, Christ and the Catholic faith as much as it is possible for so miserably inadequate a creature to love them," she wrote to Perrin. "I love the Saints through their writings. . . . I love the Catholic liturgy, hymns, architecture, rites and ceremonies. But I have not the slightest love for the Church in the strict sense of the word."[13] She was, in a word, uncompromising in her view of the church.

At one point Simone detailed her issues with the church in a thirty-two-page letter to another priest and confidant, Father Couturier. She argued that divine revelation was not limited to Christianity but rather was embodied in a great many other world religions practiced in India, Babylonia, Greece, Egypt, Druid civilizations, and China, long before the advent of Christianity. One notable exception in her list of religions was Judaism. Perhaps biased by her Jewish atheist parents, Simone wrote very critically of the religion of her ancestors. So critically, in fact, many scholars have accused her of anti-Semitism. "I have never been able to understand how it is possible for a reasonable mind to look on the Jehovah of the Bible and the Father who is invoked in the Gospel as one and the same being," she wrote. "The influence of the Old Testament and of the Roman Empire, whose tradition was continued by the Papacy, are to my mind the two essential sources of the corruption of Christianity."[14] Statements such as this one guaranteed that Simone would never be allowed as an official member of the Catholic Church, and it's not a surprise that on more than one occasion she was labeled a heretic.

The fact is, this "spiritual freelancer," as Gray calls Simone, wove together threads from a multitude of diverse cultures in order to come to an understanding of God that, while suitable to her, was very much outside the norms of church doctrine. As Gray notes, just as a wide variety of thinkers influenced Simone's philosophy, from Plato and Descartes to Spinoza, Pascal, and Kant, her understanding of God and religion cannot be traced to a single source.

Why then, one might ask, is Simone Weil so important to include in a compilation of Christian women? After all, she wasn't officially a Christian, at least as sanctioned by the Roman Catholic Church. Yet Simone Weil gives us much to ponder. Her questions and statements may startle, they may cause unease, but they also dig deeply into issues of social, ethical, and spiritual importance—issues that are as critical today as they were in the early part of the twentieth century. As biographer Stephen Plant so succinctly states, "Weil belongs to those Christian thinkers who leave aside peripheral issues and take us instead to the few most important questions about God and about life."[15] To dismiss Simone Weil's ideas because they make us uncomfortable, or because they don't fit neatly into our own definition of Christianity, would be a disservice not only to her but to ourselves as well.

44

Mother Teresa

A Pencil in God's Hand

(1910 – 1997)

She sat hunched on the edge of the bed, bending low over the emaciated figure, murmuring softly and gazing into his half-closed eyes as her gnarled fingers worked the rosary beads. The man was days from death. She'd discovered him lying half naked in the gutter, delirious with fever, his face gaunt, lips cracked, eyes glazed with pain. She had brought him back to the Missionaries of Charity, like she had hundreds of other outcasts, where he could die with dignity.

Beginnings

At age eighteen, Agnes Gonxha Bojaxhiu announced to her mother that she intended to join the Sisters of Our Lady of Loreto to serve as a missionary in India. Initially her mother refused consent, but when it became clear that Agnes would not relent, her mother retreated to her bedroom, shutting the door behind her. When she emerged twenty-four hours later, she offered Agnes her blessing with these words: "Put your hand in His—in His hand—and walk all the way with Him."[1] On December 1, 1928, Agnes set sail for India under her new name: Sister Mary Teresa. She never saw her mother again.

Because of her reluctance to talk with reporters or even her official biographers about her youth (she preferred instead to focus solely on her mission to serve the poor), we know little about Mother Teresa's early years in Albania. We do know that the years of her childhood were rife with political turbulence as Albania struggled for independence from Serbia. Her father, a successful merchant and entrepreneur, was committed to Albanian nationalism, a position that his family believed contributed to his sudden death (they suspected poisoning) as he was returning home from a political convention.

Agnes was only eight years old when her father died. "Home," she would state later, "is where the mother is." Her mother often opened the Bojaxhiu home to people in need of food and shelter, and Mother Teresa remembered her mother's response to her brother's question about the strangers who shared their table: "Some of them are our relations, but all of them are our people."[2]

Patience and Persistence

Sister Teresa, as she was called in the early years of her ministry, began her service in the Calcutta convent as a geography teacher before becoming headmistress in 1937. She spent nineteen years as a Loreto nun, rarely venturing outside the convent walls, aside from an annual retreat to Darjeeling. It was en route to this retreat, on September 10, 1946, that Sister Teresa, then thirty-six years old, experienced what she came to refer to as "the call within a call." Settled into her seat while traveling the four hundred miles from Calcutta to the foothills of the Himalayas, she experienced a clear mystical encounter with Jesus. "It was in that train, I heard the call to give up all and follow Him into the slums—to serve Him in the poorest of the poor," she said later. "I knew it was His will and that I had to follow Him. There was no doubt that it was going to be His work."[3] On the Missionaries of Charity's entrance registrar, the record of all who join the congregation, Mother Teresa later noted under her own name: "Entrance into the Society—10 September 1946." She celebrated September 10 as "Inspiration Day," the official start of the Missionaries of Charity, for the rest of her life.[4]

Simply hearing the call, of course, didn't necessarily entail that it would automatically and immediately come to fruition. In fact, Mother Teresa waited nearly two years to the day before she was granted permission from Rome to leave Loreto and launch her new mission. And she did not always wait patiently during those long months. She wrote numerous letters to her mentor and spiritual director, Father Van Exem, to Archbishop Périer, and to the cardinal prefect of the Sacred Congregation of Religious Rome, detailing the specificities of her call and her plan for putting it into action. She was not beneath outright begging, but time and time again her pleas were answered the same way: she was told to wait. "I told her she had to live only in the present and not at all in the future and be the perfect Nun," Father Van Exem wrote to Archbishop Périer.[5]

Mother Teresa struggled to obey both her superiors and Jesus himself. While she sought to put the calling out of her mind, she also wrestled with the fear that in doing so, she was disregarding Jesus' clear calling for her life. She simply could not suppress the desire to fulfill his command, despite the fact that she was fully aware this calling should unfold in his time. She was determined yet impatient. "Like the woman in the Gospel here I come again—to beg you to let me go," she wrote again to the archbishop. "Forgive me if I tire you with so many letters, forgive this child of yours—who is longing with many desires to give up all to God, to give herself in absolute Poverty to Christ in His suffering poor. . . . Please, Your Grace, do let me go soon."[6] Later, after only approval from Rome remained, she wrote this to Archbishop Périer:

Don't you think it is time for us to make a more fervent appeal to Rome? It is nearly four months that you sent my letter—Why are they not answering? Please, Your Grace, let us make a stronger appeal to Rome, for I must go—and go quickly. . . . Souls are being lost in the slums and in the streets, the Sacred Heart of Jesus is more and more suffering—and here I am waiting—for just only one "Yes" which the Holy Father I am sure would give, if he knew of it.[7]

Finally, on August 8, 1948, Mother Teresa received the news from Rome: Pope Pius XII had granted her permission to leave Loreto and begin her new mission to serve the poorest of the poor. Nine days after receiving the letter, Mother Teresa walked out of the convent toward the Calcutta slums. She wore a simple white sari and carried five rupees in her pocket.

"I Have Come to Love the Darkness"

One would assume that serving the poorest of the poor in the slums of Calcutta would be the most arduous and challenging work of Mother Teresa's life, but we know from her letters, which were published after her death, that this was not the case. We know now that Mother Teresa faced a far graver struggle during the second half of her life as she battled the demons of doubt and an unrelenting estrangement from God. She described this personal turmoil as a "terrible darkness," a "terrible emptiness," and a "feeling of absence of God." She wrote often about this pain to the archbishop and to her spiritual mentors, begging for their prayers and guidance.

At one point, at the suggestion of her spiritual director, Mother Teresa wrote a letter to Jesus himself:

In my soul I feel just that terrible pain of loss—of God not wanting me—of God not being God—of God not really existing (Jesus, please forgive my blasphemies—I have been told to write everything). . . . In my heart this is not faith—not light—not trust—there is so much pain—the pain of longing, the pain of not being wanted. . . . I want

311

God with all the powers of my soul—and yet there between us—there is a terrible separation.[8]

Even in the midst of complete darkness and seeming hopelessness, Mother Teresa gave herself fully to God. In that same intimate letter to Jesus, she pleaded with him to do as he wished. "Don't mind my feelings—Don't mind even, my pain," she wrote. "If my separation from You—brings others to You and in their love and company You find joy and pleasure—why Jesus, I am willing with all my heart to suffer all that I suffer—not only now—but for all eternity."[9]

This letter and the many she wrote to her spiritual directors exemplify the extraordinary depth of Mother Teresa's faith. Those who worked with her, knew her personally, or even connected only briefly with her always commented on her persistent joy, her gentle demeanor, and her beaming smile. The irony is that she was not pretending to feel this joy—it was genuine, a flame fanned by her connection with the most destitute of India.

Instead of stifling her missionary zeal, Mother Teresa's desperate inner struggles increased her compassion and fueled her dedication to India's poor. She endeavored to shine the light of Jesus' love into their existence. The poor gave her something as well, as she explained in a 1961 letter to friend and spiritual mentor Father Joseph Neuner: "When outside—in the work—or meeting people—there is a presence—of somebody living very close—in me. I don't know what this is—but very often even every day—that love in me for God grows more real."[10] This correspondence marked a dramatic turning point for Mother Teresa as she began to understand her darkness as a gift that allowed her to share very personally and intimately in Christ's suffering. "For the first time in 11 years—I have come to love the darkness," she wrote to Father Neuner. "For I believe now that it is a part, a very, very small part of Jesus' darkness and pain on earth. . . . Today really I feel a deep joy—that Jesus can't go anymore through the agony—but that He wants to go through it in me."[11] The darkness did not diminish, but Mother Teresa eventually felt a peace, an answer, that carried her through to the end of her life.

The Small Things

Mother Teresa's ministry was not without controversy. Her critics accused her of applying a Band-Aid to a cancer, of being naive about the root causes of poverty, and of not being political or radical enough. "Mother Teresa takes care of the poorest of the poor but never deals with why they are poor," said a Catholic charities official in a newspaper article. "She deals only with the disease [of poverty] and not with preventing it," said another aid worker.[12] Yet her intention from the start was to demonstrate compassion one person at a time. It wasn't that she didn't think globally; she simply chose to act deliberately in small ways and with small gestures: a cool cloth on a feverish forehead, a murmured prayer, a warm smile and comforting hand. This is the very reason she chose the name Mary Teresa, emphasizing that she strove to emulate Thérèse of Lisieux, who had praised the way to holiness through small acts, rather than the more dramatic Teresa of Ávila. "There are many people who can do big things," she said, "but there are few people who will do the small things."[13]

Mother Teresa told the story of a dying man half eaten by worms who was picked up from the gutter and brought to the Home for the Dying in Kalighat. "I have lived like an animal in the street, but I am going to die as an angel, loved and cared for," the man told the nuns who cleaned his ravaged body. Mother Teresa didn't need to know how the man had ended up destitute on the street. She didn't need to know how or why he had been abandoned. She was concerned with only one small thing: to offer the dying man dignity and peace. After the nuns had removed the worms from his body, Mother Teresa reported that the man smiled broadly before making a final declaration: "Sister, I'm going home to God," and he died.[14]

Although she dedicated forty years of her life to the Missionaries of Charity and saved thousands from destitution in the streets of Calcutta and around the globe, Mother Teresa always maintained that the work was God's alone—she was simply his instrument. "I don't claim anything of the work. It's His work," she said in a 1989 interview for *Time* magazine. "I'm like a little pencil in His hand. That's all. He does the thinking. He does the writing. The pencil has nothing to do [with] it. The pencil has only to be allowed to be used."[15] She died on September 5, 1997, fulfilling the parting words her mother had offered nearly seventy years earlier. Through thick darkness, loneliness, and despair, against nearly insurmountable challenges, Mother Teresa had kept her hand firmly in God's and walked all the way with him.[16]

45

Mahalia Jackson

Queen of Gospel

(1911−1972)

She followed her aunt to the segregated coach, her heavy, rope-tied suitcase bumping against her knees as she made her way down the narrow aisle. Sliding into the worn seat, the stench from the engine thick in the air, she tried to make herself comfortable for the three-day journey that lay ahead. The women curled up close to each other during the night, covering themselves with the woolen throw they had packed for the unheated car. Because the dining car was off-limits to blacks, the two women ate sandwiches, homemade pie, and fruit from the basket they had brought for the trip.

The girl stared out the window as the Illinois Central emerged from the prairie into the predawn gray of the city. With her suitcase in her hand and almost one hundred dollars pinned to her bra—money she'd scrimped from her work as a laundress in New

Orleans—sixteen-year-old Mahalia Jackson stepped foot onto the streets of the South Side of Chicago.

The Voice Heard to the End of the Block

Mahalia Jackson was born in 1911, the third of six children. She lived with thirteen family members in a New Orleans "shotgun shack," a tiny house with just four rooms lined up in a row, one after the other. Her father worked as a dockman, hauling bales of cotton on and off barges on the riverfront. After supper he earned a few extra dollars as a barber, and on Sundays he preached at the local Baptist church. As a child Mahalia often gathered spare sticks from the riverbank, which she carried back to the house on her head, to be used for cooking and as firewood during the winter.

When her mother died, her father sent five-year-old Mahalia and her ten-year-old brother, William, to live with her aunt Duke. After school she scrubbed cypress-wood floors with lye, stuffed mattresses with corn husks and Spanish moss, and wove chair seats from sugarcane and palm fronds. When she was in the eighth grade she also found additional work as a laundress, which allowed her to save a bit of extra money.

The center of Mahalia's universe was her family and the Mount Moriah Baptist Church, where she sang Wednesday and Friday evenings and four times on Sundays. Even as a young child Mahalia knew she possessed a special gift—an uncommonly powerful voice that could be heard outside the church and all the way to the end of the block.

Music was woven into her everyday existence in New Orleans. Mahalia especially remembered the jubilant funeral processions that took place weekly on the city streets. "After the burial, the band would strike up these religious songs, and the people from all over the city would meet at the cemetery and return, dancing in the streets to 'When the Saints Go Marching In,'" Mahalia recalled to her biographer, Jules Schwerin. "So that's how a lot of our songs that I sing today has that type of beat, because it's my inheritance, things that I've always been doing, born and raised-up and seen, that went on in New Orleans."[1]

Singing for Fish and Bread

When she was just off the train in Chicago, one of Mahalia's first goals was to find a church. She joined the Greater Salem Baptist Church and soon began to tour with the Johnson Singers, Chicago's first professional gospel group. They sang in neighborhood churches for as little as $1.50 a night, money that came from the distribution plate that was passed around after the concert. She referred to herself as a "fish and bread singer" and often stayed at the minister's house after her evening performance. She'd eat supper in his kitchen while he divided up the night's earnings, minus her room and board.

To make ends meet, Mahalia earned an additional twelve dollars a week as a chambermaid in a local rooming house. Later she opened her own beauty parlor, which she expanded into a profitable florist business. She combined her singing services with her flower sales, convincing mourners who insisted she sing at the funerals of their loved ones to buy flower arrangements from her shop as well.

By 1938 Mahalia was married, had made her first recordings with Decca Records, and was traveling around the Midwest and Northeast, singing to increasingly large audiences. A number of influential figures, including her husband, Ike, tried to convince her to broaden her repertoire to include blues, theater, and other secular genres, but Mahalia refused. She vowed to sing only gospel, which she called "the staff of life" and the means by which she communicated with God. "Sometimes you feel like you're so far from God, and then you know those deep songs have special meaning," she explained to her biographer. "They bring back the communication between yourself and God."[2] Her refusal to acquiesce eventually led to her divorce. "We came apart over gospel singing," she said.[3] She later married a widower but divorced him as well in 1967.

'Buked and Scorned

As Louis "Studs" Terkel, a popular Chicago DJ, browsed in a Michigan Boulevard record store one day, he heard the recording of an unfamiliar but powerful voice singing a gospel number entitled "I'm Goin' to Tell God about It One of These Days." Intrigued, Terkel tracked down Mahalia and watched her perform in the Baptist churches around Chicago. "Watching her in a church . . . her relationship to the congregation was something to experience," Terkel said. "You didn't forget—the call and response, the give and take; she didn't sing with her voice alone; it's the body, the hands, the feet."[4] Terkel invited Mahalia into his studio for a live interview and continued to play her only recording at the time—the song he'd heard in the Michigan Boulevard record store—again and again, introducing her voice to the world beyond the black church community.

In 1948, Mahalia recorded "Move On Up a Little Higher" for Apollo Records, which sold millions of copies and became the highest-selling gospel single in history. After that, Mahalia was in great demand, making frequent radio and television appearances and eventually performing at Carnegie Hall in 1950 to a racially segregated audience. By 1954 she had her own gospel program on CBS television. She began to tour extensively, earning up to a thousand dollars for a single concert. Because she'd been cheated one too many times, she insisted on payment in cash before the end of each performance, slipping the wad of bills into her bra before returning to the stage for her final numbers.

Although white audiences responded enthusiastically to her concerts and television appearances, Mahalia faced racism and segregation at every turn, particularly when she toured in the South. Restaurants would not serve her, gas stations would not fill her lavender Cadillac, and restrooms were never available. While on the road, she often slept in her car. "To find a place to eat and sleep in a colored neighborhood meant losing so much time," she recalled.[5] Even in her hometown of Chicago she was not immune to racial threats. After she purchased a single-level house in a predominantly white neighborhood in Chicago's South Side, her living room windows were hit with air-rifle pellets.

Mahalia made her debut on *The Ed Sullivan Show* in 1956, and in 1958 she performed with Duke Ellington and his band at the Newport Jazz Festival. The two released an album together the same year under Columbia Records entitled *Black, Brown and Beige*. By the end of the decade she had achieved international fame, with a performance schedule that included singing at President John F. Kennedy's inauguration.

Mahalia's fame and her personal struggle with racism made her a natural advocate for the civil rights movement. As early as 1956, civil rights leaders called on her to lend both her powerful voice and financial support to the rallies, marches, and demonstrations, and by the early 1960s, gospel music and spirituals had become the soundtrack to the civil rights movement, with Mahalia Jackson at the forefront. She was invited by Martin Luther King Jr. to sing in front of 250,000 protesters at the second march on Washington in 1963, the largest demonstration in the history of the nation. At King's request, she opened her set with "I've Been 'Buked and I've Been Scorned," one of her trademark songs. Just five years later, she sang at King's funeral and later recorded an album of his favorite songs, *The Best Loved Hymns of Dr. M. L. King*.

Well loved and respected though she was, Mahalia had a dark side too. She was known for her stubbornness, her fiery temper, and her stinginess, even long after she was earning a substantial salary. Her longtime pianist, Mildred Falls, who had accompanied Mahalia since the early 1950s, suffered the consequences. Mildred died in Chicago in the 1970s, penniless and rejected by the one person who should not have abandoned her. Abysmally underpaid by Mahalia for years, Mildred was dropped by the singer in favor of other accompanists when she complained about her low salary. "You couldn't talk to Mahalia about Mildred's situation," recalled John Sellers, a friend of the family. "When Mahalia had money, nobody could talk to her." She wouldn't accept criticism of her behavior from anyone—"not from Mildred, or me, or any of her husbands," John said. "She had the habit of sayin': 'I'm Mahalia Jackson, you hear?!'"[6] While Mahalia regularly earned between seven hundred and three thousand dollars a night, Mildred was paid two hundred dollars a week plus expenses. When Mildred requested an additional one hundred dollars a week, Mahalia fired her.

Making a Joyful Noise

In spite of near-constant enticement to expand her repertoire beyond gospel, Mahalia rarely strayed into secular genres. She enrolled in only one music class in her life, and when the instructor suggested she sing slower and sweeter to appeal to more white folks, she refused, walking out of the classroom and never returning for another lesson. Her style—dramatic, loud, and demonstrative—was her own, and she sang for one reason only: to "make a joyful noise unto the Lord." She chastised critics who considered gospel simple or lacking in artistry: "Some people are a little ashamed of gospel songs and folk songs, because it doesn't take a lot of long study, and they are simple songs of people's hearts. They think that if a song comes from the heart, then maybe it's too easy. Well, I don't agree with them! No one can hurt the gospel because the gospel is strong, like a two-headed sword is strong."[7]

The same could be said about Mahalia Jackson herself. Throughout her life she remained as strong as a two-headed sword—determined to make it on her own as a young girl living on the South Side of Chicago, determined to use her gifts for God, determined to sing about her Savior alone. Mahalia Jackson sang out her love for Jesus in a voice bold, vibrant, and strong. Nothing or no one—not poverty or racism, temptation or scorn—could quiet her joyful noise for the Lord.[8]

46

Edith Schaeffer

A Wonderful Paradox

$(1914-2013)$

She stuffed three of her father's books and a couple of other heavy objects into the pillowcase, slung the sack over her shoulder, and trudged up the stairs. At the top, she bowed solemnly before an imaginary cross and then, with great drama, flung the pillowcase out of her hands and watched it tumble with a ruckus down the stairs, where it landed in a heap at the bottom. The burden of sin had been rolled off! The two sisters cheered triumphantly before clomping down the stairs to reenact their favorite game, which they called "playing Pilgrim's Progress." Except to Edith Rachel Seville, playing Pilgrim's Progress wasn't a game. Even as a young child she longed for a real "Pilgrim's Progress moment"—an event she could point to with conviction as the moment of her transformation. "I wanted a before-and-after story," she later admitted in her autobiography.[1] The problem was, Edith couldn't remember a time when she had not believed the truth of the Bible. For as long as she could recall, she had always believed in, trusted, and loved her God.

Born to Be a Missionary

Edith Seville was born the fourth child of missionaries in Wenzhou, China. As a young girl she often "played church" with her Chinese playmates, which, like her reenactment of *Pilgrim's Progress*, she considered much more than a game. Edith felt responsible for conveying the gospel truth, and she carried out her mission with determination, insisting that her young friends pray with her and listen to her sermons. Still, she was aware of the challenges that lay before her. As she walked through town with her nursemaid, they often passed a pagoda along the Wenzhou city wall where the Chinese disposed of their newborn baby girls. The whimpers of the starving infants only fueled Edith's passion to evangelize. She was convinced that once the Chinese people knew Jesus, they would no longer throw away their baby daughters.

The Seville family returned to America for what they expected to be a yearlong furlough in 1919, but they were forced to stay when Edith's mother failed the medical examination that was required for their return to China. The family settled in Newburgh, New York, after her father accepted the call as pastor of the Westminster Independent Presbyterian Church. Although Edith was still convicted of the gospel truth, she worried that her attraction to fine clothing and the latest fashions made her too worldly. She felt that she didn't "measure up" as a "spiritual Christian," and she secretly wondered if the fact that she lacked a definitive and dramatic conversion moment indicated that she was somehow less than worthy or unworthy.

In the midst of this uncertain period, Edith attended a lecture by a leader in the Unitarian Church whose topic was entitled, "How I Know That Jesus Is Not the Son of God, and How I Know the Bible Is Not the Word of God." The more the man preached, the angrier Edith got, until finally she sat on the edge of the pew, poised to jump to her feet the moment the man finished. Just as she opened her mouth to launch into her argument, Edith heard a quiet voice from the other side of the church. A young man had risen to his feet, not to argue with the Unitarian preacher, but simply to state his own faith. "That," Edith's friend whispered into her ear, "is Fran Schaeffer."

The two dated for six months until, on New Year's Eve 1932, Fran broke up with Edith. "He had decided he was growing too fond of me, and that we'd better break up the relationship because probably the Lord wanted him to go where no woman could follow," wrote Edith years later. She added parenthetically, "I'm not sure just what he visualized that place to be like, nor where it might be; and nor does he!"[2] Two hours later, Fran called back. He was miserable; he couldn't live without her. The two were married three years later, a few weeks after Francis's college graduation.

Trusting through Fog

Not long after they were married, Francis entered the seminary, and when he stood on the platform to accept his diploma, Edith prayed the words she would pray throughout her entire life: "Please, Lord, give Fran a tongue of fire to preach your Word. Never let the fire cool off."[3] She considered praying for her husband while he preached to be her primary responsibility, and she prayed that his message would touch not only others but himself. "It was very, very possible and practical for me to continue no matter what, even if we had just had a 'fight' of some sort before he spoke . . . very possible and practical for me to 'sit under the word of God' really forgetting *anything* personal, to listen to what was coming forth, and to be thankful Fran was 'hearing this,' as well as to 'hear it' myself," she wrote in her autobiography *The Tapestry*.[4]

That said, as her son-in-law Udo Middelmann noted in his eulogy, Edith was "in no way . . . the typical pastor's or missionary wife." She supported her husband through three years of seminary by working as a seamstress, tailoring men's suits, sewing ball gowns and wedding dresses, and fashioning cowhide belts that were sold in high-end New York City boutiques. She also, as Middelmann noted, "turned her active mind to work with her husband . . . teaching seminary wives to think and to question, to create and make of life something of integrity, as her husband so wanted her to do."[5]

In 1948, when the Independent Board for Presbyterian Foreign Missions sent Francis, Edith, and their two young children to Europe, they never anticipated that a six-month trip would turn into the rest of their lives. Edith described that time as living in a fog, yet they persevered in trying to determine God's will. "I am impressed by the constantly repeated opportunity in life to trust the Lord in a fog," Edith wrote, "or to go from a secure place in what seems a sunny garden into a fog-covered path leading to the unknown!"[6]

Perseverance and trust continued to play key roles in the Schaeffers' missionary work overseas. When Edith and Francis were accused of exerting too much religious influence and were asked by the Swiss government to leave their post in Champéry, Switzerland, they did not forfeit their mission. While Edith struggled to reconcile this staggering blow with her understanding of God's will, she was also more determined than ever to trust God. "Rather than trying to get human help, we could simply ask God to help us," she suggested to her family at the time. "We have been saying that we want to have a greater reality of the supernatural power of God in our lives and in our work. It seems to me we are being given an opportunity right now to demonstrate God's power."[7] Edith, Francis, and their children (they had four now: Priscilla, Susan, Deborah, and Frank, who was two) knelt on the floor and prayed for guidance and direction. Two months later, an available chalet was found in the Alpine village of Huemoz, Switzerland. The Schaeffers made the down payment, and L'Abri was born.

A Spiritual Shelter

Francis and Edith founded L'Abri, which is the French word for "shelter," as a safe, comfortable place where questions could be asked and answers might be found. They saw their home as a spiritual shelter where people could come for help. Today the L'Abri International

Fellowship is comprised of multiple branches in eleven countries serving thousands of visitors each year. But back in May of 1955, L'Abri began with one questioning college student, a friend of the Schaeffers' oldest daughter, Priscilla.

When Priscilla telephoned her mother to ask if her friend, a young cosmopolitan girl brimming with questions about faith, spirituality, and life, could visit for the weekend, Edith hesitated. They'd been in the chalet only one month. The hot-water boiler was broken, the furnace wasn't working, and the wood stoves smoked terribly. "In other words," Edith admitted, "I felt things were too 'messy' to have a society girl who had been described as beautiful and impeccably dressed. Pride nearly brought a negative answer. Then—compassion and the realization that there might not be another weekend made me say, 'Of course, just explain our circumstances.'"[8]

That weekend, questions were discussed into the late hours of the evening as the family and a few college-age guests roasted hot dogs around the fire and read from the Bible by the light of an oil lantern. "Did we have a sense of having 'arrived'? No, a million times no," Edith said. In fact, according to her, she and Francis never felt like they had achieved their mission. They always lived moment to moment, "having things to be thankful for, things to rejoice about with excitement, things to regret and ask forgiveness for."[9]

L'Abri was conceived as an open Christian community where visitors, Christian and non-Christian, could stay as long as they wished, attend Francis's lectures—many of which were the basis for his subsequent books—and discuss life's ultimate questions with fellow seekers. There was only one rule: conversation should revolve around ideas rather than organizations or people. Discussion was not categorized by subject matter or discipline, so conversation meandered over many topics, including art, music, literature, science, philosophy, medicine, law, current events, and religions.

Word of L'Abri spread slowly, but by the 1960s guests numbered more than one hundred at a time. Edith was known for her Sunday afternoon high tea and for maintaining a seamless five-star-hotel level of comfort for their guests, but graceful hospitality was not her only claim to fame. In addition to her work at L'Abri, she also published seventeen books between 1969 and 2000, including her autobiography *The Tapestry*, as well as *What Is a Family?* and *The Hidden Art of Homemaking*, which have been influential in the Christian patriarchy and biblical womanhood movements.

In an essay published in the *Huffington Post* the day his mother died, Frank Schaeffer described Edith as "a wonderful paradox . . . an evangelical conservative fundamentalist who treated people as if she was an all-forgiving progressive liberal of the most tolerant variety."[10] Barry Hankins, professor of religion and history at Baylor University and author of the biography *Francis Schaeffer and the Shaping of Evangelical America*, described Edith similarly. "On one hand, she held a very traditional, biblical view about women's subservient role," Hankins said in Edith Schaeffer's *New York Times* obituary. "On the other . . . she embodied marriage equality. She would never use the term, of course, but in some ways she was the model of a sort of evangelical feminism."[11]

Edith Schaeffer made a tremendous contribution to Christian history as both an author and a founding partner of the L'Abri International Fellowship. Her perseverance amid hardship, her unwavering trust in God, and her personal faith leave the most lasting and inspiring impression. She was the first to admit that she and her husband never planned anything like L'Abri. Nor did they ever expect to write three dozen books between them or minister to thousands around the globe. She always claimed they took only one step at a time, asking God each step of the way for honesty and sincerity in desiring his will. Living one moment at a time, trusting God's will, and persevering to the best of her ability were the basic tenets of Edith Schaeffer's faith. She offered these guideposts, these spiritual stepping-stones, to the thousands who read her words and crossed the threshold of her Swiss chalet. And she continues to offer them to us as well.

47

Fannie Lou Hamer

A Political Activist Who Lived by Love

(1917–1977)

The group made their way through the angry crowd of gun-toting white men and snarling dogs. They sang "Go Tell It on the Mountain" and "This Little Light of Mine" to bolster their resolve as they walked up the stairs and through the doors of the courthouse. "What do you want?" snapped the clerk in the voter registration office, glancing disdainfully at the women and men lined up before him. "We're here to register," announced a woman standing at the front of the group.

Just days prior, the same woman had raised her hand in a meeting at her local church in Ruleville, Mississippi, to volunteer as one of eighteen African Americans who would travel twenty-six miles in a borrowed bus to the courthouse in Indianola. The woman was forty-four years old, wife of a sharecropper, and mother of two adopted daughters. She had been the first in the room to raise her hand; the others had followed her brave lead. Fannie Lou Hamer was determined to obtain the right to vote.

Years later, Fannie reflected on how dangerous her decision was. At the time—1962 in rural Mississippi—African Americans who attempted to register to vote typically faced serious threats, ranging from verbal harassment and the loss of their jobs to physical beatings and lynching. "I guess if I'd had any sense I'd a been a little scared," Fannie said later. "The only thing they could do to me was kill me and it seemed like they'd been trying to do that a little bit at a time ever since I could remember."[1]

Fannie Lou Hamer didn't actually register to vote that August day in 1962. She flunked the registrant's examination, which required that she read and interpret section 16 of the Mississippi state constitution, a section dealing with de facto laws. Registrars had the liberty to pick whichever constitutional passage they wanted for each test, which explains why whites easily passed and blacks rarely did. That day was the first time Fannie, who had a sixth-grade education, had ever laid eyes on her own state's constitution. As she put it, she knew "as much about [de] facto law, as a horse knows about Christmas Day."[2] But despite this initial failure, Fannie resolved to return to the courthouse as many times as it took until she passed the test.

Hate Was Not an Option

Fannie Lou Townsend was born the youngest of twenty children in Montgomery County, Mississippi. Her father, Jim, was a sharecropper who served as a minister and worked as a bootlegger on the side. Upon Fannie's arrival, her parents were paid fifty dollars by the plantation owner, a reward for producing another future field hand.

By age six, Fannie was working the fields, picking sixty pounds of cotton each week. By the time she was thirteen, she was able to pick between two and three hundred pounds of cotton a day. When the cotton crops didn't yield enough, the Townsends earned a living by "scrapping cotton," walking up to twenty miles a day in their bare feet to each plantation in the area to request leftovers from the landowners. Fannie's mother would have her family scrap the leftover cotton they acquired, picking the plant until it was clean. Sometimes they scrapped enough in a single day for a five-hundred-pound bale, which they would haul to the gin and turn in for cash.

Throughout her life Fannie reiterated the impact her mother had on her as a child. "She went through a lot of suffering to bring twenty of us up, but she still taught us to be decent and to respect ourselves, and that is one of the things that has kept me going," she said.[3] Fannie's faith was the other strong factor. Although she joined the Strangers Home Baptist Church at age twelve and was baptized in the Quiver River, much of what she learned about the Gospels she learned from her mother, who taught her children that hate was never an option. Even during her political activism days, after Fannie had been held for a week in jail and ruthlessly beaten by the guards, she refused to speak with malice against the perpetrators. "Ain't no such of a thing as I can hate and hope to see God's face," she said time and time again.[4]

"I Went There to Register for Myself"

Sometime in the 1940s (there were no marriage records for Southern blacks at the time, so the exact year is not known), Fannie married Perry (Pap) Hamer, and the couple moved to W. D. Marlow's plantation in Ruleville. The couple did not have children of their own but instead adopted and raised two girls who could not be cared for by their own families. In 1961 Fannie was the victim of a crime that made childbearing impossible: she was sterilized against her will. When she was admitted to the hospital to have a small abdominal cyst removed, she awoke from the surgery to learn she had been given a hysterectomy as well, a scenario that was not uncommon in the South during the 1930s through the 1960s.

Pap farmed and Fannie worked as the plantation timekeeper. She was responsible for maintaining employment records and recording the number of bales picked by each field hand and the amount of pay due to each worker. Fannie's sixth-grade education and her aptitude for both math and reading enabled her to land such a rare job and excel at it.

To make ends meet, especially during the winter, the Hamers also ran her late father's bootlegging liquor operation, and Fannie frequently did domestic chores in the owner's house for extra cash. Even that minimal financial stability came to an end, however, when Fannie boarded the bus bound for the courthouse in Indianola. Despite the fact that she wasn't actually able to register to vote, when she finally made it back to the plantation that night, Fannie was met by her enraged boss, who demanded that she withdraw her voter registration application or leave the farm. Fannie refused. "Mr. Dee, I didn't go down there to register for you," she declared. "I went there to register for myself."[5] After serving eighteen years as his loyal employee, Fannie fled the farm that night, forced to leave her husband and daughters behind.

Everywhere Fannie went, violence followed. Ten days after her eviction from the plantation, sixteen bullets were fired into the neighbor's home where Fannie was staying, fortunately not harming any of the inhabitants. That same night, shots were fired at the home of another woman who had attempted voter registration. Two young women in the house were gravely wounded, sustaining multiple gunshot wounds to the head, neck, legs, and arms.

Finally, after two months on the run, Fannie decided to return to Ruleville. She was not able to get her job back, and her husband had subsequently been fired by Marlow as well. Instead, she found new and unexpected employment as a local leader with the Student Nonviolent Coordinating Committee (better known as SNCC), the organization leading the voter registration campaign. Fannie's mission was clear: she was quickly becoming a well-known political activist.

A National Political Activist Is Born

It didn't take Fannie long to return to the Indianola courthouse. On December 4, 1962, she took the voter registration exam again, telling the clerk, "I'll be here every thirty days until I become a registered voter."[6] This time Fannie was prepared—she had studied the Mississippi constitution with the help of the SNCC volunteers—and she passed the test. Of course, when she went to vote the following August in a primary election, Fannie was informed she was ineligible because she had not paid the poll tax for two years—obviously because she had not been registered.

The SNCC officials recognized a leader in Fannie. As biographer Kay Mills notes, "Fannie Lou Hamer had a presence. She was smart. And as a poor black southern sharecropper, she represented the soul of the people whom the movement wanted to represent. . . . She had a personal story, which would only grow more compelling the more she endured. And she had a voice with which to tell it. Virtually everyone whose path crossed hers remembered first and foremost her singing and her speaking."[7]

However, her new role as a political activist was not without serious risks. On June 9, 1963, Fannie was on her way back from Charleston, South Carolina, with other activists from a literacy workshop when the group was arrested on a false charge and jailed in Winona, Mississippi. Fannie was beaten by the police, almost to the point of death. While in her cell, she overheard officers in the booking room plotting to kill the activists and dispose of their bodies in the nearby Big Black River. Fortunately, volunteers at the SNCC headquarters tracked down the missing activists and succeeded in getting them released from jail. It took Fannie more than a month to recover from her injuries. On December 2, an all-white jury found Montgomery County Sheriff Earle Patridge, Police Chief Thomas Herrod, and three other officers involved in the incident not guilty.

Fannie walked out of the Winona jail and away from the travesty of the trial more determined than ever to become a first-class citizen and make that right available to every African American person in America. In 1964 she helped found the Mississippi Freedom Democratic Party (MFDP), which challenged the legitimacy of Mississippi's all-white delegation to that year's Democratic convention. She appeared before the convention's credentials committee and told her story about trying to register to vote in Mississippi, a speech that was televised by most major news broadcasts, despite President Lyndon Johnson's attempts to preempt it with an impromptu press conference. That same year Fannie ran for Congress in Mississippi, to demonstrate to the people that a "Negro can run for office," she said.[8]

The MFDP was not successful in its bid for seats. In fact, when the Democratic Party suggested a compromise that would offer the MFDP two nonvoting seats in exchange for other concessions, the MFDP refused to concede. Fannie sharply rebuked Democrat senator Hubert Humphrey, who was running for vice president at the time, for suggesting the compromise:

> Do you mean to tell me that your position is more important than four hundred thousand black people's lives? Senator Humphrey, I been praying about you; and I been thinking about you, and you're a good man, and you know what's right. The trouble is, you're afraid to do what you know is right. You just want this job [as vice president], and I know a lot of people have lost their jobs, and God will take care of you, even if you lose this job. But Mr. Humphrey, if you take this job, you won't be worth anything. Mr. Humphrey, I'm going to pray for you again.[9]

After her bold challenge of Humphrey, Fannie was not asked to participate in future meetings.

Although the MFDP failed to win a seat at the Atlantic City Democratic National Convention in 1964, four years later in Chicago it was successful. Fannie Lou Hamer received a thunderous standing ovation when she became the first African American to take a seat as an official delegate at a national-party convention since the Reconstruction era following the Civil War. She was also the first woman ever from Mississippi to do so.

For more than fifteen years Fannie Lou Hamer worked tirelessly to pave the way for African Americans to vote, to run for political office, and to be treated, in her own words, as first-class citizens. However, despite the fact that she is best known today as a civil rights leader, her most lasting contribution might very well be her legacy of love.

Throughout her entire lifetime Fannie was a victim of the most pervasive, violent kind of hatred. This was a woman beaten nearly to death at the hands of white men; terrorized by her own neighbors; and relentlessly scorned, demeaned, threatened, and bullied. Yet because her love for her fellow humans was connected so closely with her faith, she never succumbed to hatred or bitterness. "You have to love 'em," Fannie told fellow civil rights activist Unita Blackwell the first time she met her.[10] Her statement wasn't empty political rhetoric but evidence of the way she lived out her faith in the face of daunting obstacles and enormous hardships. Whether confronting a belligerent voter registration official, lying bloody and beaten on the cold floor of a jail cell, or standing triumphant as a delegate before a national audience, Fannie Lou Hamer lived out love day by day.

48

Madeleine L'Engle

Writing toward the Why

$(1918-2007)$

Madeleine L'Engle quit writing on her fortieth birthday. When a publishing house rejected her book, she declared it "an obvious sign from heaven." In a dramatic gesture, she covered her typewriter in her study and then paced the room, sobbing. "The rejection on my fortieth birthday seemed an unmistakable command: Stop this foolishness and learn to make cherry pie," she wrote. The trouble was, while she walked in circles around the study weeping, she was also already busily working out a novel in her head about failure. Realizing that she was still "writing," Madeleine made a decision in that moment that would change the course of her life: "I uncovered the typewriter. In my journal I recorded this moment of decision, for that's what it was. I had to write. It was not up to me to say I would stop, because I could not. . . . If I never had another book published, and it was very clear to me that this was a real possibility, I still had to go on writing."[1]

Four years later, after it was rejected more than two dozen times, *A Wrinkle in Time* was finally published. The novel won the prestigious Newbery Medal in 1963, and as a result, Madeleine never had difficulty publishing again. She wrote more than sixty books over her lifetime, including works of fiction, nonfiction, and poetry.

Writing Responsibly

Madeleine's parents were married almost twenty years before their daughter was born in 1918. Her father, a drama and music critic for a New York City paper, and her mother, an accomplished pianist, were accustomed to enjoying an active social life, which they continued after the birth of their daughter, leaving Madeleine with a great deal of time on her hands to read and write alone in her bedroom.

School was torturous for young Madeleine. Neither the teachers nor her peers at her private girls' boarding school liked her. Ridiculed for her clumsiness in sports and deemed unintelligent by her teachers, Madeleine retreated into her own imagination. "As difficult as these experiences were at the time, their value lay in the effect they had in shaping L'Engle as a writer," biographer Donald Hettinga observes. "They forced her to develop a rich interior world, and they provided the material for a significant portion of her fiction."[2]

By the time Madeleine graduated from Smith College in 1941, she had written dozens of short stories and knew exactly what she wanted to do with her life. "I headed like a homing pigeon for New York," she wrote. "It was the place of my birth. It was where I would find music and art, theatre and publishing; it was where I belonged."[3] In New York City Madeleine also met her husband, Hugh Franklin, a successful stage actor who later became known for his role as Dr. Tyler on the soap opera *All My Children*. And it was in New York that Madeleine decided to drop her last name, Camp, in favor of her middle name, L'Engle, because she wanted to make it on her own without the influence of her father's name in publishing circles. It was a difficult decision for her. Her father had died in 1935, while Madeleine was in boarding school in South Carolina, and her mother suggested that in dropping the name Camp she was rejecting her father.

Death would become a frequent theme in Madeleine's work—so much, in fact, that some of her novels were initially rejected by publishers who claimed death played too prominent a role. "Publisher after publisher turned down *Meet the Austins* because it begins with a death," Madeleine acknowledged. "Publisher after publisher turned down *A Wrinkle in Time* because it deals too overtly with the problem of evil."[4] She insisted that her responsibility as a writer was to present reality accurately, and for her, reality included both the good and the bad, the beautiful and the ugly. "A writer who writes a story which has no response to what is going on in the world is not only copping out himself but helping others to be irresponsible, too," she wrote.[5] Even fantasy, she argued, serves as "a search for a deeper reality, for the truth that will make us more free."[6] For Madeleine, writing fantasy was a way for her to apprehend the mysteries of God. She claimed the young adult fantasy novel *A Wrinkle in Time* was a theological book because it was a metaphor for God's love.

Madeleine didn't always consider herself a person of faith. In fact, having abandoned religion in college, she admitted that she and her husband rarely darkened a church door during the early years of their marriage. But something changed with the birth of her two biological children and the adoption of a third. "We discovered that we did not want our children to grow up in a world which was centered on man to the exclusion of God," she wrote.[7] Realizing that bedtime prayers wouldn't suffice, and guiltily acknowledging that she couldn't very well send her children to Sunday school without participating in worship herself, she and Hugh began to attend a small church in the center of Goshen, the Connecticut village where they'd moved from New York City in 1951. "As long as I don't need to say any more than that I try to live as though I believe in God, I would very much like to come to your church—if you'll let me," she told the minister.[8] Not only did the minister agree to let the conflicted skeptic through the church doors, he also made Madeleine the choir director.

Reflections on Faith and Art

Writing and faith quickly became inextricably entwined for Madeleine, and over time she came to view writing as a form of prayer. "As I understand the gift of the spirit in art, so I understand prayer, and there is very little difference for me between praying and writing," she wrote in *The Irrational Season*. "At their best, both become completely unselfconscious activities."[9] She attempted to answer many of her questions related to the existence of suffering, grief, and evil through her fiction. "It's not easy for me to be a Christian, to believe twenty-four hours a day all that I want to believe," she admitted in *Walking on Water: Reflections on Faith and Art*. "I stray, and then my stories pull me back if I listen to them carefully."[10] As she quipped in *The Summer of the Great-Grandmother*, "If I 'believe' for two minutes once every month or so, I'm doing well."[11]

Madeleine resisted the label of "Christian writer," despite the fact that she wrote dozens of nonfiction books about spirituality and faith. She preferred instead to be considered a writer who is Christian. "I have often been asked if my Christianity affects my stories, and surely it is the other way around," she admitted. "My stories affect my Christianity, restore me, shake me by the scruff of the neck, and pull this straying sinner into an awed faith."[12]

Madeleine's fiction is not overtly Christian. She doesn't mention Jesus or God by name, and, in fact, some Christians have interpreted characters like Mrs. What, Mrs. Who, and Mrs. Which in *A Wrinkle in Time* as witches and accused her of blasphemy and heresy. She has also been criticized for referring to the Bible as story and has been labeled a New Age spiritualist for her assertion that God is present in all parts of creation. Madeleine herself claimed, "There can be no categories such as 'religious' art and 'secular' art, because all true art is incarnational, and therefore 'religious.'"[13] She believed her job as a writer was to draw people to the light of Christ, not by blatantly evangelizing or hitting them over the head with theology, or by "loudly discrediting what they believe, by telling them how wrong they are and how right we are, but by showing them a light that is so lovely that they will want with all their hearts to know the source of it." She had confidence that her art—her words—would do exactly that without any overt mention of God: "What we are is going to be visible in our art, no matter how secular (on the surface) the subject may be."[14]

Madeleine L'Engle has been most criticized for her broad and encompassing view of Christianity. She's been accused of universalism, a charge she denied in *Walking on Water*: "I don't mean to water down my Christianity into a vague kind of universalism, with Buddha and Mohammed all being more or less equal to Jesus—not at all! But neither do I want to tell God (or my friends) where he can and cannot be seen!"[15] She was the first to admit that she didn't have any of it figured out, but she also insisted that God is a God of love and a God who loves all.

In the end, she refused to limit God, preferring instead to celebrate the fact that so much of him cannot be defined or known. She chastised those who, because of fear and a need for control, attempt to define him in a particular way. Madeleine found not fear or unease but comfort and consolation in this unknowable, mysterious God. "The only God worth believing in is neither my pal in the house next door nor an old gentleman shut up cozily in a coffin where he can't hurt me," she asserted. "He is the *mysterium tremendens et fascinans*"[16]—literally, "the terrible mystery." A paradox, yes, but one that made sense to Madeleine.

As Donald Hettinga notes, Madeleine L'Engle's science fiction stories are her response to this God of mystery. "I'm never surprised when I discover that one of my favourite science fiction writers is Christian," L'Engle wrote in *Walking on Water*, "because to think about worlds in other galaxies, other modes of being, is a theological enterprise."[17] At their center, her books ask deeply profound questions: What is this universe like? Why is there so much suffering? What does it mean? And the most simple and complex of all questions: Why? Not only did she work through these questions in her published works, she also grappled with them privately, filling dozens of journals, which she called her "free psychiatrist's couch," over her lifetime.

338

Story as a Way of Living Life

Madeleine L'Engle believed in the power of questioning and the power of story. Over time and with persistent asking, she learned that it's more important to ask the right questions than it is to get watertight answers.[18] And story taught her that it is indeed possible to live through fear and thrive in spite of it. When she was a young child, her father's coughing and wheezing, the result of his mustard gas–burned lungs, was a constant reminder of war and its terror. Initially she wrote as a way to escape that fear, and then ultimately as a way to understand it. "Story was in no way an evasion of life, but a way of living life creatively instead of fearfully," she said. While she was the first to admit that she wrestled with doubt, she also acknowledged that story often transformed her from a place of fearful disbelief to a place of faith. "In trying to share what I believe, I am helped to discover what I do, in fact, believe, which is often more than I realize. I am given hope that I will remember how to walk across the water."[19] And in receiving the gift of Madeleine L'Engle's stories, we too are given that hope, the hope of remembering how to walk across water.

49

Ruth Bell Graham

Keep Looking Forward

(1920–2007)

By age twelve, Ruth Bell knew exactly what she wanted to do with her life. She dreamed of becoming a missionary—an unmarried missionary in Tibet, to be exact. The plan was not unrealistic. Born to medical missionaries and raised in Qingjiang, Jiangsu, China, Ruth was more than familiar with the rigors and dangers of missionary life. Her father was a surgeon and superintendent of the 170-bed Presbyterian Hospital, three hundred miles north of Shanghai. Her mother, in addition to her domestic duties, worked in the women's clinic. Ruth recalled many nights when she lay rigid in bed, listening to gunshots echoing just outside the compound's walls. It was a precarious existence in which death was a very real threat, yet in spite of the risks, Ruth was determined to dedicate her life to Christ as a foreign missionary, and an unmarried one at that. What she did not anticipate was that God had other, very different plans for her.

"I'll Do the Leading, and You'll Do the Following"

At age thirteen Ruth was sent from China to boarding school in North Korea, after which she returned to the United States and enrolled in Wheaton College in Chicago. It was there that Ruth met Billy Graham, whom she described in letters to her parents as a "real inspiration" and "a man of one purpose [that] controls his whole heart and life."[1] Ruth was immediately smitten, and the feeling was mutual. But there was a problem. While Ruth was still determined to follow her calling as a missionary, Billy was firm. He knew his calling was as an evangelistic minister, not a missionary. He drew the line in the sand: Ruth could choose him or missionary work—the decision was hers to work out with God.

Ruth grappled with her decision for several months. While she admitted to both Billy and herself that she loved him and could not imagine life without him, she could not quell the apprehension she felt about marrying him. At one point she wrote to her parents that she believed the relationship was "of the Lord," but at the same time she expressed her deepest concerns in her journal. "If I marry Bill I must marry him with my eyes open," she wrote. "He will be increasingly burdened for lost souls and increasingly active in the Lord's work. After the joy and satisfaction of knowing that I am his by rights—and his forever, I will slip into the background. . . . In short, be a lost life. Lost in Bill's."[2]

Ruth continued to waffle even after the official engagement was announced. When she returned to Wheaton in January 1942, Billy asked if she wished to give the ring back to him. She didn't, she admitted, but she also couldn't quite abandon the idea that she was meant to be a missionary. Billy, never one for subtleties, laid out the issue clearly for her, saying, "Listen, do you or do you not think the Lord brought us together?" Ruth could not argue with that; she knew God had ordained their partnership. Then the answer for Billy was simple: "I'll do the leading, and you'll do the following."[3] The decision was made. Ruth followed Billy, and from that moment on, she never looked back.

Nineteen months later, on August 13, 1943, Ruth Bell and Billy Graham were married before 250 guests at Montreat Presbyterian Church in North Carolina. Although she was always candid about the challenges of living in the public sphere as the wife of a world-famous evangelist, she never wrote or spoke with regret about her decision to abandon missionary work in favor of marrying Billy Graham. "Make the least of all that goes and the most of all that comes," she said more than once during her lifetime. "And keep looking forward. Don't look backwards."[4]

The Goodbyes Come Like a Small Death

Just a few days after their honeymoon, Ruth got a sneak peek at her future. Although she was ill with a high fever, Billy didn't cancel his previously scheduled preaching engagement. Instead, he checked his wife into the local hospital before leaving town and sent her a telegram and a box of candy from the road. This would be the first of many occasions that Ruth, who would come to be known as the "Revival Widow" by the press, would be relegated to second priority.

Not only did she wrestle with feelings of abandonment and loneliness while Billy was on the road, she also struggled to deal with her husband's increasing fame and the spotlight that was constantly fixed on her and their children. By 1954 the family was continuously hounded by the media and the public. Tourists would drive through their Montreat neighborhood, slow in front of the Grahams' house to snap pictures, and dash across the front yard in search of souvenirs— a twig, a stone, a splinter from the rustic gate. Fans lined up by the dozen for Billy's autograph at the airport and in restaurants. Ruth especially was scrutinized by the press, from her makeup to her clothing and jewelry to the brand of her shoes. "It's an odd kind of cross to bear," she reflected in her journal. "Yet those who have not been through it would consider it some kind of glory."[5]

Ruth never got used to the limelight, and she never enjoyed it. Often at her husband's crusades she would slip quietly into the crowd to find a seat in the back of the stadium or up high near the rafters. She was always eager to escape the fans and the flashbulbs and whenever possible would flee to her hotel room with her worn leather Bible in hand. She turned to the Bible and to her own writing for solace and would often pour her true feelings, anxieties, and sorrows into her journal. In fact, Ruth published more than a dozen books of her own, including several volumes of poetry, personal reflections, and stories for children. It's in these very personal accounts that Ruth reveals her heart:

> We live a time
> secure;
> sure
> It cannot last
> for long
> then
> the goodbyes come
> again again
> like a small death,
> the closing of a door.
> One learns to live
> with pain.
> One looks ahead,
> not back,
> . . . never back,
> only before.
> And joy will come again
> warm and secure,
> if only for the now,
> laughing,
> we endure.[6]

Although Ruth never intended her poems or personal reflections for publication, her writing is particularly valuable in that it allows us an intimate glimpse of her more pensive, vulnerable side. While these writings offer us insight into her ongoing struggles, they also illustrate how much Ruth relied on God, his Word, and prayer to carry her through the most troubling times. Her prayerful and meditative writing was also a powerful antidote against the pervasive loneliness and isolation. "Sometimes I wrote to capture a moment or reflect on a thought. Sometimes I wrote because I had to. It was write or develop an ulcer. I chose to write," she admitted.[7]

Billy was on the road more than six months out of the year, often for a month or longer at a time. Yet according to their five children, Ruth never displayed her loneliness or sorrow. Her oldest daughter, GiGi, speculated that maybe Ruth cried behind closed doors, but she never saw it. She remembers only the fact that her mother kept the children busy and never complained about their father's absence. Anne, the Grahams' secondborn, remembered always seeing her mother's bedroom light on, no matter how late at night. "She'd be studying her Bible," Anne recalled. "That's how Mother coped with Daddy's being gone so much."[8]

Ministering to the Individual

Ruth may have kept a low profile compared to her world-famous husband, but she ministered to many lost souls in her own right. When Ruth traveled with Billy during his early crusades, she often struggled to discern her role. During the 1954 London crusade, for instance, Ruth hung in the shadows, wanting to help but anxious and lacking confidence. Frustrated, she wrote in her journal, "I don't know where one single contact I have made over here has resulted in one single conversion to Christ."[9] As the years passed, though, Ruth gained confidence and began to discover her own niche in ministry. Unlike her husband, who preached to thousands, Ruth thrived in ministering to a single individual at a time. She didn't fear or shy from people's problems, no matter how ugly. Instead, she befriended the outcasts—drug addicts, criminals, and prisoners—and spent hours conversing with and counseling them.

Ruth visited one such criminal, Marvin King, who was imprisoned for second-degree murder in the state prison of southern Michigan. Although he struggled to forgive himself for his crime, he was comforted by her warmth and compassion. "Ruth was a woman God chose to use in keeping the candle of hope and love burning when fate had plunged me into the abyss of guilt and despair," he said later, after he'd been granted early parole.[10] She also befriended Carol, a twenty-year-old convicted murderer who was serving a sixty-year sentence in Raleigh's Correction Center for Women. "I had a lot of people that tried to get in the jail to see me, the more or less want-to-save-your-soul type people," Carol told Ruth's biographer, Patricia Cornwell. "I was hearing so much of how I was being damned and going to hell. But Ruth wasn't like that. She wasn't judgmental. She didn't try to push me."[11]

Likewise, Ruth refused to shun even the most scandalized celebrity. In 1994, when the televangelist Jim Bakker was released from prison, she invited him to sit with her in church the first Sunday he was out of jail, and she called the Asheville newspaper and warned them not to send a reporter to church.

Ruth fulfilled a similar role as trusted advisor and counselor for her husband, much to the irritation of some of his paid staff members. It was no secret that Ruth and her father, Dr. Bell, were the two people Billy sought first for personal, leadership, and business advice. He didn't necessarily heed their advice, but he listened. For instance, Ruth was adamantly opposed to Billy's involvement in politics, and she repeatedly made her opinions on the matter clear. At one point, as they dined with President Lyndon Johnson and Lady Bird Johnson at the Democratic convention in 1964, the president asked Billy for advice about who he should choose as his running mate. Before he could respond, Ruth kicked her husband under the table—to remind him, "You are supposed to limit your advice to moral and spiritual issues."[12]

Not Just Tibet, but Everywhere

Ruth Bell Graham was content to stand in the shadows and let her husband take the stage. Her primary job, and one she did exceedingly well, was to raise their five children, shield them from the glaring spotlight, and support her husband in his worldwide ministry. Despite her calm, steady, and consistent demeanor, we know from her candid personal reflections that Ruth struggled in this role throughout her entire life. She sacrificed much in marrying a world-famous evangelist—not only her dreams and ambitions of serving as a missionary in Tibet but also her privacy and desire for a normal family life.

Yet a closer look at her subtle but important role reveals an interesting insight. Perhaps Ruth did not stray as far from her original ambition as it might seem. As Cornwell noted, Ruth's life evolved in a way she could have never imagined back when she was a Wheaton student, but her priorities never wavered. Ruth Bell Graham ministered primarily to one, but in doing so she ministered to the world.

50

Flannery O'Connor

The Observer

(1925–1964)

As the new editor of her college newspaper, Flannery O'Connor made her intentions clear to her readers:

> Although the majority of you like the "my love has gone now I shall moan" type of work, we will give you none of it. Although the minority of you prefer consistent punctuation and a smack of literary pretension, we aren't going to worry about giving it to you. In short, we will write as we feel, preserving a modicum of orthodox English and making a small effort at keeping our originality out of our spelling. If you like what we do, that's very nice. If you don't please remember the paper drive when you dispose of your copy.[1]

Flannery O'Connor was brutally honest, both in her life and in her writing. Striving for and living the truth was the single focus of her short life, and she pursued it at all costs, without any regard to what people might think. She grounded her fiction in reality, portraying the visible world through intricate sensory detail. Yet at the same time, her work included an aura of mystery. "For her, reality did not lead to mystery; it included it," biographer Kathleen Feeley observed. "The unseen was as real to her as the visible universe."[2] As Flannery herself said, "The main concern of the fiction writer is with mystery as it is incarnated in human life."[3]

Imaginative, Tough, and Alive

Flannery O'Connor was born Mary Flannery O'Connor in Savannah, Georgia, the only child of Edward O'Connor, a real estate agent, and Regina Cline. As a young girl she was painfully shy, self-reliant but distant. She spent much of her time alone in her bedroom, drawing pictures of birds, particularly chickens. When she was assigned to write a story in school, she composed essays about chickens and ducks—so often, in fact, that her third grade teacher, Sister Mary Consolata, informed the young Flannery that she never wanted to read another essay about a chicken or a duck by the girl again.

When she was ten years old Flannery wrote a collection of vignettes entitled "My Relitives," which her adoring father had typed and bound. The satirical series of family profiles was so true to reality that most of the aunts, uncles, and cousins featured in it refused to recognize or acknowledge themselves in the story. No one was spared, her mother later told a journalist. Many years after, Flannery admitted to a friend that "My Relitives" had been written "in the naturalistic vein and was not well-received."[4]

Flannery attended Catholic elementary school, and after the family moved in 1938 to Milledgeville, Georgia, she continued her education at the Peabody Laboratory School, which was affiliated with the Georgia State College for Women (GSCW). Two years after the move, when Flannery was fifteen years old, her father succumbed to a mysterious and painful death from lupus at the age of forty-five. Flannery rarely spoke of her father after his death, but her journal, written during her first year of college, revealed a rare glimpse into the spiritual insights she gleaned from the loss. "A sense of the dramatic, of the tragic, of the infinite, has descended upon us, filling us with grief, but even above grief, wonder," she wrote. "Our plans were so beautifully laid out, ready to be carried to action, but with magnificent certainty God laid them aside and said, 'You have forgotten—mine?'"[5]

Flannery split her time between drawing cartoons and writing satirical poems, essays, and stories for the *Corinthian*, GSCW's newspaper. She graduated from the accelerated three-year program with a journalism scholarship to Iowa State University. Early in her first semester at Iowa, though, Flannery decided to change her major and enroll in the elite Iowa Writers' Workshop. When she knocked on director Paul Engle's office door and began to speak, her thick Georgian accent was so indecipherable to Engle's Midwestern ear that he was forced to ask that she write her request on a notepad. In neat script, her brief note read, "My name is Flannery O'Connor. I am not a journalist. Can I come to the Writers' Workshop?"[6] The next day, when Engle read her writing samples, he deemed them imaginative, tough, and alive, and Flannery was immediately admitted into Iowa's MFA graduate writing program.

During her second year in the workshop, Flannery began work on early drafts of her first novel, *Wise Blood*, which would be published seven years later in 1952. She went on to write a second novel published in 1960, *The Violent Bear It Away*, as well as dozens of short stories, including "A Good Man Is Hard to Find," which was published in a collection in 1955 and is arguably her most famous story.

Flannery O'Connor's literary career was cut short in 1964 when, at the age of thirty-nine, she died at a hospital near her family's Milledgeville home. A rare form of lupus, the same incurable autoimmune disease that had killed her father twenty-four years earlier, took Flannery's life as well.

"Leave Evangelizing to the Evangelists"

Much has been written about the influence of Roman Catholicism and Flannery's faith in general on her fiction, and she herself was vocal on the topic in speeches and interviews and in her own letters and essays. While a thread of dark comedy runs through her work, her stories and novels are overall a dismal and despairing look at humanity.

In "A Good Man Is Hard to Find," for instance, a family en route to their vacation in Florida is sidelined by a car accident and then brutally murdered by a psychopathic killer, called the Misfit, and his henchmen. The story's message was largely misunderstood. When Flannery read "A Good Man Is Hard to Find" aloud at a party, the audience's laughter abruptly turned to horrified silence when they realized the story was heading toward the cold-blooded murder of the parents, their three children, and the grandmother. Upon leaving the party, Mark Twain biographer Van Wyck Brooks mentioned that it was a shame someone so talented would view life as "a horror story."[7] Other reviewers described her fiction as "highly unladylike . . . brutal irony . . . slam bang humor . . . and as balefully direct as a death sentence."[8] By the time she had completed a book tour, Flannery remarked that she was relieved to return to her Georgia farm and "back to the chickens who don't know that I write."[9]

Flannery insisted it was her job as a writer to present concrete reality, no matter how harsh that reality was. "The sorry religious novel comes about when the writer supposes that because of his belief, he is somehow dispensed from the obligation to penetrate concrete reality," she wrote in the essay "Novelist and Believer." "He will think that the eyes of the Church or of the bible or of his particular theology have already done the seeing for him, and that his business is to rearrange this essential vision into satisfying patterns, getting himself as little dirty in the process as possible."[10]

She took her argument one step further when she claimed that fiction—and art in general—was enough in and of itself, simply because art is a reflection of God. "We are not content to stay within our limitations and make something that is simply a good in and by itself," Flannery observed in her essay "Catholic Novelists and Their Readers." "Now we want to make something that will have some utilitarian value. Yet what is good in itself glorifies God because it reflects God. The artist has his hands full and does his duty if he attends to his art. He can safely leave evangelizing to the evangelists."[11]

The religious novelist's intentions to present a sugarcoated truth may be good, acknowledged Flannery, but they are ultimately misguided. "We see people distorting their talents in the name of God for reasons that they think are good—to reform or to teach or to lead people to the Church," she wrote. But, she added, "The novelist who deliberately misuses his talent for some good purpose may be committing no sin, but he is certainly committing a grave inconsistency, for he is trying to reflect God with what amounts to a practical untruth." She also criticized the religious novelist for attempting to package his story into an instant answer. Fiction, she argued, doesn't have an instant answer. Instead, "It leaves us, like Job, with a renewed sense of mystery."[12]

Flannery O'Connor's novels and stories are full of brutal violence, but she insisted that the violence served a purpose. "In my own stories I have found that violence is strangely capable of returning my characters to reality and preparing them to accept their moment of grace," she wrote in *Mystery and Manners*.[13] Thus, in her story "A Good Man Is Hard to Find," the grandmother gradually becomes concerned with someone other than herself, and by the final scene, she pleads with the Misfit to save himself. "In a final moment of absolute reality, all pretense is over and vision fills the void: 'the grandmother's head cleared for an instant,' and her heart embraces the criminal in a moment of perfect charity," Feeley observes.[14]

A Full Measure of Splendor

Although she was a devout Catholic, Flannery's faith wasn't without challenge. "If you want your faith, you have to work for it," she wrote in a 1962 letter to Alfred Corn, a college student who had written to Flannery about his religious doubt. "You can't fit the Almighty into your intellectual categories." Yet she believed that the limits of her intellect ironically strengthened her faith in the end. A healthy Christian skepticism, she told Alfred, "will keep you free—not free

351

to do anything you please but free to be formed by something larger than your own intellect or the intellects around you."[15]

"There are many theological implications in [Flannery's] writing," noted her friend and fellow Southern writer Caroline Gordon, "but they lie so far beneath the surface of the literal level that they do not obtrude themselves on our consciousnesses on a first, sometimes even a second reading."[16] Flannery O'Connor risked misunderstanding and misinterpretation for the sake of art and truth. She once quipped that she'd wait fifty, even one hundred years to have one of her stories read right, and she was even willing to risk that the typical reader might never fully and accurately comprehend her work.

"The novelist is required to open his eyes on the world around him and look," Flannery stated. "If what he sees is not highly edifying, he is still required to look. Then he is required to reproduce, with words, what he sees." And if what he sees is horror, what should the writer do? she asked. "Is he to change what he sees and make it, instead of what it is, what in the light of faith he thinks it ought to be? Is he . . . supposed to 'tidy up reality'?"[17] Her answer was an emphatic no.

As a Southern white woman writing during the pre–civil rights era, Flannery also depicted race relations without sugarcoating the truth, yet more often than not, blacks were minor characters in the background of most of her stories. Flannery admitted that she didn't understand her black characters the way she did her white characters. "I don't feel capable of entering the mind of a Negro," she told a student interviewer at the College of Saint Teresa in Minnesota. "In my stories they're seen from the outside."[18] Flannery's resistance to inhabiting the minds of black characters suggests one of two possibilities: that she felt an uneasy distance from an African American experience that bordered on racism, or, as writer Alice Walker suspects, Flannery respectfully resisted characterizing the consciousness of an oppression she could not possibly comprehend. Since Flannery created such deft characterizations of white perceptions of blackness, Walker's generous interpretation appears to be the most plausible.

Her job as a fiction writer, Flannery insisted, was as "an observer, first, last and always,"[19] and what she observed was a violent humanity in all its crushing reality. Her stories evoke terror. They elicit shock and horror. Some would argue that they are extreme, even excessive. Yet beneath those often brutal, raw, and grotesque observations lie themes of grace and redemption as well. "Only art could make such fiction beautiful; only reality could sustain such intense art," Feeley concludes. "Only an artist penetrated with Christianity could use such extreme means to evoke from reality its full measure of splendor."[20] Flannery O'Connor puts the burden on us, her readers. She doesn't tidy up reality; she doesn't make it easy on us. The full measure of splendor is there, it's available, and it's real. But it's up to us to open our eyes and our minds to see it.[21]

Afterword

*G*o forth without fear."
        Back in the fourteenth century when Catherine of Siena heard these words directly from God, she answered. She stepped onto a path rarely traveled by women in her time, and she embraced her God-given role as a powerful and influential political envoy.

But take note: this command was not unique to Saint Catherine alone.

Every one of the fifty women featured in this book heard God's command, "Go forth without fear," and every one listened, obeyed, and answered yes. They may not have understood the words exactly as Catherine of Siena did, they may not have received them in such a clearly articulated vision, but they heard the command. And each and every one of these fifty women stepped forth and answered his call.

The stories of these women tell us that circumstances don't matter nearly as much as obedience itself, because God calls his daughters to answer right where they are.

For some, that meant stepping out of the comfortable, the familiar, and the routine into the unexpected, the frightening, the foreign, and the unknown.

Catherine Booth feared preaching more than anything else, yet when she heard the call to rise and walk from the pew to the pulpit, she answered.

Ida Scudder never intended to follow in her parents' footsteps as a missionary, yet when she heard God call her to serve as a doctor in India, she answered.

355

Mary McLeod Bethune felt unqualified to serve in President Roosevelt's administration, yet when God called her as a voice for African American people, she answered.

Dorothy Sayers considered religious writing a departure from her "proper job," yet when God called her to write theological plays and essays, she answered.

For others, God's call demanded that they answer and act exactly where they were.

Katharina Luther impacted and influenced Martin Luther's ministry in more ways than we'll ever know simply by working tirelessly behind the scenes as a wife, mother, and businesswoman.

Susanna Wesley ministered within her own home, nurturing and shaping her children, including two sons who made a lasting mark on Christian history.

Thérèse of Lisieux chose not grand, dramatic gestures but small, ordinary acts of devotion steeped deeply in love.

Corrie ten Boom never anticipated her ministry would be born amid the horrors of a concentration camp, yet that was exactly where God called her and her sister to share God's hope.

Obedience is the common thread that weaves these fifty women together across nine centuries, dozens of countries, and myriad callings as writers, speakers, abolitionists, educators, social workers, missionaries, activists, survivors, mothers, and wives. God called, and these fifty women boldly answered.

Friends, the call doesn't stop with these fifty women. God asks *us* to answer him as well.

God calls us to go forth without fear—into the unknown, into the unfamiliar. He calls us to go forth without fear, right where we are, with exactly what we have. God doesn't require perfect skills—we see from the women in this book that he uses even our deficits. God doesn't demand flawless character—we see from the women in this book that he uses us in spite of our weaknesses and our flaws. God doesn't expect immovable, unwavering faith—we see from the women in this book that he uses us even in the midst of doubt and despair.

Look hard at the women who have walked before us. None is perfect. None is flawless. All are human. But God used them to change the world. God placed them in situations unique to their gifts, talents, and temperaments—in prisons, classrooms, brothels, homes, churches, mission fields—and asked them to go forth without fear and in trust. And they answered yes.

So these are the two questions I leave with you at the close of this book.

Where is God calling you to go forth without fear?

And will you answer yes?

Notes

Chapter 1 Hildegard of Bingen

1. Hildegard of Bingen, quoted in Sabina Flanagan, *Hildegard of Bingen, 1098–1179: A Visionary Life* (New York: Routledge, 1989), 4.

2. Ibid.

3. Ibid.

4. Flanagan, *Hildegard of Bingen*, 45.

5. Hildegard of Bingen, quoted in ibid., 7.

6. For additional sources for Hildegard of Bingen, see Heinrich Schipperges, *Hildegard of Bingen: Healing and the Nature of the Cosmos* (Princeton: Marcus Wiener, 1997); and Gabriele Uhlein, *Meditations with Hildegard of Bingen* (Santa Fe: Bear, 1983).

Chapter 2 Saint Birgitta (Bridget) of Sweden

1. Julia Bolton Holloway, *Saint Bride and Her Book: Birgitta of Sweden's Revelations* (Cambridge, England: D. S. Brewer, 2000), 3.

2. Bridget Morris, *St. Birgitta of Sweden* (Woodbridge, England: Boydell Press, 1999), 41.

3. Ibid., 42.

4. Bridget of Sweden, quoted in Morris, *St. Birgitta of Sweden*, 62–63.

5. Ibid., 65.

6. Ibid., 93.

7. Morris, *St. Birgitta of Sweden*, 98.

8. Bridget of Sweden, quoted in ibid., 114.

9. Bridget of Sweden, quoted in Marguerite Tjader Harris, ed., *Birgitta of Sweden: Life and Selected Revelations* (Mahwah, NJ: Paulist Press, 1990), 11.

10. Bridget of Sweden, quoted in Morris, *St. Birgitta of Sweden*, 117.

11. Ibid., 12.

12. For additional sources for Saint Birgitta (Bridget) of Sweden, see Edith Deen, *Great Women of the Christian Faith* (New York: Harper and Brothers, 1959); and Carol Levin, Debra Barrett-Graves, Jo Eldridge Carney, W. M. Spellman, Gwynne Kennedy, and Stephanie Witham, eds., *Extraordinary Women of the Medieval and Renaissance World: A Biographical Dictionary* (Westport, CT: Greenwood Press, 2000).

Chapter 3 Julian of Norwich

1. Grace M. Jantzen, *Julian of Norwich: Mystic and Theologian* (London: SPCK, 1987), 33.
2. Rosemary Radford Ruether, *Visionary Women: Three Medieval Mystics* (Minneapolis, MN: Fortress Press, 2002), 43.
3. Julian of Norwich, quoted in Jantzen, *Julian of Norwich*, 75.
4. Ibid., 76.
5. Ibid., 80.
6. Ibid., 91.
7. Ibid., 180.
8. Ibid., 173.
9. Julian of Norwich, *The Revelations of Divine Love* (Grand Rapids: Christian Classics Ethereal Library), 144, http://www.ccel.org/ccel/julian/revelations.pdf.
10. For an additional source for Julian of Norwich, see Anniina Jokinen, "Julian of Norwich (1342–c. 1416)," Luminarium: Anthology of English Literature, April 9, 2010, http://www.luminarium.org/medlit/julian.htm.

Chapter 4 Catherine of Siena

1. Catherine of Siena, quoted in Sigrid Undset, *Catherine of Siena* (New York: Sheed and Ward, 1954), 33.
2. Ibid., 34.
3. Catherine of Siena, quoted in Edith Deen, *Great Women of the Christian Faith* (New York: Harper and Brothers, 1959), 54.
4. Catherine of Siena, quoted in Vida D. Scudder, ed. and trans., *Catherine of Siena: As Seen in Her Letters* (New York: E. P. Dutton, 1927), 121–22.
5. Catherine of Siena, quoted in Deen, *Great Women*, 57.
6. Ibid., 58.
7. Catherine of Siena, quoted in Undset, *Catherine of Siena*, 214.
8. Ibid., 215.
9. Ibid., 268.
10. For an additional source for Catherine of Siena, see Carole Levin, Debra Barrett-Graves, Jo Eldridge Carney, W. M. Spellman, Gwynne Kennedy, and Stephanie Witham, eds., *Extraordinary Women of the Medieval and Renaissance World: A Biographical Dictionary* (Westport, CT: Greenwood Press, 2000).

Chapter 5 Margery Kempe

1. Margery Kempe, *The Book of Margery Kempe*, ed. Lynn Stanley (New York: W. W. Norton, 2001), 8.
2. Louise Collins, *Memoirs of a Medieval Woman: The Life and Times of Margery Kempe* (New York: Harper and Row, 1964), 41.
3. Kempe, *Book of Margery Kempe*, 51–52.
4. Ibid., 50.
5. Ibid., 51.
6. Margery Kempe, quoted in Collins, *Memoirs*, 191.
7. Ibid., 93.
8. Kempe, *Book of Margery Kempe*, 157.
9. For additional sources for Margery Kempe, see Valentina Castagna, *Re-Reading Margery Kempe in the 21ˢᵗ Century* (Bern, Switzerland: Peter Lang AG, International Academic, 2011);

and Anniina Jokinen, "Margery Kemp (c. 1373–1438)," Luminarium: Anthology of English Literature, April 9, 2010, http://www.luminarium.org/medlit/margery.htm.

Chapter 6 Katharina Luther

1. Roland H. Bainton, *Women of the Reformation in Germany and Italy* (Minneapolis, MN: Augsburg, 1971), 23.
2. Ibid., 24.
3. Ibid., 26.
4. Ibid., 27.
5. Warren W. Wiersbe, *50 People Every Christian Should Know: Learning from Spiritual Giants of the Faith* (Grand Rapids: Baker Books, 2009), 11.
6. Katharina Luther, quoted in Bainton, *Women of the Reformation*, 38.
7. Martin Luther, quoted in Bainton, *Women of the Reformation*, 40.
8. Katharina Luther, quoted in Bainton, *Women of the Reformation*, 37.
9. Martin Luther, quoted in Bainton, *Women of the Reformation*, 27.

Chapter 7 Teresa of Ávila

1. Teresa of Ávila, quoted in Cathleen Medwick, *Teresa of Avila: The Progress of a Soul* (New York: Alfred A. Knopf, 1999), xii.
2. Medwick, *Teresa of Avila*, 20.
3. Teresa of Ávila, quoted in ibid., 20.
4. Theodore K. Rabb, *Renaissance Lives: Portraits of an Age* (New York: Pantheon Books, 1993), 99–100.
5. Teresa of Ávila, quoted in Rabb, *Renaissance Lives*, 101.
6. Ibid., 103.
7. Teresa of Ávila, quoted in Medwick, *Teresa of Avila*, 104.
8. For an additional source for Teresa of Ávila, see Megan Don, *Falling into the Arms of God: Meditations with Teresa of Avila* (Novato, CA: New World Library, 2005).

Chapter 8 Anne Askew

1. Elaine V. Beilin, ed., *The Examinations of Anne Askew* (New York: Oxford University Press, 1996), xv.
2. Anne Askew, quoted in Beilin, *Examinations*, 93.
3. Quoted in Beilin, *Examinations*, xxv.
4. Beilin, *Examinations*, xxiv.
5. Anne Askew, quoted in Beilin, *Examinations*, 103–4.
6. Ibid., 49.
7. Ibid., 30.
8. Ibid., 54.
9. Elaine V. Beilin, "A Woman for All Seasons: The Reinvention of Anne Askew," quoted in Pamela Joseph Benson and Victoria Kirkham, eds., *Strong Voices, Weak History: Early Women Writers and Canons in England, France, and Italy* (Ann Arbor: University of Michigan Press, 2005), 342.

Chapter 9 Anne Hutchinson

1. Winnifred King Rugg, *Unafraid: A Life of Anne Hutchinson* (Boston: Houghton Mifflin, 1930), 59.

2. Hugh Peter, quoted in Deborah Crawford, *Four Women in a Violent Time* (New York: Crown, 1970), 144–46.

3. Eve LaPlante, *American Jezebel: The Uncommon Life of Anne Hutchinson, the Woman Who Defied the Puritans* (New York: HarperCollins, 2004), 13.

4. Anne Hutchinson, quoted in ibid.

5. Anne Hutchinson, quoted in Rugg, *Unafraid*, 177.

6. Anne Hutchinson, quoted in LaPlante, *American Jezebel*, 120–21.

7. John Winthrop, quoted in LaPlante, *American Jezebel*, 125.

8. Thomas Dudley, quoted in LaPlante, *American Jezebel*, 126.

9. John Winthrop, quoted in LaPlante, *American Jezebel*, 244.

Chapter 10 Anne Bradstreet

1. Anne Bradstreet, quoted in Elizabeth Wade White, *Anne Bradstreet: The Tenth Muse* (New York: Oxford University Press, 1971), 120.

2. Anne Bradstreet, "Upon a Fit of Sickness," October 22, 2002, http://www.annebradstreet.com/upon_a_fit_of_sickness.htm.

3. Jeannine Hensley, ed., *The Works of Anne Bradstreet* (Cambridge, MA: Belknap Press, 1967), xiv.

4. Adrienne Rich, in foreword of Hensley, *Works*, xiv–xv.

5. White, *Anne Bradstreet*, 133.

6. Anne Bradstreet, quoted in Hensley, *Works*, 257.

7. Ibid., 292–93.

8. Ibid., 240.

9. Ibid., 243–44.

10. Ibid., 244.

11. Ibid.

12. White, *Anne Bradstreet*, 305.

13. Anne Bradstreet, quoted in Hensley, *Works*, 245.

Chapter 11 Margaret Fell

1. Margaret Fell, quoted in Isabel Ross, *Margaret Fell: Mother of Quakerism* (New York: Longmans, Green, 1949), 12.

2. George Fox, quoted in Bonnelyn Young Junze, *Margaret Fell and the Rise of Quakerism* (Stanford, CA: Stanford University Press, 1994), 126.

3. Margaret Fell, quoted in Ross, *Margaret Fell*, 128.

4. Ibid., 172–73.

5. Quoted in Ross, *Margaret Fell*, 173.

6. Margaret Fell, quoted in Ross, *Margaret Fell*, 173.

7. Ibid., 176.

8. Ibid., 22.

9. William Penn, quoted in Junze, *Margaret Fell*, 24.

10. Margaret Fell, quoted in Ross, *Margaret Fell*, 381.

Chapter 12 Susanna Wesley

1. Samuel Wesley, quoted in Rebecca Lamar Harmon, *Susanna: Mother of the Wesleys* (Nashville: Abingdon Press, 1968), 51.

2. Harmon, *Susanna*, 45.

3. Susanna Wesley, quoted in Harmon, *Susanna*, 45.

4. Samuel Wesley, quoted in Harmon, *Susanna*, 45.

5. Anne Adams, "Susanna Wesley: Mother of Methodism," History's Women: The Unsung Heroines, http://www.historyswomen.com/womenoffaith/SusannahWesley.html.

6. Susanna Wesley, quoted in Harmon, *Susanna*, 47.

7. Ibid., 45.

8. Ibid., 60.

9. Ibid., 62.

10. Samuel and Susanna Wesley, quoted in Harmon, *Susanna*, 56.

11. Susanna Wesley, quoted in Harmon, *Susanna*, 59–60.

12. Ibid., 79.

13. Ibid., 89.

14. Ibid., 164.

Chapter 13 Hannah More

1. Charles Howard Ford, *Hannah More: A Critical Biography* (New York: Peter Lang, 1996), 43.

2. Hannah More, quoted in Ford, *Hannah More*, 32.

3. Ford, *Hannah More*, 42.

4. Ibid., 54.

5. Samuel Johnson, quoted in Ford, *Hannah More*, 54.

6. Jonas Hanway, quoted in Ford, *Hannah More*, 59.

7. Mary Alden Hopkins, *Hannah More and Her Circle* (New York: Longmans, Green, 1947), 223.

8. William Wilberforce, quoted in Mark K. Smith, "Hannah More: Sunday Schools, Education, and Youth Work," *The Encyclopedia of Informal Education*, 2002, http://www.infed.org/thinkers/more.htm.

9. Hannah More, quoted in Smith, "Hannah More."

10. William Wilberforce, quoted in Ford, *Hannah More*, 175.

11. Smith, "Hannah More."

12. Hopkins, *Hannah More*, 220.

13. Hannah More, quoted in D. W. Bebbington, *Evangelicalism in Modern Britain: A History from the 1730s to the 1980s* (London: Routledge, 1989), 12.

Chapter 14 Phillis Wheatley

1. Henry Louis Gates Jr., *The Trials of Phillis Wheatley: America's First Black Poet and Her Encounters with the Founding Fathers* (New York: Basic Civitas Books, 2003), 6.

2. Ibid., 29–30.

3. Vincent Carretta, *Phillis Wheatley: Biography of a Genius in Bondage* (Athens, GA: University of Georgia Press, 2011), 10.

4. Ibid., 14.

5. Ibid., 40.

6. Phillis Wheatley, quoted in Carretta, *Phillis Wheatley*, 43–44.

7. Gates, *Trials*, 71.

8. Phillis Wheatley, "On Being Brought to America from Africa," Poetry Foundation, http://www.poetryfoundation.org/poem/174733.

9. Gates, *Trials*, 75–78.

10. Carretta, *Phillis Wheatley*, 60.

11. William H. Robinson, *Phillis Wheatley and Her Writings* (New York: Garland, 1984), 44–45.

12. Quoted in Carretta, *Phillis Wheatley*, 96.

13. Ibid., 39.

14. Carretta, *Phillis Wheatley*, 173.

15. For an additional source for Phillis Wheatley, see Vincent Carretta, ed., *Complete Writings: Phillis Wheatley* (New York: Penguin Group, 2001).

Chapter 15 Elizabeth Fry

1. June Rose, *Elizabeth Fry: A Biography* (New York: St. Martin's Press, 1980), 12.

2. Elizabeth Fry, quoted in Rose, *Elizabeth Fry*, 20.

3. Ibid., 23.

4. Ibid., 33.

5. Ibid., 53.

6. Ibid., 58.

7. Ibid., 62.

8. Ibid., 134.

Chapter 16 Jarena Lee

1. Jarena Lee, "The Life and Religious Experience of Jarena Lee, a Coloured Lady, Giving an Account of Her Call to Preach the Gospel," in *Classic African American Women's Narratives*, ed. William L. Andrews (New York: Oxford University Press, 2003), 19.

2. Ibid., 21.

3. Ibid., 27.

4. Ibid., 27–28.

5. Ibid., 33.

6. Ibid., 34.

7. Anna Carter Florence, *Preaching as Testimony* (Louisville, KY: Westminster John Knox Press, 2007), 45.

8. Ibid., 44.

9. Lee, "Life and Religious Experience," 36.

10. Ibid., 37.

11. Florence, *Preaching as Testimony*, 39.

12. Ibid., 40.

13. Lee, "Life and Religious Experience," 37.

Chapter 17 Ann Hasseltine Judson

1. Gordon Langley Hall, *Golden Boats from Burma* (Philadelphia: Macrae Smith, 1961), 45.

2. Hannah More, quoted in ibid., 26.

3. Diane Severance, "Ann Judson: 1st American Woman Missionary," Christianity.com, http://www.christianity.com/church/church-history/timeline/1801-1900/ann-judson-1st-american-woman-missionary-11630365.html.

4. Hall, *Golden Boats from Burma*, 123.

5. "Ann Judson: A Life of Self-Denial" (Pensacola, FL: Chapel Library, 2012), http://www.truthfulwords.org/biography/annjudson.pdf.

6. Ibid., 7.

7. Ann Judson, quoted in Severance, "Ann Judson."

Chapter 18 Mary Lyon

1. Elizabeth Alden Green, *Mary Lyon and Mount Holyoke: Opening the Gates* (Hanover, NH: University Press of New England, 1979), 10.
2. Ibid, 26.
3. Mary Lyon, quoted in Green, *Mary Lyon*, 87.
4. Ibid., 117.
5. Ibid., 146.
6. Ibid., 143.
7. Ibid., 95.
8. Diane Severance, "Mary Lyon's Vision for Christian Women," Christianity.com, http://www.christianity.com/church/church-history/timeline/1801-1900/mary-lyons-vision-for-christian-women-11630442.html.
9. Mary Lyon, quoted in Green, *Mary Lyon*, 143–44.
10. Eliza Hubbell, quoted in Severance, "Mary Lyon's Vision."
11. Mary Lyon, quoted in Green, *Mary Lyon*, 338.
12. Ibid.
13. Mary Lyon, quoted in "History," Mount Holyoke, 2014, http://www.mtholyoke.edu/about/history.

Chapter 19 Sojourner Truth

1. Sojourner Truth, *Narrative of Sojourner Truth: A Bondswoman of Olden Time, Emancipated by the New York Legislature in the Early Part of the Present Century; with a History of Her Labors and Correspondence, Drawn from Her "Book of Life"* (Boston, 1875), 61.
2. Ibid., 65.
3. Ibid., 66.
4. Ibid., 67.
5. Ibid., 69.
6. Sojourner Truth, quoted in "Sojourner Truth: Abolitionist and Women's Rights Advocate," *Christianity Today*, August 8, 2008, http://www.christianitytoday.com/ch/131christians/activists/sojourner.html?start=1.
7. Nell Irvin Painter, *Sojourner Truth: A Life, a Symbol* (New York: W.W. Norton, 1996), 128–29.
8. Boston *Liberator*, quoted in Painter, *Sojourner Truth*, 139.
9. Painter, *Sojourner Truth*, 140.
10. Sojourner Truth, quoted in "Sojourner Truth."
11. Truth, *Sojourner Truth's Narrative*, 178.
12. Ibid., 308.
13. Berenice Lowe, "Michigan Days of Sojourner Truth," Sojourner Truth Institute, http://www.sojournertruth.org/Library/Archive/MichiganDaysOfSojourner.htm.
14. For an additional source for Sojourner Truth, see "This Far by Faith: African-American Spiritual Journeys: Sojourner Truth," PBS, http://www.pbs.org/thisfarbyfaith/people/sojourner_truth.html.

Chapter 20 Phoebe Palmer

1. Phoebe Palmer, quoted in Harold E. Raser, *Phoebe Palmer: Her Life and Thought* (Lewiston, NY: Edwin Mellen Press, 1987), 38–39.
2. Ibid., 36.

3. Phoebe Palmer, quoted in "Phoebe Palmer (1807–1874) and Holiness Theology," TeachUSHistory.org, http://www.teachushistory.org/second-great-awakening-age-reform /approaches/phoebe-palmer-1807-1874-holiness-theology.

4. Phoebe Palmer, quoted in "Phoebe Palmer: Mother of the Holiness Movement," *Christianity Today*, August 8, 2008, http://www.christianitytoday.com/ch/131christians/movers andshakers/palmer.html.

5. Phoebe Palmer, quoted in Raser, *Phoebe Palmer*, 47.

6. Raser, *Phoebe Palmer*, 92.

7. Phoebe Palmer, quoted in "Phoebe Palmer: Mother of the Holiness Movement."

8. Quoted in Raser, *Phoebe Palmer*, 119.

9. Richard Wheatley, *The Life and Letters of Mrs. Phoebe Palmer* (New York: W. C. Palmer, 1881), 31–32.

10. Ibid., 157.

11. Ibid., 622.

12. Ibid., 623.

Chapter 21 Harriet Beecher Stowe

1. Harriet Beecher Stowe, quoted in Joan D. Hedrick, *Harriet Beecher Stowe: A Life* (New York: Oxford University Press, 1994), 193.

2. Ibid.

3. Ibid., 45.

4. Hedrick, *Harriet Beecher Stowe*, 88.

5. Harriet Beecher Stowe, quoted in Hedrick, *Harriet Beecher Stowe*, 99.

6. Ibid., 139.

7. Calvin Stowe, quoted in Hedrick, *Harriet Beecher Stowe*, 138.

8. Gayle Kimball, *The Religious Ideas of Harriet Beecher Stowe: Her Gospel of Womanhood* (New York: Edwin Mellen Press, 1982), 15.

9. Harriet Beecher Stowe, quoted in Hedrick, *Harriet Beecher Stowe*, 193.

10. Ibid., 205.

11. Ibid., 208.

12. Quoted in Hedrick, *Harriet Beecher Stowe*, 282.

13. Harriet Beecher Stowe, quoted in Hedrick, *Harriet Beecher Stowe*, 284.

Chapter 22 Florence Nightingale

1. Florence Nightingale, quoted in Mark Bostridge, *Florence Nightingale: The Making of an Icon* (New York: Farrar, Straus and Giroux, 2008), 51.

2. Ibid., 92.

3. Florence Nightingale, quoted in Lucy Ridgely Seymer, *Florence Nightingale* (New York: MacMillan, 1950), 30.

4. Florence Nightingale, quoted in Gillian Gill, *Nightingales: The Extraordinary Upbringing and Curious Life of Miss Florence Nightingale* (New York: Ballantine Books, 2004), 330.

5. Gill, *Nightingales*, 381.

6. For additional sources for Florence Nightingale, see Marjie Bloy, "Florence Nightingale: 1820–1910," The Victorian Web, January 3, 2012, http://www.victorianweb.org/history/ crimea/florrie.html; and Mary Lewis Coakley, "The Faith Behind the Famous: Florence Nightingale," *Christianity Today*, January 1990, http://www.christianitytoday.com/ch/1990/ issue25/2537.html?start=1.

Chapter 23 Harriet Tubman

1. Frederick Douglass, quoted in Clifford Kate Larson, *Bound for the Promised Land: Harriet Tubman, Portrait of an American Hero* (New York: Ballantine Books, 2004), 16.
2. Larson, *Bound*, 53.
3. Harriet Tubman, quoted in Catherine Clinton, *Harriet Tubman: The Road to Freedom* (New York: Little, Brown, 2004), 31.
4. Harriet Tubman, quoted in Larson, *Bound*, 84.
5. Ibid., 88.
6. Harriet Tubman, quoted in Clinton, *Harriet Tubman*, 91.
7. Thomas Garrett, quoted in Clinton, *Harriet Tubman*, 91.
8. Clinton, *Harriet Tubman*, 173.
9. Harriet Tubman, quoted in Clinton, *Harriet Tubman*, 209.
10. Harriet Tubman, quoted in Larson, *Bound*, 280.
11. Ibid., 289.
12. For an additional source for Harriet Tubman, see Sarah Bradford, *Harriet Tubman: The Moses of Her People* (Bedford, MA: Applewood Books, 1993).

Chapter 24 Antoinette Brown Blackwell

1. Elizabeth Cazden, *Antoinette Brown Blackwell: A Biography* (Old Westbury, NY: Feminist Press, 1983), 80.
2. Antoinette Brown Blackwell, quoted in Cazden, *Antoinette Brown Blackwell*, 80.
3. Ibid., 3.
4. Lucy Stone, quoted in Cazden, *Antoinette Brown Blackwell*, 31.
5. Antoinette Brown Blackwell, quoted in Cazden, *Antoinette Brown Blackwell*, 83.
6. Luther Lee, quoted in Cazden, *Antoinette Brown Blackwell*, 84.
7. Antoinette Brown Blackwell, quoted in Cazden, *Antoinette Brown Blackwell*, 89.
8. Ibid., 127.
9. Ibid., 162.
10. For an additional source for Antoinette Brown Blackwell, see Carol Lasser and Merrill Marlene Deahl, *Friends and Sisters: Letters Between Lucy Stone and Antoinette Brown Blackwell* (Chicago: University of Illinois Press, 1987).

Chapter 25 Josephine Butler

1. Josephine Butler, quoted in A. N. Wilson, *Eminent Victorians* (London: BBC Books, 1989), 175.
2. George Butler, quoted in Joseph Williamson, *Josephine Butler—The Forgotten Saint* (Leighton Buzzard, Bedfordshire, England: Faith Press, 1977), 14.
3. Lisa Severine Nolland, *A Victorian Feminist Christian: Josephine Butler, the Prostitutes and God* (Carlisle, Cumbria, England: Paternoster, 2004), 56–57.
4. Josephine Butler, quoted in Williamson, *Josephine Butler*, 23.
5. Ibid., 25.
6. Josephine Butler, quoted in Dan Graves, "Josephine Butler Championed Women," June 2007, http://www.christianity.com/church/church-history/timeline/1901-2000/josephine-butler-championed-women-11630685.html.
7. Josephine Butler, quoted in Williamson, *Josephine Butler*, 34.
8. Ibid., 30–31.
9. Ibid., 96.

10. For an additional source for Josephine Butler, see Glen Petrie, *A Singular Iniquity: The Campaigns of Josephine Butler* (New York: Viking Press, 1971).

Chapter 26 Catherine Booth

1. Catherine Bramwell-Booth, *Catherine Booth: The Story of Her Loves* (London: Hodder and Stoughton Limited, 1970), 35.

2. Catherine Booth, quoted in ibid., 36.

3. William Booth, quoted in Bramwell-Booth, *Catherine Booth*, 63.

4. Catherine and William Booth, quoted in Bramwell-Booth, *Catherine Booth*, 142–43.

5. Catherine Booth, quoted in Bramwell-Booth, *Catherine Booth*, 178.

6. William and Catherine Booth, quoted in Roy Hattersley, *Blood and Fire: William and Catherine Booth and Their Salvation Army* (New York: Doubleday, 2000), 113.

7. Catherine Booth, quoted in Bramwell-Booth, *Catherine Booth*, 188.

8. Ibid., 331–32.

9. William Booth, quoted in Bramwell-Booth, *Catherine Booth*, 230.

10. Bramwell-Booth, *Catherine Booth*, 416.

11. Catherine Booth, quoted in ibid., 435.

12. For additional sources for Catherine Booth, see "History of the Salvation Army," The Salvation Army, http://www.salvationarmyusa.org/usn/history-of-the-salvation-army; and Pamela J. Walker, *Pulling the Devil's Kingdom Down: The Salvation Army in Victorian Britain* (Berkeley, CA: University of California Press, 2001).

Chapter 27 Hannah Whitall Smith

1. Hannah Whitall Smith, quoted in Marie Henry, *Hannah Whitall Smith* (Minneapolis, MN: Bethany House, 1984), 30.

2. Ibid., 33.

3. Ibid., 34.

4. Hannah Whitall Smith, *The Christian's Secret of a Happy Life* (Grand Rapids: Revell, 2012), 82.

5. Hannah Whitall Smith, quoted in Henry, *Hannah Whitall Smith*, 76.

6. Ibid., 88.

7. Hannah Whitall Smith, *The God of All Comfort* (Grand Rapids: Christian Classics Ethereal Library), 143, http://www.ccel.org/ccel/smith_hw/comfort.pdf.

Chapter 28 Clara Swain

1. Clara Swain, *A Glimpse of India* (New York: James Pott, 1909), 36, http://openlibrary.org/books/OL23530335M/A_glimpse_of_India.

2. Ibid., 96–97.

3. Ibid., 79.

4. Ibid., 73.

5. Ibid., 46.

6. Ibid., 68–69.

7. Ibid., 222.

8. Ibid., 269.

9. Ibid., 294.

10. Ibid., 111–12.

11. Ibid., 115.

12. For additional sources for Clara Swain, see Dan Graves, "No Rest for a Weary Clara Swain," Christianity.com, May 2007, http://www.christianity.com/church/church-history/time line/1801-1900/no-rest-for-a-weary-clara-swain-11630553.html; Mrs. Robert Hoskins, *Clara A. Swain, M.D.: First Medical Missionary to the Women of the Orient* (Boston: Women's Foreign Missionary Society, Methodist Episcopal Church, 1912), http://archive.org/details/claraaswain mdfi00socigoog; and the Clara Swain Mission Hospital website, http://cshbareilly.in/index.jsp.

Chapter 29 Amanda Berry Smith

1. Amanda Berry Smith, *An Autobiography: The Story of the Lord's Dealings with Mrs. Amanda Smith, The Colored Evangelist* (Chicago: Meyer and Brother, 1893), 18.
2. Ibid., 30.
3. Ibid., 78.
4. Ibid., 80.
5. Ibid., 103.
6. Ibid., 183.
7. Ibid., 184.
8. Chris Armstrong, "Poor, Black, and Female: Amanda Berry Smith Preached Holiness in the Teeth of Racism," Grateful to the Dead, November 7, 2010, http://grateful tothedead.wordpress.com/2010/11/07/poor-black-and-female-amanda-berry-smith-preached-holiness-in-the-teeth-of-racism.
9. Smith, *Autobiography*, 117.
10. Ibid., 118.
11. Ibid.
12. Ibid., 116–17.
13. Ibid., 117.
14. Ibid.

Chapter 30 Lottie Moon

1. International Mission Board, "Lottie Moon Christmas Offering," http://www.imb.org/main/give/page.asp?StoryID=5523&.
2. Erich Bridges, "Lottie Moon Mission Offering Climbs to $149.3 Million," International Mission Board, June 5, 2013, http://www.imb.org/main/news/details.asp?StoryID=11925&LanguageID=1709#.UxYQAPldWSo.
3. John Allen Moore, "Lottie's Biography," IMB, http://www.imb.org/main/give/page.asp?StoryID=5527&LanguageID=1709.
4. Julia Toy, quoted in Moore, "Lottie's Biography."
5. Lottie Moon, quoted in Moore, "Lottie's Biography."
6. Catherine B. Allen, "The Legacy of Lottie Moon," *International Bulletin of Missionary Research*, October 1, 1993, http://www.thefreelibrary.com/The+legacy+of+Lottie+Moon.-a014550858.
7. Lottie Moon, quoted in Moore, "Lottie's Biography."
8. Ibid.
9. Ibid.
10. Ibid.
11. R. J. Willingham, quoted in Moore, "Lottie's Biography."
12. Lottie Moon, quoted in Moore, "Lottie's Biography."
13. Ibid.
14. Ibid.

Chapter 31 Fanny Crosby

1. Fanny Crosby, *Fanny Crosby's Life Story* (New York: Everywhere Publishing, 1903), 25.
2. Ibid., 13–14.
3. Ibid., 29.
4. Ibid., 41.
5. Ibid., 17.
6. Ibid., 123.
7. Robert J. Morgan, *Then Sings My Soul: 150 of the World's Greatest Hymn Stories* (Nashville: Thomas Nelson, 2003), 165.
8. John Hall, quoted in ibid.
9. Crosby, *Fanny Crosby's Life Story*, 126–27.
10. Keith Schwanz, "Satisfied: Women Hymn Writers of the 19th-Century Wesleyan/Holiness Movement" (Grantham, PA: Wesleyan/Holiness Clergy, 1998), http://www.whwomenclergy.org/booklets/satisfied/php.
11. Fanny Crosby, *Fanny Crosby's Story of Ninety-Four Years*, ed. S. Trevena Jackson (New York: Fleming H. Revell, 1915), 173.
12. Ira Sankey, *My Life and the Story of the Gospel Hymns and of Sacred Songs and Solos* (Philadelphia: Sunday School Times, 1907), 258, http://www.archive.org/stream/mylifeandstoryg00sankgoog#page/n10/mode/2up.
13. Crosby, *Fanny Crosby's Story of Ninety-Four Years*, 97–98.
14. Ibid., 132.
15. For an additional source for Fanny Crosby, see Edith Blumhofer, *Her Heart Can See: The Life and Hymns of Fanny J. Crosby* (Grand Rapids: Wm. B. Eerdmans, 2005).

Chapter 32 Pandita Ramabai

1. Pandita Ramabai, *Pandita Ramabai through Her Own Words: Selected Works*, comp. and ed. Meera Kosambi (New Delhi, India: Oxford University Press, 2000), 300.
2. Ibid., 299.
3. Ibid., 248.
4. Ibid., 302.
5. Ibid., 304.
6. Ibid., 307.
7. Ibid., 308.
8. Pandita Ramabai, quoted in Keith J. White, "Jesus Was Her Guru," *Christianity Today*, July 1, 2005, http://www.christianitytoday.com/ch/2005/issue87/5.12.html?start=3.
9. Ramabai, *Pandita Ramabai*, 310.
10. Pandita Ramabai, quoted in Helen S. Dyer, *Pandita Ramabai: The Story of Her Life* (London: Morgan and Scott, 1923), 87–88, http://archive.org/stream/cu31924024067294/cu31924024067294_djvu.txt.
11. Pandita Ramabai quoted in White, "Jesus Was Her Guru."

Chapter 33 Amy Carmichael

1. Amy Carmichael, quoted in Elisabeth Elliot, *A Chance to Die: The Life and Legacy of Amy Carmichael* (Grand Rapids: Fleming H. Revell, 1987), 59.
2. Ibid., 141.
3. Ibid., 142.
4. Ibid., 79.

5. Elliot, *Chance to Die*, 126.

6. Amy Wilson Carmichael, *Things as They Are: Mission Work in Southern India* (London: Morgan and Scott, 1905), 188, http://www.gutenberg.org/files/29426/29426-h/29426-h.htm.

7. Elliot, *Chance to Die*, 198.

8. Amy Carmichael, quoted in Elliot, *Chance to Die*, 189.

9. Ibid., 304.

10. Ibid., 311.

11. Ibid., 322.

12. Quoted in Elliot, *Chance to Die*, 327.

13. Ibid.

14. For additional sources for Amy Carmichael, see Phyllis Berry, "Amy Carmichael and the Origin of the Dohnavur Fellowship," Mission Frontiers, August 1999, http://www.mission frontiers.org/issue/article/a-living-legacy; Helen Kooiman Hosier, *100 Christian Women Who Changed the 20th Century* (Grand Rapids: Revell, 2000); and Elizabeth R. Skoglund, *Amma: The Life and Words of Amy Carmichael* (Grand Rapids: Raven's Ridge Books, 1994).

Chapter 34 Ida Scudder

1. Dan Graves, "Ida Scudder Changed Her Mind," Christianity.com, http://www.christian ity.com/church/church-history/timeline/1801-1900/ida-scudder-changed-her-mind-1163 0634.html.

2. Hilda Olson, quoted in Dorothy Clarke Wilson, *Dr. Ida: The Story of Dr. Ida Scudder of Vellore* (New York: McGraw-Hill, 1959), 286.

3. Ida Scudder, quoted in Graves, "Ida Scudder."

4. Christian Medical College Vellore, http://www.cmch-vellore.edu/pdf/patients/CMC,%20in%20service%20of%20the%20nation%20since%201900.pdf.

Chapter 35 Thérèse of Lisieux

1. Thérèse of Lisieux, quoted in Vita Sackville-West, *The Eagle and the Dove: A Study in Contrasts: St. Teresa of Avila, St. Thérèse of Lisieux* (Garden City, NY: Doubleday, Doran, 1944), 117.

2. Ibid.

3. Ibid., 117.

4. Ibid., 104.

5. Ida Gorres, *The Hidden Face: A Study of St. Thérèse of Lisieux* (San Francisco: Ignatius Press, 1959), 112.

6. Thérèse of Lisieux, quoted in Albert H. Dolan, *An Hour with the Little Flower* (Chicago: Carmelite Press, 1926), 12–13.

7. Thérèse of Lisieux, quoted in ibid., 17.

8. Thérèse of Lisieux, quoted in Sackville-West, *Eagle and the Dove*, 126.

9. Sackville-West, *Eagle and the Dove*, 126.

10. For an additional source for Thérèse of Lisieux, see John Clarke, trans., *Story of a Soul: The Autobiography of Saint Thérèse of Lisieux* (Washington, DC: ICS Publications, 1996).

Chapter 36 Mary McLeod Bethune

1. Mary McLeod Bethune, quoted in Rackam Holt, *Mary McLeod Bethune: A Biography* (Garden City, New York: Doubleday, 1964), 122.

2. "Determining the Facts: Mary McLeod Bethune," National Park Service, http://www. nps.gov/nr/twhp/wwwlps/lessons/135bethune/135facts1.htm.

3. Aubrey Williams, quoted in "Determining the Facts."

4. Mary McLeod Bethune, quoted in "Determining the Facts."

5. Mary McLeod Bethune, quoted in Holt, *Mary McLeod Bethune*, 205.

6. Mary McLeod Bethune, quoted in Audrey Thomas McCluskey and Elaine M. Smith, eds., *Mary McLeod Bethune: Building a Better World* (Bloomington, IN: Indiana University Press, 1999), 54.

7. Ibid., 59–61.

8. Ibid., 61.

Chapter 37 Faye Edgerton

1. Ethel Emily Wallis, *God Speaks Navajo* (New York: Harper and Row, 1968), 22.

2. Faye Edgerton, quoted in Wallis, *God Speaks Navajo*, 13.

3. Ibid., 55.

4. Ibid., 69.

5. Ibid., 70.

6. Ibid., 79.

7. Wallis, *God Speaks Navajo*, 101.

8. Ibid., 103.

9. Ibid., 107.

10. Ibid., 106.

11. Roger Deal, quoted in Dan Graves, "Faye Edgerton Gave God's Word to the Navajo," Christianity.com, May 2007, http://www.christianity.com/church/church-history/time line/1801-1900/faye-edgerton-gave-gods-word-to-the-navajo-11630622.html.

Chapter 38 Edith Stein

1. Edith Stein, quoted in Waltraud Herbstrith, *Edith Stein: A Biography* (New York: Harper and Row, 1985), 103.

2. "Teresa Benedict of the Cross Edith Stein (1891–1942)," The Vatican, http://www. vatican.va/news_services/liturgy/saints/ns_lit_doc_19981011_edith_stein_en.html.

3. Edith Stein, quoted in ibid.

4. Edith Stein, quoted in Herbstrith, *Edith Stein*, 7.

5. Edith Stein, *The Collected Works of Edith Stein (Life in a Jewish Family: 1891–1916)*, eds. Dr. L. Gelber and Romaeus Leuven (Washington, DC: ICS Publications, 1986), 260.

6. Edith Stein, quoted in Herbstrith, *Edith Stein*, 25.

7. Herbstrith, *Edith Stein*, 31.

8. Edith Stein, quoted in Herbstrith, *Edith Stein*, 54.

9. Ibid., 64.

10. Ibid., 66.

11. Herbstrith, *Edith Stein*, 95.

12. Edith Stein, quoted in Herbstrith, *Edith Stein*, 95.

13. Edith Stein, quoted in "Teresa Benedict."

14. Edith Stein, quoted in Herbstrith, *Edith Stein*, 87.

Chapter 39 Corrie ten Boom

1. Corrie ten Boom, *Prison Letters* (Old Tappan, NJ: Fleming H. Revell, 1975), 80.

2. Ibid., 90.

3. Corrie ten Boom, *The Hiding Place* (Uhrichsville, Ohio: Barbour, 1971), 136–37.
4. ten Boom, *Prison Letters*, 10.
5. ten Boom, *Hiding Place*, 139.
6. ten Boom, *Prison Letters*, 11.
7. ten Boom, *Hiding Place*, 176.
8. Ibid., 177.
9. Ibid., 185.
10. Ibid., 190.
11. Ibid., 193.
12. Ibid., 210–11.
13. For additional sources for Corrie ten Boom, see Ellen de Koon Stamps, *My Years with Corrie* (Old Tappan, NJ: Fleming H. Revell, 1978); and the Corrie ten Boom Museum website, http://www.corrietenboom.com.

Chapter 40 Dorothy Sayers

1. *Daily Telegraph*, quoted in James Brabazon, *Dorothy Sayers* (New York: Charles Scribner's Sons, 1981), 164.
2. Dorothy Sayers, quoted in ibid., 193.
3. Brabazon, *Dorothy Sayers*, 171.
4. Dorothy Sayers, quoted in Barbara Reynolds, *Dorothy L. Sayers: Her Life and Soul* (New York: St. Martin's Press, 1993), 319.
5. Dorothy Sayers, quoted in Brabazon, *Dorothy Sayers*, 232.
6. Dorothy Sayers, quoted in Reynolds, *Dorothy L. Sayers*, 331.
7. Ibid., 338–39.
8. Ibid., 333.
9. Dorothy Sayers, quoted in Brabazon, *Dorothy Sayers*, 262.
10. Ibid., 263.
11. For additional sources for Dorothy Sayers, see Alzina Stone Dale, ed., *Dorothy L. Sayers: The Centenary Celebration* (New York: Walker, 1993); and "Dorothy Sayers: Mystery Writer and Apologist," *Christianity Today*, August 8, 2008, http://www.christianitytoday.com/ch/131christians/musiciansartistsandwriters/sayers.html.

Chapter 41 Dorothy Day

1. Dorothy Day, *Loaves and Fishes* (Maryknoll, NY: Orbis Books, 1997), 5.
2. Dorothy Day, *The Long Loneliness* (New York: Harper and Brothers, 1952), 37–38.
3. Ibid., 136.
4. Ibid., 149.
5. Day, *Loaves and Fishes*, 13.
6. Dorothy Day, quoted in Jim Forest, "Servant of God Dorothy Day," The Catholic Worker Movement, http://www.catholicworker.org/dorothyday/ddbiographytext.cfm?number=72.
7. Dorothy Day, quoted in Jim Forest, *Love Is the Measure: A Biography of Dorothy Day* (Mahwah, NJ: Paulist Press, 1986), 91–92.
8. Ibid., 102.
9. Dorothy Day, quoted in Jim Forest, "Servant of God."
10. Ibid.
11. Dorothy Day, quoted in William D. Miller, *All Is Grace: The Spirituality of Dorothy Day* (Garden City, NY: Doubleday, 1987), 98.

12. For additional sources for Dorothy Day, see Robert Coles, *Dorothy Day: A Radical Devotion* (Reading, MA: Addison-Wesley, 1987); and William D. Miller, *Dorothy Day: A Biography* (New York: Harper and Row, 1982).

Chapter 42 Gladys Aylward

1. Quoted in Alan Burgess, *The Small Woman* (New York: E. P. Dutton, 1957), 22.
2. Jeannie Lawson, quoted in Burgess, *Small Woman*, 50.
3. Ibid., 54.
4. Gladys Aylward, quoted in Burgess, *Small Woman*, 89.
5. Ibid., 101.
6. Ibid., 149.
7. Gladys Aylward, quoted in "Gladys Aylward: 'I Wasn't First Choice for What I've Done in China,'" HistoryMakers, http://www.historymakers.info/inspirational-christians/gladys-aylward.html.
8. For additional sources for Gladys Aylward, see John M. Fritzius, "Gladys Aylward (1902–1970): Missionary to China," Tlogical.net, http://www.tlogical.net/bioaylward.htm; and "Gladys Aylward's Impossible Mission to China," Christianity.com, http://www.christianity.com/church/church-history/timeline/1901-2000/gladys-aylwards-impossible-mission-to-china-11630754.html.

Chapter 43 Simone Weil

1. Simone Weil, quoted in Francine Du Plessix Gray, *Simone Weil* (New York: Penguin Group, 2001), 87.
2. Émile Chartier, quoted in Stephen Plant, *Simone Weil* (Liguori, MO: Triumph, 1996), 4.
3. Simone Weil, quoted in Gray, *Simone Weil*, 20.
4. Ibid., 40–41.
5. Ibid., 98.
6. Simone Weil, *The Simone Weil Reader*, ed. George A. Panichas (New York: David McKay, 1977), 14.
7. Ibid., 15.
8. Ibid.
9. Ibid., 16.
10. Ibid., 11, 13.
11. Plant, *Simone Weil*, 23.
12. Simone Weil, quoted in Gray, *Simone Weil*, 191.
13. Ibid., 177.
14. Ibid., 146.
15. Plant, *Simone Weil*, 84.

Chapter 44 Mother Teresa

1. David Scott, *A Revolution of Love: The Meaning of Mother Teresa* (Chicago: Loyola Press, 2005), 43.
2. Kathryn Spink, *Mother Teresa: A Complete Authorized Biography* (San Francisco: HarperCollins, 1997), 7–8.
3. Mother Teresa, *Come Be My Light*, ed. Brian Kolodiejchuk (New York: Doubleday, 2007), 40.
4. Ibid., 43.
5. Ibid., 79.
6. Ibid., 93.

7. Ibid., 119.
8. Ibid., 193.
9. Ibid., 194.
10. Ibid., 211.
11. Ibid., 214.
12. Scott, *Revolution of Love*, 97–98.
13. Mother Teresa, quoted in ibid., 52.
14. Mother Teresa, *The Joy in Loving: A Guide to Daily Living with Mother Teresa*, comp. Jaya Chaliha and Edward Le Joly (New York: Viking, 1996), 75.
15. Mother Teresa, quoted in Edward W. Desmond, "Interview with Mother Teresa," *Time*, 1989, http://www.servelec.net/mothertheresa.htm.
16. For an additional source for Mother Teresa, see Anne Sebba, *Mother Teresa: Beyond the Image* (New York: Doubleday, 1997).

Chapter 45 Mahalia Jackson

1. Mahalia Jackson, quoted in Jules Schwerin, *Got to Tell It: Mahalia Jackson, Queen of Gospel* (New York: Oxford University Press, 1992), 25.
2. Mahalia Jackson, quoted in Schwerin, *Got to Tell It*, 27.
3. Ibid., 47.
4. Louis "Studs" Terkel, quoted in Schwerin, *Got to Tell It*, 65.
5. Mahalia Jackson, quoted in Schwerin, *Got to Tell It*, 112.
6. John Sellers, quoted in Schwerin, *Got to Tell It*, 121.
7. Mahalia Jackson, quoted in Schwerin, *Got to Tell It*, 26.
8. For an additional source for Mahalia Jackson, see "Mahalia Jackson: The Queen of Gospel," http://www.mahaliajackson.us.

Chapter 46 Edith Schaeffer

1. Edith Schaeffer, *The Tapestry: The Life and Times of Francis and Edith Schaeffer* (Waco, TX: Word Books, 1981), 100.
2. Ibid., 144.
3. Ibid., 200.
4. Ibid., 204.
5. Udo Middelmann, "Edith Schaeffer: New Yorker at Heart," A Journey through NYC Religions, April 10, 2013, http://www.nycreligion.info/?p=9388.
6. Schaeffer, *Tapestry*, 276.
7. Ibid., 410.
8. Ibid., 428–29.
9. Ibid., 433.
10. Frank Schaeffer, "A Tribute to My Evangelical Leader Mom—Edith Schaeffer, RIP," *The Huffington Post*, March 30, 2013, http://www.huffingtonpost.com/frank-schaeffer/a-tribute-to-my-evangelic_b_2983906.html.
11. Paul Vitello, "Edith Schaeffer, Definer of Christian Family Values, Dies at 98," *New York Times*, April 6, 2013, http://www.nytimes.com/2013/04/07/world/europe/edith-schaeffer-98-dies-defined-christian-values.html.

Chapter 47 Fannie Lou Hamer

1. Fannie Lou Hamer, quoted in Chana Kai Lee, *For Freedom's Sake: The Life of Fannie Lou Hamer* (Urbana, IL: University of Illinois Press, 1999), 26.

2. Ibid., 29.

3. Fannie Lou Hamer, quoted in Kay Mills, *This Little Light of Mine: The Life of Fannie Lou Hamer* (New York: Penguin Books, 1993), 17.

4. Fannie Lou Hamer, quoted in Lee, *For Freedom's Sake*, 13.

5. Ibid., 32.

6. Ibid., 37.

7. Mills, *This Little Light*, 41.

8. "Fannie Lou Hamer (1917–1977): Testimony before the Credentials Committee, Democratic National Convention," American RadioWorks, http://americanradioworks.publicradio.org/features/sayitplain/flhamer.html.

9. Fannie Lou Hamer, quoted in Mills, *This Little Light*, 125.

10. Ibid., 17.

Chapter 48 Madeleine L'Engle

1. Madeleine L'Engle, *A Circle of Quiet: The Crosswicks Journal, Book One* (New York: HarperCollins, 1972), 21–22.

2. Donald R. Hettinga, *Presenting Madeleine L'Engle* (New York: Twayne, 1983), 4.

3. Madeleine L'Engle, quoted in ibid., 7.

4. L'Engle, *Circle of Quiet*, 20.

5. Ibid., 98.

6. Madeleine L'Engle, quoted in Hettinga, *Presenting Madeleine L'Engle*, 11.

7. L'Engle, *Circle of Quiet*, 34.

8. Ibid.

9. Madeleine L'Engle, *The Irrational Season: The Crosswicks Journal, Book Three* (New York: HarperCollins, 1977), 122.

10. Madeleine L'Engle, *Walking on Water: Reflections on Faith and Art* (New York: Farrar, Straus and Giroux, 1980), 106.

11. Madeleine L'Engle, *The Summer of the Great-Grandmother: The Crosswicks Journal, Book Two* (New York: HarperCollins, 1974), 142.

12. L'Engle, *Walking on Water*, 106.

13. Ibid., 25.

14. Ibid., 122.

15. Ibid., 32.

16. L'Engle, *Summer*, 142.

17. L'Engle, *Walking on Water*, 134–35.

18. Ibid., 15.

19. Ibid., 187.

Chapter 49 Ruth Bell Graham

1. Ruth Bell Graham, quoted in Patricia Cornwell, *Ruth, a Portrait: The Story of Ruth Bell Graham* (New York: Doubleday, 1997), 75.

2. Ibid., 86.

3. Billy Graham, quoted in Cornwell, *Ruth, a Portrait*, 91.

4. Ruth Bell Graham, quoted in Elizabeth R. Skoglund, *Found Faithful: The Timeless Stories of Charles Spurgeon, Amy Carmichael, C. S. Lewis, Ruth Bell Graham, and Others* (Grand Rapids: Discovery House, 2003), 302.

5. Ibid., 133.

6. Ruth Bell Graham, *Sitting by My Laughing Fire* (Waco, TX: Word Books, 1977), 153.

7. Ruth Bell Graham, *Footprints of a Pilgrim: The Life and Loves of Ruth Bell Graham* (Nashville: Word, 2001), 20.

8. Anne Graham, quoted in Cornwell, *Ruth, a Portrait*, 169.

9. Ruth Bell Graham, quoted in Cornwell, *Ruth, a Portrait*, 120.

10. Marvin King, quoted in Cornwell, *Ruth, a Portrait*, 246.

11. Quoted in Cornwell, *Ruth, a Portrait*, 247.

12. Ruth Bell Graham, quoted in Cornwell, *Ruth, a Portrait*, 206.

Chapter 50 Flannery O'Connor

1. Flannery O'Connor, quoted in Kathleen Feeley, *Flannery O'Connor: Voice of the Peacock* (Brunswick, NJ: Rutgers University Press, 1972), 20.

2. Feeley, *Flannery O'Connor*, 6.

3. Flannery O'Connor, "Catholic Novelists and Their Readers," CatholicCulture.org, http://www.catholicculture.org/culture/library/view.cfm?recnum=9118.

4. Flannery O'Connor, quoted in Brad Gooch, *Flannery: A Life of Flannery O'Connor* (New York: Little, Brown, 2009), 39.

5. Ibid., 72.

6. Ibid., 117.

7. Van Wyck Brooks, quoted in Gooch, *Flannery*, 264.

8. Quoted in Gooch, *Flannery*, 265.

9. Flannery O'Connor, quoted in Gooch, *Flannery*, 264.

10. Flannery O'Connor, quoted in Robert H. Brinkmeyer Jr., *The Art & Vision of Flannery O'Connor* (Baton Rouge: Louisiana State University Press, 1989), 19.

11. O'Connor, "Catholic Novelists."

12. Ibid.

13. Flannery O'Connor, *Mystery and Manners: Occasional Prose*, eds. Sally and Robert Fitzgerald (New York: Farrar, Straus and Giroux, 1969), 112.

14. Feeley, *Flannery O'Connor*, 73.

15. Flannery O'Connor, quoted in Brinkmeyer, *Art & Vision*, 24.

16. Caroline Gordon, in foreword of Feeley, *Flannery O'Connor*, xii.

17. O'Connor, "Catholic Novelists."

18. Flannery O'Connor, quoted in Gooch, *Flannery*, 336.

19. Ibid.

20. Feeley, *Flannery O'Connor*, 176–77.

21. For an additional source for Flannery O'Connor, see Rosemary M. Magee, ed., *Conversations with Flannery O'Connor* (Jackson, MS: University of Mississippi Press, 1987).

Michelle DeRusha is the author of *Spiritual Misfit: A Memoir of Uneasy Faith.* She also writes a monthly column on religion and spirituality for the *Lincoln Journal Star* and is a regular contributor to *The High Calling* and other online journals. She writes about faith in the everyday on her blog, MichelleDeRusha.com, and lives with her husband and their two boys in Lincoln, Nebraska.

Connect with writer and speaker

Michelle DeRusha

at **MichelleDeRusha.com.**

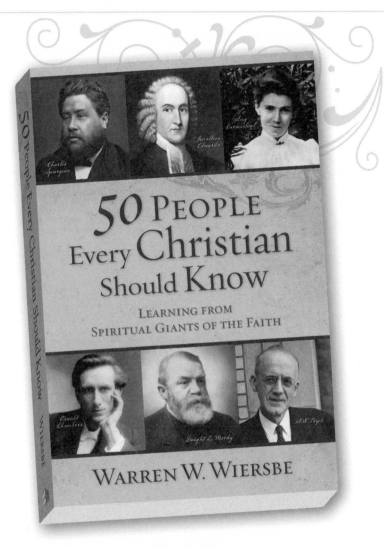